THE HIDDEN LIFE OF RENAISSANCE ART

Secrets and Symbols in Great Masterpieces

THE HIDDEN LIFE OF
RENAISSANCE ART

Secrets and Symbols in Great Masterpieces

CLARE GIBSON

**BARNES
& NOBLE**

NEW YORK

EDITOR: Sara Hunt
ART EDITOR: Deborah Hayes

ISBN-13: 978-0-7607-9326-8
ISBN-10: 0-7607-9326-3

Printed and bound in China

1 3 5 7 9 10 8 6 4 2

Page 1: Raphael's 1510–11 fresco The School of Athens *(detail; see pages 162–66) is a masterpiece of Western art that combines a virtuoso demonstration of portraiture and perspective with ingenious and intriguing symbolism.*

Page 2: This detail from The Miracle of the Relic of the True Cross on the Rialto Bridge *(c.1496; see pages 174–77), by Vittore Carpaccio, provides a view of the famous bridge over the Grand Canal in Venice, Italy, when it was a wooden drawbridge, lined with shops. (It would be another century before the stone bridge that still stands was constructed.)*

Page 3: Detail from Minerva Chasing the Vices from the Garden of Virtue *(see pages 127–131).*

Below: Piero di Cosimo (1462–1522) painted a series of depictions of the Greek mythological hero Perseus. In this 1515 scene, Perseus is portrayed in his winged sandals flying to the rescue of Andromeda, who is trapped by a terrifying monster.

For Emily and Keith Wood

CONTENTS

INTRODUCTION

With Rome's fall, the most excellent craftsmen, sculptors, painters, and architects were likewise destroyed, leaving their crafts and their very persons buried and submerged under the miserable ruins and the disasters which befell that most illustrious city. Painting and sculpture were the first to go to ruin, since they are arts that serve more to delight us than anything else...

Giorgio Vasari, *The Lives of the Artists* (1568)

Let your eyes linger on the word "Renaissance," and what springs to mind? Chances are that your mind's eye will have envisaged a painting by Leonardo da Vinci (*The Mona Lisa* or *The Last Supper*, perhaps), a sculpture by Michelangelo Buonarroti (*David*? *La Pietà*?), or maybe the dome with which Filippo Brunelleschi crowned Florence Cathedral. Small wonder, if so, for these breathtaking achievements are some of the glories of the extraordinary flowering of European culture that marked an emphatic moving-away from the conformity of the Middle Ages and a significant stride toward the Modern age. Yet while such iconic examples of Italian painting, sculpture, and architecture have become world-renowned icons of this era of astounding achievement, their dazzling fame has all too often obscured a fascinating hidden life whose roots and shoots extend far beyond the confines of post-medieval Italy.

WHAT, WHY, WHEN, AND WHERE?

According to Giorgio Vasari (1511–74), the Italian artist and architect whose *Le vite de' più eccellenti architetti, pittori, et scultori Italiani* (*The Lives of the Most Eminent Architects, Painters, and Sculptors of Italy*, or *The Lives of the Artists* for short, of 1550 and 1568) is an invaluable, if idiosyncratic, source of information, the roots of the Renaissance stretch back to ancient Rome, whose divinely inspired artists had achieved perfection in their work. The fall of Rome to the barbarian hordes had cast Europe into the Dark Ages, culturally speaking, Vasari explained, and it would not be until the fourteenth century (*trecento* in Italian) that this divine spirit would again begin to stir in Italy, bursting into life during the fifteenth century (*quattrocentro*), and reaching its apogee during the sixteenth century

Above: *A self-portrait of Giorgio Vasari, Italy's first and most famous art historian.* **Top:** *Leonardo da Vinci's* The Last Supper *is among the most celebrated masterpieces of Western art.*

(*cinquecento*), as represented by the work of Michelangelo (1475–1564), Vasari's hero.

In describing this "progress of art's rebirth and the state of perfection to which it has again ascended in our own times," Vasari, an Italian writing in his native tongue, did not use the French word *renaissance* (whose Italian equivalent is *rinascimento*). This was, in fact, coined by the nineteenth-century French historian Jules Michelet and affirmed by the German cultural scholar Jakob Burckhardt in his influential work *Civilization of the Renaissance in Italy* (1867). And although the name has stuck, more than a century later, the exact whats, whys, whens, and wheres of the Renaissance are still being debated.

They may quibble about the details, but most art historians agree on what constitutes the big Renaissance picture, with many attributing the start of this reconnection with the Greco–Roman spirit of

Classical antiquity to the Italian writers Dante Alighieri (1265–1321, see pages 178 to 181) and Petrarch (1304–74), whose Latin epic poem *Africa* focused on the Second Punic War and whose allegorical poems the *Trionfi* recalled Roman triumphal processions. All concur that the driving force behind the Renaissance was initially generated by an admiration for the literature of the Greek-influenced Roman Empire and the desire to read as much of it as possible, facilitated by scholars' familiarity with Latin, the language of ancient Rome and the lingua franca, or common tongue, of educated people all over Europe. So it was that the constricting scholasticism of the Middle Ages, a narrow, contemplative school of thought that was based largely on the writing of the Christian Church Fathers, was gradually supplanted by humanism, whose outlook, inspired and colored by Classical knowledge and values, focused far more freely on individualism and human potential.

With the intellectual emphasis increasingly being on independent learning, active experimentation, and secular interests, the consequences included great advances in scientific, mathematical, and geographical knowledge, as well as the broadening of scholarship to include the study of ancient Greek, Islamic, and other "pagan" civilizations. And while the fall of Constantinople (then the capital of the Byzantine Empire, and today the Turkish city of Istanbul) to the Ottoman Turks in 1453 was lamented as a disaster for Christendom, it contributed profoundly to European cultural life by triggering an influx of learned refugees carrying precious manuscripts, artifacts, instruments, and other products of sophisticated Eastern wisdom to the Western world.

The art of the Renaissance was fueled by the growth and spread of this knowledge-hungry, convention-challenging, boldly experimental mindset, rather than by the unthinking emulation of Greco–Roman styles (and, indeed, hardly any examples of Classical painting remained to be inspected, while what little sculpture and architecture had survived was limited in number). And once it had taken root in the fertile soil of Italy—the Roman Empire's heartland, after all—this Renaissance mindset rapidly developed a life and impetus of its own, encouraged by Johann Gutenberg's invention of movable type, and thus of the printing press, which spread knowledge and news of advances throughout Europe by means of typeset pages and engraved woodcut images at a rapid rate after 1455. The movement of ambitious, in-demand architects and artists between courts and countries, as well as their collaboration on major building projects in Rome and elsewhere, similarly fostered the dissemination and exchange of ideas.

Although different dates and descriptions pertain to the various parts of Europe whenever the Renaissance is discussed, it appears that the elegant, linear outlines, bright colors, exquisitely rendered naturalism, religious and chivalric themes that characterized the International Gothic style of art that prevailed in Europe from the late fourteenth century gave way to the art of the Early Renaissance from around 1420, starting in Florence, Italy. Art and artists consequently

Top: A moving depiction of the Greek myth of Danaë by the Venetian-school artist Titian (c.1485–1576).
Right: Michelangelo's sensitive and lifelike Pietà, *the body of Jesus in the arms of his grieving mother.*

having flourished as a result of the interest and funds lavished on them by rich and cultured patrons—among them the trendsetting cream of society, including religious and secular rulers, as well as the merely wealthy—the high point of the Italian Renaissance, the High Renaissance, is regarded as dating from 1500 to 1527, when Rome was sacked by the troops of the Holy Roman Emperor Charles V (1500–58). Following this enforced break in continuity, it was Mannerism (the *maniera nuova*, or "new style," which sought to depict ideals of beauty through the distortion of human proportions) that prevailed until 1600. And while some art historians may term it the "Second Renaissance," most today consider Mannerism to be distinct from the art of the Renaissance.

A further distinction can be made between the Italian Renaissance and the Northern Renaissance, as the cultural rebirth that occurred in northwestern Europe, notably in France, Germany, and the Low Countries (which correspond to modern-day Belgium and The Netherlands) was called, in whose art different preoccupations, themes, and techniques are evident, as the following pages illustrate.

*Below: Michelangelo's breathtaking Sistine Chapel frescos are characterized not just by their beauty and color, but by the anatomical detail of the figures. **Opposite:** Portrait of a Man with a Medal of Cosimo the Elder, 1474–75, by Botticelli.*

RENAISSANCE REALISM

Despite the differences in approach that can be discerned throughout Europe during the Renaissance, the one common thread that seems to run though the art of the continent at this time, linking England with Poland, and Scandinavia with Spain, is realism. Vasari praised the realism achieved by the Classical artists, and stated,

I am convinced that anyone who will discreetly ponder this matter will agree with me…that the origin of these arts was Nature herself, that the inspiration or model was the beautiful fabric of the world, and that the Master who taught us was that divine light infused in us by a special act of grace which has not only made us superior to other animals, but even similar…to God Himself.

It was to nature, or rather, to the people whom they saw with their own eyes, that the artists of the Renaissance turned first in their quest to paint their subjects as realistically, and thus plausibly, as possible, the intention being to evoke a profound sense of emotional recognition, connection, and empathy in the viewers of their works.

While the artists of the Italian Renaissance, perhaps in response to their relatively easy access to Roman sculpture, were fascinated by human anatomy, and especially by musculature—as is evident, for instance, in Michelangelo's frescos on the ceiling of the Sistine Chapel (1508–12)—those of the Northern Renaissance were notable for their uncompromising, "warts-and-all" approach to facial features, as well as for their increasing interest in both anecdotal scenes and true-to-life landscapes.

Close observation of natural models was therefore an essential prerequisite of realistic rendering, but Renaissance artists also experimented with, and eventually perfected, certain techniques that gave the perception of reality, including centrally arranged, symmetrical compositions; perspective (the art of translating the three dimensions of reality into two dimensions to give the impression of spatial depth); subtle palettes and types of brushwork (to achieve, for example, shadows, shading, *sfumato*, "smoky," and *chiaroscuro*, or light-and-shade, effects); and the use of oil paints (which enabled the creation of lifelike illusions of depth, detail, and luminosity through the application of layers of color).

Ultimately, however, it was the naturalistic appearance of their human subjects' bodies, combined with the convincing depiction of expressions, gestures, and body language, that captured the "dignity," animation, and dynamism of humankind, conveyed to viewers the nature of painted individuals' characters, feelings, and interaction, and thereby told a compelling story.

STORIES AND SECRETS

In his *Della pittura* (*On Painting*) of 1435, Leon Battista Alberti (1404–72), a noted Italian architect and prolific writer on the arts, stressed how vital it was that a picture should tell a story (*istoria* in Italian), so that the viewer should be left in no doubt as to its meaning. Alberti's contemporaries, the artists of the Renaissance, utilized a range of media and methods in their attempts to attain this aim. Some, they developed themselves, including such tricks of perspective as the modification of color and tone, foreshortening, and receding parallel lines leading to vanishing points, which, if successful, gave the impression that a scene depicting a past or imaginary event was being viewed in the present, through a window. Others, they inherited from their medieval predecessors, including the sequential-narrative form of composition, which may be compared to a comic strip in that the same character repeatedly appears in different situations within the same image.

And with most art being created as a focus for piety or to impress others, it was doubly important that those who looked at a painting instantly understood what was being depicted. This was often achieved by the inclusion of centuries-old—even archetypal—symbols and attributes drawn from a commonly recognized iconography that served to represent or identify when depicted in an appropriate context. In this way, devout viewers would know that a dove pictured above the figure of Christ symbolized the Holy Ghost, for instance, while the same bird portrayed alongside a voluptuous nude woman in a secular scene would be understood by those blessed with a little Classical learning to be the attribute of Venus, the Roman goddess of sensual love.

Yet some artists deliberately set out to encode hidden messages in their works, subtle communications that would only be understood by those in the know, an enlightened elite. Sometimes these took the form of *imprese*, or personal emblems, artfully incorporated into an apparently incidental feature (see, for example, Sandro Botticelli's *The Wedding Feast*, pages 140 to 143). Other symbols, among them anamorphic images (such as the distorted skull that can be seen in Hans Holbein's *The Ambassadors*, see pages 200 to 203), provided an opportunity for the artist to display his skill, as well as baffle the uninitiated viewer. Finally, the significance of still further, apparently incongruous, details—like the six toes on Joseph's left foot in Raphael's *The Marriage of the Virgin*, see pages 26 to 28—remains impenetrable, if, indeed, they were intended to have any covert meaning at all.

JOIN THE INITIATED!

Renaissance art may give you the thrilling sense of gazing through a window into another, magical world, but unless you understand its visual language, most of the information and wisdom encoded in its masterpieces will forever remain a mystery to you. So let *The Hidden Life of Renaissance Art* open your eyes to the symbols and secrets that teem below the surface, giving you a greater understanding of Renaissance society's piety, philosophies, values, endeavors, and achievements, as well as a rewarding insight into the thought processes of some the world's greatest geniuses.

Thanks to art, instead of seeing one world, our own, we see it multiplied and as many original artists as there are, so many worlds are at our disposal.
Marcel Proust, *Remembrance of Things Past: The Past Recaptured* (1913–27)

EXPRESSIONS OF PIETY

Set your affections on things above, not on things on the earth.

The New Testament Book of Colossians 3:2

Above: The Feast in the House of Levi (1573) *was one of the largest canvases of the sixteenth century, and was originally intended as a depiction of the Last Supper. Its artist, Paulo Veronese, was consequently investigated by the Roman Catholic Inquisition as to why there were apparently irrelevant and suggestive details in the painting.* **Top:** *A detail from Michelangelo Buonarroti's fresco* The Conversion of St. Paul, 1542–50 *(see pages 71–73).*

Almost all of the artworks created during the Middle Ages were religious. And while different genres and themes, including allegories, Classical subjects, portraits, and history paintings, became increasingly popular throughout Europe during the Renaissance era, Christian art continued to predominate.

Why this preference for sacred subjects? The simple answer is that with artists requiring payment for their work, the only lay individuals blessed with sufficient disposable income to commission paintings, who also craved the prestige conferred on patrons of art, and, moreover, understood that they were expected to set an example to their "inferiors," were society's leaders—monarchs, members of the aristocracy, and, increasingly, local nobility and wealthy merchants. And in an age in which visible devoutness was a prerequisite for social acceptance, let alone success, it was necessary to be seen to be a devoted Christian. But the most frequent commissioners of religious art by far were corporate bodies with a strong, if not overriding, interest in religion, such as the Italian *scuole* (charitable lay confraternities), religious orders, and representatives of the Roman Catholic Church's hierarchy, most notably the pope himself.

So while the ostensible purpose of religious works of art was to act as a focus for public or private prayer and devotion when hanging in a church, chapel, cell, or chamber, their very presence proclaimed the profound piousness, artistic discernment, and spending power of the person or people who had paid for them, whose "donor portraits" were often ingeniously incorporated into such devotional images.

PIETY IN THE AGE OF THE PLAGUE

Although commissioning works of art celebrating the glory of God undeniably bought social advantages, such cynical secular considerations were typically eclipsed by the sincere desire to ensure the salvation of one's soul.

The collective faith of ordinary people during the fourteenth and fifteenth centuries had not wavered since the Middle Ages, when Western Europe effectively corresponded to Christendom. And during the medieval period, Christendom had literally been at war with the "infidels" of Islam, fighting the Crusades in the Holy Land from the eleventh to the thirteenth centuries, while those who questioned the teaching of the all-powerful Church at home were persecuted as heretics. Satan, it seemed, was everywhere, and a combination of constant vigilance, instant stamping-out of evident evil, purity of mind, good works, and regular church-going was the only way to keep him at bay, and one's soul safe.

The Renaissance era may have seen certain bold individuals, notably Martin Luther (1483–1546), the German instigator of the Protestant Reformation, challenging the corruption that they saw within the Church, and questioning some of its teachings, but Western Europeans' fundamental trust in Christ and the redemption that Christianity promised remained unshaken. And as Christians, they believed that at the Last Judgment, they would be judged according to their behavior on earth. If found wanting, or sinful, they would be condemned to spend eternity suffering the unspeakable agonies of hell, where they would be at the brutal mercy of Satan and his devilish helpers; but if judged to have lived a good Christian life, they could expect to join God in heaven, where they would live in bliss forever after.

The Church stressed that the importance of finding favor with God through constantly being virtuous in thought, word, and deed (and being obedient to the Church's decrees) was paramount—after all, a human being's lifespan in earthly years is as nothing when compared with eternity—but humans are humans, no one is perfect, and lapses, or transgressions, often occurred. So from 1348, when the Black Death, or plague, arrived in the Mediterranean regions from China via the Crimea, those who had reckoned on having years ahead of them in which to mend their wicked ways or repent of their sins realized that there was a very real chance that their lives would be snuffed out in an instant should they fall victim to this terrible disease, and that hell probably awaited them. Indeed, by 1400, it is estimated that Europe's population had been cut by half, and although the pandemic of 1348 to 1350 was by far the most devastating, sporadic outbreaks of the plague occurred until the eighteenth century. Seeing men, women, and children sicken and die before their eyes, and whole communities wiped out within a matter of days, with no real understanding of either cause or cure, must have been a petrifying experience that left survivors traumatized. According to Philip Ziegler, writing in *The Black Death* (1969), "The terrors of the Black Death drove man to seek a more intense, a more personal relationship with the God who thus scourged him, it led him out of the formal paths of establishment religion…." And it also led to different ways of presenting religious art.

Above and below: *During the last two decades of the fifteenth century, Botticelli sketched almost one hundred scenes illustrating Dante's* Divine Comedy. *These hellish details are from the* Inferno: *above, Lucifer, and below, seducers and flatterers.*

HUMANIZING HOLINESS

The paintings that decorated churches during the Middle Ages appear rather crude to the modern eye. Although the limited media and materials that were available to medieval artists were partly responsible, this simplicity was also intentional. For in an age when very few people could read (only the most privileged members of society were literate), a church's wall paintings acted as a storybook, showing in pictures what could not be conveyed through the written word. In this way, ordinary church-goers became familiar with the tales told in the Bible, and also with the symbols and attributes that came to make up the iconography of Christianity. Not only were most of these perpetuated by Renaissance artists, but they are so deeply ingrained in the collective Christian consciousness that such scenes as a naked man and woman flanking a serpent-entwined apple tree still instantly suggest Adam and Eve and the Fall of humankind, as related in the Old Testament Book of Genesis.

Symbolically speaking, the vocabulary of devotional art changed little during the Renaissance, especially when the origin of certain seminal images was Biblical, such as the white dove that signifies the Holy Ghost (see Piero della Francesca's *Baptism of Christ*, pages 42 to 44, for further details). Similarly, portrayals of saints retained the attributes (traditional emblems, objects, or features) that had long helped to identify them when unsophisticated artistic tools and techniques made it difficult to distinguish one painted person from another—St. Agnes's lamb and long hair, for instance, or the instrument that had been responsible for a martyr's gruesome torture or death, like the wheel to which St. Catherine had been tied, with which she was invariably depicted.

What did change, however—partly in reflection of the reality- and human-oriented world view of the Franciscan order—was the style in which holy personages were painted, with the stiff, unnatural representations of the medieval, Byzantine-influenced era giving way to ever-more realistic figures, whose true-to-life expressions and gestures had the power to evoke a profound emotional response in viewers who were increasingly able to identify with them as people (especially if their features were those of a local beauty or bigwig or if the painted backdrop resembled the surrounding neighborhood). And that this was one of the most sought-after aims of painters of devotional scenes was confirmed by Leon Battista Alberti, who, writing in his *Della pittura* (*On Painting*), stated that it was crucial that a work of art "captures the eye of whatever learned or unlearned person is looking at it and moves his soul."

In addition, artists widened the scope of their source material to include scenes drawn from non-Biblical texts, such as the Apocrypha (or Pseudepigrapha), Jewish texts that, in the Roman Catholic tradition, are appended to the books of the Old Testament; the New Testament Apocryphal Gospels, which elaborate on the life of Christ, the Virgin, and many other early Christian characters; and, perhaps most importantly of all for illustrative purposes, Jacobus de Voragine's *The Golden Legend*, a thirteenth-century collection of anecdotal tales that added life and color to otherwise dull, worthy, and somewhat one-dimensional saintly personalities.

Kneeling before such paintings as Luca Signorelli's *The Martyrdom of St. Sebastian* (see pages 77 to 79), faced with the harrowing evidence of the saint's suffering, while at the same time knowing that his exemplary faith and fortitude had earned him a place in heaven, would have rein-

Below: These expressive, life-sized panels depicting the instantly recognizable Adam and Eve were painted by Albrecht Dürer in 1507. The figures are lifelike and animated, while Adam's active masculinity and Eve's passivity are partly conveyed by the difference in their skin tones.

forced a mystical sense of connection with this saintly being. And because this painting may, on one level, be interpreted as symbolizing resistance to infection by the plague, heartfelt prayers and pleas for immunity would have been directed toward Sebastian through his portrait. Indeed, those saints who were credited with particular powers of protection and patronage were the recipients of fervent prayers from appropriate groups of individuals: the citizens of Venice addressed themselves to St. Mark, for instance; goldsmiths' guilds venerated St. Eligius; those with sore throats implored St. Blaise for relief; and members of religious orders addressed their founders, such as St. Francis and St. Dominic.

Apart from Christ himself, the Virgin Mary was the most generally, and frequently, depicted figure in the devotional art of the Renaissance, for it was believed that as the mother of God, she had the divine ear, that she would take pity on those who petitioned her aid with prayer, and that as a tender-hearted soul, she would therefore intercede with God for them. With her cult blossoming early in this era, every aspect of her life was portrayed—from her immaculate conception to her assumption and coronation as queen of heaven (see *The Coronation of the Virgin*, pages 38 to 41)— with the emphasis being on her sweetness (as in "Madonna of Humility" portrayals, for example, which show her sitting on the ground), the joy and agony of her motherhood, and, significantly, her love of humankind. Indeed, it was during the medieval and Early Renaissance periods that Mary was increasingly depicted as the Virgin of Mercy (or Misericordia), sheltering vulnerable humans under her voluminous blue mantle or praying to her son on their behalf at the Last Judgment.

Above: La Sacra Conversazione, *by Lorenzo Lotto (also known as* Madonna and Child with Saints and an Angel, 1527–28)*. Lotto was heavily influenced by Giorgione in his portrayal of the Holy Family in an intimate and secular setting.* ***Below:*** *Botticelli's painting of St. Augustine of Hippo (1480) features a devout-looking man at his desk, with writing and reading materials and a bishop's miter.*

POPULAR SAINTS

Certain saints make frequent appearances in Renaissance art. Some of the most popular are listed below, along with the physical characteristics and attributes that may provide helpful clues in identifying them. Note that palm branches (and crowns) typically signify martyrs, and that haloes signal holiness.

Agatha *Appearance:* a young woman wearing costly-looking clothes. *Attributes:* severed breasts on a plate; pincers; a torch or fire.

Agnes *Appearance:* a young girl with long hair. *Attributes:* a lamb; an olive branch; a sword; fire. See *The Adoration of the Mystic Lamb*, pages 55 to 58.

Ambrose *Appearance:* an older man dressed as a bishop, with a miter and crozier. *Attributes:* a beehive; a book; writing instruments; a whip.

Andrew *Appearance:* an older man, with white hair and a beard. *Attributes:* a fishing net; a rope; a cross saltire (an "X"-shaped cross).

Antony of Egypt *Appearance:* an old man with a beard in a monastic robe. *Attributes:* a bell; a pig; a tau cross.

Antony of Padua *Appearance:* a man in Franciscan garb. *Attributes:* the Christ Child; a kneeling donkey; a flaming heart or fire; a lily; a cross; a book.

Augustine of Hippo *Appearance:* an older man dressed as a bishop, with a miter and crozier, or wearing a black habit. *Attributes:* books; writing instruments; a shell; an angel; a child; a flaming heart. See *The Vision of St. Augustine*, pages 83 to 86.

Barbara *Appearance:* a young woman with long hair. *Attributes:* a tower, perhaps with three windows; a ciborium; a cannon. See *The Adoration of the Mystic Lamb*, pages 55 to 58.

Bartholomew *Appearance:* a dark-haired, bearded man carrying a piece of his own flayed skin. *Attribute:* a knife.

Benedict *Appearance:* an old man with a white beard, wearing a black or white Benedictine habit. *Attributes:* a broken tablet; a broken sieve; a raven; a thorn bush.

Bernard *Appearance:* a man wearing a white Cistercian habit. *Attributes:* a dragon; a beehive; three miters.

Blaise *Appearance:* a man dressed as a bishop, with a miter and crozier. *Attributes:* a pig; carding combs; crossed candles.

Catherine of Alexandria *Appearance:* a young woman with long hair, often richly dressed, sometimes wearing a crown. *Attributes:* a wheel, sometimes broken or spiked; a sword; a ring.

Catherine of Siena *Appearance:* a young woman wearing a white or black-and-white nun's habit; sometimes displaying stigmata. *Attributes:* a lily; a book; a skull; a rosary; a crucifix; a crown of thorns; a ring.

Cecilia *Appearance:* a young woman with long hair. *Attributes:* musical instruments, especially organs; a lily; a rose.

Christopher *Appearance:* a large man wading through water. *Attributes:* a flowering or sprouting staff; the Christ Child on his back.

Clare *Appearance:* a gray nun's habit, with a knotted belt. *Attributes:* a monstrance; a lily; a cross; a lamp.

Cosmas and Damian *Appearance:* two young twin men. *Attributes:* identical red doctors' hats and robes; ointment containers; medical instruments.

Dominic *Appearance:* a black-and-white Dominican habit. *Attributes:* a black-and-white dog; a star; a rosary; a lily; a book.

Dorothy *Appearance:* a young woman with long hair. *Attributes:* a basket containing roses and apples; a crown of roses. See *The Adoration of the Mystic Lamb*, pages 55 to 58.

Eligius *Appearance:* a man wearing bishops' regalia, including a miter, and carrying a crozier, or wearing a smith's cap and apron. *Attributes:* pincers; hammer and anvil; golden chalice.

Eustace *Appearance:* a man wearing a soldier's uniform. *Attributes:* a stag with a crucifix between its antlers; hunting dogs; a brass bull. See *The Vision of St. Eustace*, pages 80 to 82; *Portrait of a Knight*, pages 167 to 169.

Below: A white-robed St. Bernard has a vision of the Virgin in this scene by Filippino Lippi (1480–86). **Right:** *In* The Mystical Marriage of St. Catherine of Siena *(1511), Fra Bartolommeo depicts the saint's spiritual union with God.*

Francis *Appearance:* a monk in a Franciscan habit and knotted belt; stigmata visible on his hands. *Attributes:* a crucifix; birds and animals; a lily.

George *Appearance:* a soldier on horseback. *Attributes:* a lance, sometimes broken; a dragon; a white flag with a red cross on it; a sword.

Giles *Appearance:* an older man, with a beard, wearing a white Benedictine habit. *Attributes:* a deer; an arrow; a lily.

Gregory the Great *Appearance:* an older man dressed as a pope, with a papal tiara and crozier. *Attributes:* a dove; Christ and the instruments of his Passion. See *The Coronation of the Virgin*, pages 38 to 41.

Helena *Appearance:* an older woman wearing a crown and costly-looking clothes. *Attributes:* a large cross; nails; a model of a church. See *The Miracle of the Relic of the True Cross on the Rialto Bridge*, pages 174 to 177.

Hubert *Appearance:* a man dressed as a huntsman or as a bishop. *Attributes:* a stag with a crucifix between its antlers; hunting dogs; a hunting horn. See *Portrait of a Knight*, pages 167 to 169.

James the Greater *Appearance:* an older man with a beard, sometimes wearing pilgrims' garb, including a cloak and hat; sometimes on horseback. *Attributes*: a pilgrim's staff and purse; a scallop shell; a sword. See *The Agony in the Garden*, pages 45 to 48.

James the Less *Appearance:* a young, bearded man similar in appearance to Jesus. *Attributes:* a fuller's club; a hatter's bow.

Jerome *Appearance:* an older man with a white beard, either nearly naked or wearing a cardinal's red hat and garb. *Attributes:* a stone; a skull; an hourglass; a crucifix; a book; writing instruments; a lion; a model of a church. See *The Meditation of St. Jerome*, pages 87 to 90.

John the Baptist *Appearance:* a baby or child; a dishevelled-looking man with dark hair and a beard,

Above: St. Lucy, *by Domenico Beccafumi, 1521.*
Below: Titian's St. Mark Enthroned, *1510.*

wearing a camel-hair or sheepskin tunic; his decapitated head on a dish. *Attributes:* a reed staff or cross; a lamb, sometimes bearing a cross; the Latin words *Ecce Agnus Dei*, "Behold, the Lamb of God"; an ax; water or a river; a baptismal cup; a honeycomb. See *The Virgin of the Rocks*, pages 32 to 34; *The Baptism of Christ*, pages 42 to 44; *The Descent into Limbo*, pages 52 to 54; *The Coronation of the Virgin*, pages 38 to 41; *The Allegory of the Old and New Testaments*, pages 132 to 136.

John the Evangelist *Appearance*: a young, clean-shaven man; an older man with a beard. *Attributes:* a book or scroll; writing instruments; an eagle; a cup or chalice containing a snake or snakes; a cauldron; a palm branch. See *The Agony in the Garden*, pages 45 to 48; *The Altarpiece of the Seven Sacraments*, pages 59 to 61; *St. John the Evangelist at Patmos*, pages 68 to 70.

Joseph of Nazareth *Appearance:* an older man with a white beard. *Attributes:* the Virgin and Child; a staff, sometimes with a lily, fleur-de-lis, white flower, or dove on top; carpentry tools. See *The Marriage of the Virgin*, pages 26 to 28.

Jude (Thaddeus) *Appearance:* a bearded man. *Attributes*: an ax; a club; a lance.

Julian *Appearance:* a young man, sometimes on a horse. *Attributes:* a stag; a falcon; a boat; a sword.

Lucy *Appearance:* a young woman with long hair, sometimes with a wounded throat. *Attributes:* two eyes on a dish; a candle or lamp; a sword; an ox.

Luke *Appearance:* a mature man. *Attributes:* a book or scroll; writing instruments; a winged ox; a painter's palette and brush.

Margaret of Antioch *Appearance:* a young woman with long hair. *Attributes:* a crucifix; a dragon; a pearl rosary.

Mark *Appearance:* an older man, with dark hair and a beard. *Attributes:* a book or scroll; writing instruments; a lion, often winged.

Martha   *Appearance:* a modestly dressed woman. *Attributes:* a bunch of keys; a ladle and dish or pot; an aspergillum; a dragon. See *The Conversion of the Magdalene*, pages 65 to 67.

Martin   *Appearance:* a man dressed as a Roman soldier, riding a horse, or as a bishop. *Attributes:* a cloak; a sword; a beggar; a goose.

Mary of Egypt   *Appearance:* an older woman cloaked in her long hair. *Attributes:* three loaves of bread.

Mary Magdalene   *See below.*

Mary Magdalene

Appearance: an attractive woman with long hair, often richly dressed and in red; an old woman cloaked in her hair. She may appear alone, or with the resurrected Christ in a *Noli Me Tangere* scene, or in depictions of the Crucifixion with the Virgin Mary, among others.

Attributes: a jar or pot, often alabaster; a mirror; jewelry; a skull; a crown of thorns; a crucifix; a whip; a book.

As featured in: *The Conversion of the Magdalene*, pages 65 to 67; *The Altarpiece of the Seven Sacraments*, pages 59 to 61.

Right: *Fiorentino's Descent from the Cross, 1523. Mary Magdalene is dressed in red, on her knees among the abject mourners.*
Below: *Titian's Noli Me Tangere, c.1512.*

Matthew   *Appearance:* a mature man, often bearded. *Attributes:* a book or scroll; writing instruments; a purse; an angel or winged male; a sword; an ax.

Maurice   *Appearance:* a black man dressed as a soldier. *Attributes:* a white flag with either a red cross or an eagle on it.

Nicholas   *Appearance:* an older man dressed as a bishop, with a miter and crozier. *Attributes:* an anchor; three moneybags or golden balls; three children in a vessel.

Paul   *Appearance:* an older man with short hair and a beard. *Attributes:* a book; a sword. See *The Conversion of St. Paul*, pages 71 to 73.

Peter   *Appearance:* an older man with short, white hair and a beard; often wearing yellow, blue, or green robes. *Attributes:* a fishing boat, net, or fish; a cockerel; crossed keys; chains; a papal tiara; a papal crozier; a book; an inverted cross. See *The Agony in the Garden*, pages 45 to 48; *The Coronation of the Virgin*, pages 38 to 41.

Philip   *Appearance:* a mature man, sometimes bearded. *Attributes:* a cross; a dragon; loaves of bread. See *St. Philip Exorcizing the Demon From the Temple of Mars*, pages 74 to 76.

Sebastian   *Appearance:* a young man, often nearly naked, tied to a tree. *Attributes:* arrows; bows. See *The Martyrdom of St. Sebastian*, pages 77 to 79.

Simon   *Appearance:* a mature man. *Attributes*: a book; a saw; a cross.

Stephen   *Appearance:* a young, clean-shaven man wearing a deacon's dalmatic and stole. *Attributes:* a stone or stones; a censer. See *The Adoration of the Mystic Lamb*, pages 55 to 58.

Theodore   *Appearance:* a man wearing a soldier's uniform, sometimes on horseback. *Attributes:* a spear or shield; a dragon.

Thomas   *Appearance:* a young, clean-shaven man. *Attributes:* a set-square or T-square; a belt; a dagger; a spear.

Ursula   *Appearance:* a long-haired young woman, richly dressed. *Attributes:* other young women; a crown; ermine; a pilgrim's staff; arrow(s); a white flag with a red cross on it; a ship. See *The Legend of St. Ursula*, pages 91 to 93.

Veronica   *Appearance:* an older woman wearing a veil or turban. *Attributes:* a cloth bearing the image of Christ's face.

Above: Germany's Albrecht Dürer (1471–1528) was the most important figure of the Northern Renaissance. His 1506 altarpiece The Feast of the Rose Garlands *was painted during a stay in Venice and is among his more Italian-influenced works. He has included himself on the far right of the painting, as the long-haired man leaning against a tree in the background.*

THE REFORMATION

The learning and scholarship encouraged by humanism led to a broadening and deepening of Biblical analyses, resulting in parallels being drawn between Old and New Testament characters and events (see, for instance, Dirck Bouts's *Abraham and Melchizedek*, pages 23 to 25), and even between the Bible and the mythical tales of Classical mythology (with Joachim Patenier's *Charon Crossing the River Styx*, see pages 108 to 111, fusing the Christian and Greco–Roman visions of the afterlife, for instance). Yet humanism also contributed directly to one of the biggest upsets of the medieval status quo: the Reformation initiated by Martin Luther in 1517, when he pinned his Ninety-Five Theses to the door of Wittenberg Castle's church.

Luther, a learned Augustinian friar, had been appalled, on visiting Rome in 1510, to see indulgences being sold, along with other flagrant examples of what he considered to be corrupt practices on the part of the Roman Catholic Church. His initial denunciation of such customs led to his challenging of the Church's interpretation of the Bible and ultimately its very authority, symbolized by the pope, its figurehead. Luther's arguments struck a chord in many Northern European regions, and inspired a number of prominent sympathizers—secular rulers among them—to follow his lead. (Tellingly, long before 1517, the targets of many of the critical artistic allegories of Northern Europe were representatives of the Roman Catholic Church.) England became a Protestant nation (in 1533), while after decades of strife, the Peace of Augsburg (1555) finally allowed Lutheran worship in the Holy Roman Empire (the region that equates to modern-day Germany).

The sober simplicity of the Bible-based, faith-focused Protestant vision pervades the art of the Northern Renaissance, with a profound religious element being discernible even in such straightforward portraits as Maerten van Heemskerck's *Pieter Jan Foppeszoon and His Family* (see pages 196 to 199), as well as in more overtly religious paintings like Hans Holbein's *Allegory of the Old and New Testaments* (see pages 132 to 136). Indeed, one of the hallmarks of Northern Renaissance art is the eloquent expression of complicated concepts through the use of subtle symbolism.

Lot and His Daughters

Albrecht Dürer

c.1496/1499, oil on panel, National Gallery of Art, Washington, DC

The annihilation of the cities of Sodom and Gomorrah offered Christian artists of the Renaissance—including the German painter Albrecht Dürer—an interesting alternative way of portraying the fate of incorrigible sinners and the salvation of the righteous to the more usual depictions of the Last Judgment or the infernal torments of hell. And although this fire-and-brimstone tale is related in the Old Testament Book of Genesis, references in the New Testament to the cities' destruction being "an ensample [sic] unto those that after should live ungodly," and to Lot being a "just" and "righteous" man who was "vexed with the filthy conversation of the wicked" (2 Peter 2:6–8), serve to sanction its relevance to devout Christians.

When Abraham complied with God's instruction to leave Haran for the Promised Land, his nephew Lot joined him, with Abraham eventually settling in Canaan, and Lot, on the plain of Jordan, in the city of Sodom, despite the men there being "wicked and sinners" (Genesis 13:13). God had already announced his intention of destroying Sodom to Abraham when two angels accepted Lot's hospitality, whereupon all of Sodom's menfolk surrounded his house, demanding that he hand them over for their sexual gratification, and then refusing Lot's offer of his two virgin daughters instead. After blinding the predatory Sodomites, the angels instructed Lot to leave, along with his wife and daughters. This Lot did, whereupon God ordered him to "Escape for thy life; look not behind thee" (Genesis 19:17), while conceding that his party could head for the city of Zoar rather than the mountains. As soon as Lot entered Zoar, God "rained upon Sodom and upon Gomorrah brimstone and fire from the Lord out of heaven" (Genesis 19:24). Lot and his daughters were safe, but his wife was no longer with them, for she had looked back, and had been turned into a pillar of salt in punishment for her disobedience.

*See also **Abraham and Melchizedek** (pages 23–25).*

Plumes of smoke rise into the sky from the burning city of Gomorrah. Gomorrah's name was forever after teamed with that of Sodom as a shorthand term for doomed dens of depravity. "And he looked toward Sodom and Gomorrah, and toward all the land of the plain, and beheld, and, lo, the smoke of the country went up as the smoke of a furnace" (Genesis 19:28). In symbolic terms, fire represents both punishment and purification.

The figure of Lot's wife is still recognizably female. Towers of salt remain a feature of the Dead Sea shoreline, and at least one is said to be Lot's wife.

Genesis (13:10) describes the plain of Jordan as being so well watered before the destruction of Sodom and Gomorrah that it could be compared to the "garden of the Lord", i.e., the Garden of Eden. Called the "salt sea" in Genesis 14:3, today this body of water is known as the Dead Sea, for its high mineral content—dominated by salt at 35 percent—is fatal to organic life.

One of Lot's daughters balances a bundle of possessions on her head. Her red dress is the color of blood, and thus of life, and may refer to her fecundity.

The box that Lot's other daughter is carrying has a lock, and therefore clearly contains such valuable items as money or jewelry that must be safeguarded from thieving hands. This box represents the family's material wealth.

A distaff, which was once used by women for spinning yarn from wool, represents womanhood and industrious homemaking, or woman's work, in the context of Christianity.

After leaving Zoar for the mountains, Lot's daughters feared that they would never again meet any men, and that they would therefore remain childless.

They therefore rendered Lot insensible with wine (maybe poured from the flagon that hangs from Lot's staff) and slept with him, the products of these incestuous unions being baby sons named Moab and Ben-ammi (or Ammon), the ancestors of the Moabites and Ammonites.

Lot's garment is lined with sheepskin. Genesis tells us that he had flocks of sheep, which represent the faithful in Christian art.

Lot appears to be carrying a basket of eggs, which represent fertility and the potential for new life, and may consequently allude to his numerous future descendents.

The Three Archangels and Tobias

Francesco Botticini

c.1470, tempera on panel, Galleria degli Uffizi, Florence, Italy

So powerful is the sense of movement and purpose conveyed by Francesco Botticini in the painting that once hung above the Cappini altar in Florence's Santo Spirito Church that you would be forgiven for mistaking it for a scene taken directly from the Scriptures. In fact, despite symbolic reference being made to many episodes that occur in the Old and New Testaments, *The Three Archangels and Tobias* is essentially a fanciful triple portrait of three archangels: Michael, Raphael, and Gabriel. Archangels, whose tasks include communicating God's will to humans, are said to belong to the third hierarchy of angels, along with princedoms and angels; the first comprising the orders of seraphim, cherubim, and thrones; and the second being made up of dominions, virtues, and powers. Three archangels are named in the Bible—Michael, Gabriel, and Raphael—and Jewish tradition makes mention of four more: Uriel, Chamuel, Jophiel, and Zadiel.

While Michael is a warrior and dispenser of justice, and Gabriel, an announcer of momentous births, Raphael is considered a guardian angel and healer. This characterization is largely due to the tale told in the Apocryphal, or Deuterocanonical, Book of Tobit. According to this, Tobit—a good man of Nineveh who had been struck blind—sent his son, Tobias, to collect money owed to him from Gabael, in Rages, part of Media, accompanied by Raphael in the guise of a mortal man named Azarias. It was Raphael who advised Tobias to cut the heart, liver, and gall bladder out of a fish that had attacked him and then to banish a demon afflicting Sara, his future wife, by burning the heart and liver, and finally, to restore his father's vision by rubbing fish gall over his eyes. Raphael's perceived powers of protection were believed to be so potent that before a beloved son departed on a potentially perilous trip, Renaissance fathers often commissioned paintings of him and Tobias, with the specification that Tobias should be given their offspring's features.

*See also **The Coronation of the Virgin** (pages 38–41).*

His shining armor, steely gray wings, and drawn sword identify this resolute-looking figure as Michael, the angelic leader of the heavenly host in the battle against evil and the vanquisher of Satan. His drawn sword also signifies his role as the uncompromising enforcer of God's will and the unswayable administrator of divine justice.

The lily is the attribute of Gabriel, symbolically doubling up as the messenger's staff (or scroll) traditionally carried by this archangelic herald and a floral reference to the chastity of the Virgin Mary, to whom Gabriel announced the news that she would conceive a son.

The Book of Tobit tells us that when Tobias and Raphael set off for Media, the young man's dog went with them. A canine companion is therefore nearly always depicted alongside Tobias. Dogs invariably denote fidelity in Christian art, but are regarded with distaste as unclean scavengers in Hebrew convention.

The golden orb that Michael, a divine representative, holds aloft in his left hand symbolizes the world, or the universe, and God's absolute dominion over it. As the weigher of souls at the Last Judgment, Michael may alternatively carry scales.

Raphael is generally portrayed wearing traveling garb, which may include a pilgrim's staff, a water container, a moneybag, and sandals, as here. He was regarded as the guardian angel of pilgrims, travelers, merchants, and young people.

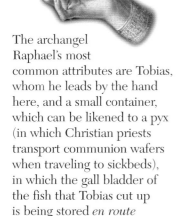

The archangel Raphael's most common attributes are Tobias, whom he leads by the hand here, and a small container, which can be likened to a pyx (in which Christian priests transport communion wafers when traveling to sickbeds), in which the gall bladder of the fish that Tobias cut up is being stored *en route* to Nineveh.

Although all three archangels' wings and haloes mark them out as angelic beings, Botticini has made a clear distinction between each archangel by tailoring the appearance of their wing feathers to their responsibilities. Raphael's wings are made up of peacock feathers, whose "eyes" may allude to the curing of Tobit's blindness and the restoration of his sense of sight.

Botticini has used artistic license in his rendering of the fish that, according to Tobit 6:2, leaped out of the River Tigris and "would have devoured him [Tobias]." For not only is this specimen far too small to have swallowed a young man (it is thought that a crocodile was the "fish" in question), but the Book of Tobit relates that Tobias and the angel cut up the fish and set aside the heart, liver, and gall before roasting the remnants and eating them. Only then did they resume their journey. A fish is one of the most ancient symbols of Christ himself and can additionally signify conversion and baptism.

Abraham and Melchizedek

Dirck Bouts

1464–68, oil on panel,
St. Peter's, Leuven, Belgium

irck Bouts's *Last Supper*, or *Holy Sacrament*, triptych, and particularly his blending of local faces and features with religious subject matter, must have delighted the leading lights of Leuven (or Louvain), a city in the duchy of Brabant (now in Belgium) that the cloth trade had made prosperous. Indeed, Bouts was appointed city painter in the same year as he completed this commission for the altarpiece of St. Peter's Church on behalf of the Confraternity of the Holy Sacrament.

Abraham and Melchezidek is one of the four smaller images that flank the triptych's central painting (*The Last Supper*), being paired with *The Feast of the Passover* in opposition to *The Gathering of the Manna* and *Elijah in the Desert*. The scenes depicted by this quartet, which were selected by two theology professors at Leuven University, are all drawn from the Old Testament and are all considered precursors to the Last Supper in some way, and thus also to the institution of the Christian sacrament of the Eucharist.

The story of the meeting of Abram (as the Hebrew patriarch Abraham was originally called) and Melchizedek can be read in Genesis 14:18–24. There it is told how after Abraham "smote" and vanquished Chedorlaomer (or Kedorlaomer), king of Elam, and his allies, Melchizedek, king of Salem—which many scholars believe to mean Jerusalem—went out to meet him, and offered him bread and wine as he blessed him, saying, "Blessed be Abram of the most high God, possessor of heaven and earth." Not only does the New Testament Book of Hebrews, in discussing this episode, compare Melchizedek to the "Son of God" (Hebrews 7:3), but explains that Melchizedek was worthy of Abraham's gift of a tenth of the spoils on account of "first being by interpretation King of righteousness, and, after that also King of Salem, which is, King of peace" (Hebrews 7:2), in other words, God's representative on earth. In Bouts's painting, the figure of Melchizedek can therefore be loosely linked with Christ.

See also **Lot and His Daughters** (pages 18–19); Abraham detail, *The Descent into Limbo* (page 54).

The king of Sodom is mentioned as being present at the meeting of Melchizedek and Abraham, and the richly dressed man accompanying the priest-king may therefore represent him. The faces of the two soberly garbed men behind him are so full of character that they were probably painted from life, and are most likely likenesses of two members of the Confraternity of the Holy Sacrament, the pious brotherhood that paid Bouts for his artistry and then donated their purchase to St. Peter's.

Although Genesis informs us that the encounter occurred in the valley of Shaveh, Bouts has depicted it as taking place in the countryside of the Low Countries, which is quite hilly around Leuven, with the cityscape in the background being unmistakably Flemish. It is possible that the ecclesiastical edifice that dominates all else is St. Peter's Church itself (whose towers had not yet been built), and that Bouts included the town hall (whose construction was completed in 1468) to its right.

Having come fresh from the battlefield, Abraham is portrayed as a warrior, wearing armor, and with a sheathed sword strapped to his side.

Melchizedek's headdress seems to combine a crown with a miter, no doubt because Genesis describes him as being both a king and "the priest of the most high God." In the messianic psalm 110 (verse 4), as well as in Hebrews 5:6 and 5:10 and elsewhere, the priestly order of Melchizedek is spoken of in association with Jesus Christ, the messiah of Christianity, the parallel being made explicit in Hebrews 6:20.

A reading of Genesis 14:18 tells us that Melchizedek "brought forth bread and wine," which Bouts has depicted in the hands of the priest-king, at the very center of the image. Those familiar with the iconography of Christianity would instantly make a link between the bread and wine offered by Melchizedek and the bread and wine that Jesus identified as being his body and blood and gave to his disciples to consume at the Last Supper. Indeed, every time that the faithful of Leuven took communion at the altar below Bouts's triptych, they would have been reminded of Christ's exhortation, "this do in remembrance of me" (Luke 22:19).

When Abraham heard that Chedorlaomer and his army had looted Sodom and Gomorrah and had kidnapped Lot, he rushed to rescue his nephew, taking with him 318 of his "trained servants." Bouts has portrayed some of Abraham's men bringing up the rear on the road behind their leader, many of them wearing fifteenth-century-style clothes, armor, and liveries.

The Marriage of the Virgin

Raphael

1504, oil on panel, Pinacoteca di Brera, Milan, Italy

The marriage of the Virgin Mary was a popular subject in medieval and Renaissance art, particularly in the central Italian region of Umbria, for the cathedral at Perugia believed itself to be the proud possessor of the mother of Christ's wedding ring. And because Raphael was trained by Perugino (Pietro Vanucci, c.1445–1523), a leading proponent of the Umbrian School who had himself tackled the *Sposalizio* ("marriage" in Italian) between 1500 and 1504, it is not surprising that he should have represented the theme in a similar fashion when commissioned by the Albizzini family to create a devotional image for the chapel of St. Joseph in San Francesco of the Minorities Church, in the Città del Castello, near Perugia.

Apart from certain Apocryphal texts, the main source for artists seeking information on the *Sposalizio* was the *The Golden Legend*, by the Italian friar Jacobus de Voragine (c.1229–98). When Mary, it was said, who was living at the Temple in Jerusalem, reached the age of fourteen, it was decided that she should marry. Competition for her hand was so fierce that the high priest sought divine help in making a decision. He accordingly instructed each of Mary's suitors to leave a rod, or staff, at the Temple overnight, announcing that should one flower, this would identify its owner as Mary's future husband. The next morning, the rod of Joseph, an older man, was alone in having burst into bloom, whereupon the Holy Ghost, in the form of a dove, alit upon it in divine confirmation that Mary should marry Joseph.

Writing in his *The Lives of the Artists* (1568), Giorgio Vasari notes that this painting "clearly reveals the growth of Raphael's skill as he refined Pietro's style and then surpassed it. In this work, a temple is drawn in perspective with so much love and attention that it is amazing to see the difficult problems Raphael sought to confront in such an exercise." Indeed, it is primarily his temple that makes Raphael's treatment so exceptional.

See also **Humanizing Holiness** (pages 12–13).

Mary gracefully extends her right hand so that Joseph can place a wedding ring on her finger. Although wedding rings are usually worn on the "ring finger," that is, the finger adjacent to the little finger, the finger in question can be on the left or right hand. The left was often favored because it was believed to be connected to the heart (which was once thought to be the seat of the emotions) by the *vena amoris* (the Latin for "vein of love"). The right hand, by contrast, was otherwise preferred to the "sinister" left because it represented "righteousness," and the convention in many Roman Catholic countries is for wedding rings to be worn on this hand.

During the second half of the sixteenth century, Protestant women initiated a switch to the left hand.

Mary was said to be so perfect that every man longed to make her his wife.

According to Apocryphal sources, Mary was one of seven virgins attached to the Temple who were given the coveted task of weaving a new veil for it. Here, some of the virgins watch the wedding of one of their number, just as they are said to have witnessed the miraculous flowering of Joseph's rod.

Raphael has depicted the Temple in Jerusalem as being Classical in style, and with sixteen sides, and it is thought that he was inspired to do so through an exchange of ideas with Donato Bramante (?1444–1514), who was born near Raphael's home town of Urbino and whom Raphael succeeded as architect of St. Peter's Basilica in Rome in 1514. Indeed, this painting and Bramante's Tempietto in Rome not only look familiar, but share a completion date of 1504. The ancient models for what, in Renaissance art, became the archetypal "pagan" temple were such circular structures as the Roman Temple of Vesta in Tivoli.

RAPHAEL URBINAS (Latin for "Raphael of Urbino"), MDIIII ("1504")—in other words, Raphael's signature and the year in which he finished the painting—appear to have been hewn in stone above the doorway to the Temple.

Raphael's masterly handling of perspective draws the viewer's eye from Mary and Joseph's hands and over the shoulder of the high priest, then traveling along the line described by the path and up the Temple steps to the doorway-framed sky, the painting's vanishing point. Symbolically speaking, this doorway may represent a gateway to God, while the steps that lead up to it may signify ascension to the spiritual realm. Christ's words to his disciples may also be significant: "I am the door: by me if any man enter in, he shall be saved" (John 10:9).

Joseph's beard marks him out as older than his fresh-faced rivals. The haloes above the bridal couple's heads highlight their sanctity.

Raphael has painted Joseph with bare feet, possibly in accordance with God's exhortation to Moses to "put off thy shoes from off thy feet, for the place whereon thou standest is holy ground" (Exodus 3:5), the suggestion being that the Temple grounds are sacred, as is the sacrament of marriage (especially when one of the marriage partners is the future mother of Christ). Look closer, and you will see that Joseph has six toes, which, according to an article in the *BMJ* (the erstwhile *British Medical Journal*), is a sign of "postaxial polydactyly," a genetic trait exhibited by at least one of Raphael's models. An alternative theory is that this sixth toe was not drawn from life, but was fashioned by Raphael to convey a covert message.

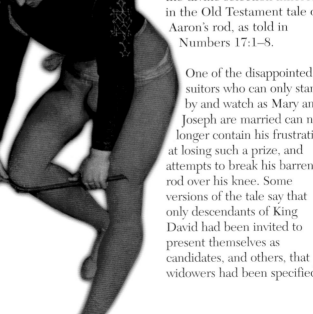

Joseph's rod is flowering, the only one amid those held by the crowd of men behind him to do so. The spontaneous blooming of his rod can be likened to the chaste Mary's miraculous conception of Jesus and her eternally pure, unsullied beauty, which is why lilies, her traditional attribute, irises (or a fleur-de-lis, their stylistic equivalent), or any white flower may be depicted at the apex of his staff; alternatively, a dove, the symbol of the Holy Ghost, may surmount it. (And a further link between Joseph's rod and Mary's virginity can be found in the Latin language, for while *virga* means "a rod," *virgo* denotes a virgin.) Joseph's floral staff also has echoes of the divine selection inherent in the Old Testament tale of Aaron's rod, as told in Numbers 17:1–8.

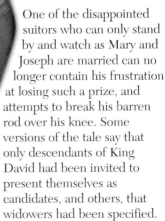

One of the disappointed suitors who can only stand by and watch as Mary and Joseph are married can no longer contain his frustration at losing such a prize, and attempts to break his barren rod over his knee. Some versions of the tale say that only descendants of King David had been invited to present themselves as candidates, and others, that widowers had been specified.

The Journey of the Magi to Bethlehem

Benozzo di Lese di Sandro Gozzoli

c.1460, fresco, Palazzo Medici-Riccardi, Florence, Italy

His politically motivated banishment from Florence in 1433 was a low point in the life of Cosimo de' Medici (1389–1464), the scion of an influential banking family. Yet by the time that this dazzling fresco was created, he had established himself as the virtual ruler of the nominally republican city, with plenty of male heirs to take his place. And a mere decade after his return, Cosimo clearly felt secure enough to commission Florentine architect Michelozzo di Bartolommeo (1396–1472) to build a new city palace—the Palazzo Medici—which was completed in the same year as fellow Florentine Benozzo Gozzoli's fresco cycle for the *palazzo*'s private chapel.

The fresco shown here is one of three, each painted on a different wall and each depicting one of the magi ("wise men" in Latin) who, according to the Gospel of St. Matthew (2:1–11), made their way to Bethlehem to worship the newborn Jesus. Over the millennia, this New Testament episode was embellished and reshaped, so that the magi were said to have numbered three, and rather than having been astrologer–priests, they became a trio of kings named Caspar, Balthazar, and Melchior.

In their popular incarnation as Jesus-adoring royals, the magi appealed to rich patrons of the arts who wished to advertise their wealth, as well as their piety, for the theme legitimized the display of costly clothes, expensive possessions, extensive retinues, and such impressive incidental details as the pursuit of "noble" pastimes like hunting, all of which can be seen here. The Medici were furthermore members of the Compagnia dei Magi ("Company of the Magi"), a lay brotherhood that made a stately procession through the Florentine streets on January 6, Epiphany, or the Three Kings' feast day, so that many elements of this painting may have been true to life. Indeed, not only can the faces of the most prominent Medici themselves be spotted on the left, but art historians believe that the likenesses of many of their friends, allies, and retainers were included in this mass portrait.

See also **The Medici Family** (pages 159–60), *Primavera* (pages 122–26), *The Wedding Feast* (pages 140–43).

The procession's starting point was a fortress occupying a commanding hilltop position in the distance. This has been identified as Cafaggiolo Castle, which dates from the fourteenth century and is situated to the north of Florence.

A Medici property, it was remodeled by Michelozzo di Bartolommeo at the same time as he was working on the Palazzo Medici.

The golden letters on his hat spell out the words OPUS BENOTII, which, loosely translated from the Latin, mean "the work of Benozzo." This annotation suggests that we are looking at the artist's self-portrait (middle-ground, left).

In front of Benozzi, his distinctive nose and jaw are hallmarks of the features of Lorenzo de' Medici (1449–92). Cosimo's grandson, aged around eleven here, would mature into Lorenzo *Il Magnifico* ("the Magnificent").

Standing next to Lorenzo is his brother Giuliano (1453–78), who was around seven years of age when Gozzoli immortalized his image. Giuliano would be murdered by his family's political enemies in 1478.

This is a portrait of Cosimo de' Medici himself (foreground, left). Then around seventy years of age, he had four years of life left to him.

The color of
Cosimo's mount,
and the length of its ears in
relation to those of the
thoroughbred horses that
others are riding, mark it out
as a donkey, or ass. It is said
that Cosimo really did ride a
donkey in order to signal his
essentially humble character,
as though he were a peasant
rather than one of the richest
men in Europe. He was,
however, following the highest
of examples, for Jesus had
elected to ride a donkey on his
entrance into Jerusalem: "And
Jesus, when he had found a
young ass, sat thereon; as it
is written" (John 12:14), the
reference being to the
prophecy contained in the Old
Testament Book of Zechariah
(9:9) "...behold, thy King
cometh unto thee: he is just,
and having salvation; lowly,
and riding upon an ass…"

Piero de' Medici
(1416–69),
Cosimo's heir,
precedes his
father a little
as they follow
the king. Piero
was the patron who instructed
Gozzoli, and who probably
suggested that the artist model
his work on the much-
admired *The Adoration of the
Magi* (1423), by Gentile de
Fabriano (*c*.1370–1427),
which had been commissioned
for Florence's Santa Trinità
Church by the Strozzi family,
rivals of the Medici. (As the
caller of the shots, it was
no doubt also Piero who
demanded that Gozzoli make
his original headdress, whose
outline is still evident, larger.)

A repetitive motif of rings—
denoting diamond rings—
each containing a letter that,
in sequence, spell out the
Latin word *semper* ("always")
is picked out in gold on the
red trappings of Piero's
mount. This was an *impresa*,
or personal emblem, of the
Medici family, signifying that
the dynasty would forever
remain unbreakably strong.

Piero's servant wears
the Medici livery,
which incorporates the
family colors of white,
green, and red (which, some
believe, together represent
the cardinal virtues of faith,
hope, and charity), as well as
their diamond-ring emblem.

His crown, white-
and-gold garb, and
youthful good looks
identify this figure
as the youngest, and
thus the most junior,
of the three kings,
who is usually
named as Caspar (although
Melchior is sometimes
specified instead). Caspar
may also represent youth
and the continent of Europe.

Oranges and orange trees
often feature in images
associated with the Medici
family, whose coat of arms
bore six red balls. If these
stylized heraldic devices
represent golden coins, they
may have referred to the
family trade of banking, or, if
they denote pills, to a former
medical business. With
oranges sometimes going
under the Latin name of
malus medicus ("medicinal
apple"), the pun is
unmistakable.

The gift with which Caspar is traditionally associated is frankincense, and the viewer can assume that the ornate container being raised aloft by the young king's retainer contains this aromatic resin, a symbol of divinity. This scene decorates the east wall; the angle of the hooves of the horses on the far right indicates that the viewer should now turn to the south wall, devoted to Balthazar and his attendants, and then to the west wall, Melchior's section.

The Virgin of the Rocks

Leonardo da Vinci

c.1491–1508, oil on panel, National Gallery, London, England

Question marks have always been associated with the "London version" of Leonardo da Vinci's *The Virgin of the Rocks*, long before *The Da Vinci Code* (2003) became a worldwide publishing phenomenon. For even disregarding the cryptic visual codes and audacious conspiracies suggested by U.S. writer Dan Brown, who wove this image into his best-selling thriller, a veil of mystery has obscured the exact circumstances of its creation, not least when infrared reflectography revealed a dramatically different underdrawing.

Regarding its history, it is thought that it is a reworking of an earlier painting of the same theme (which today hangs in the Louvre, in Paris, France) that was commissioned in 1483 by the Confraternity of the Immaculate Conception for an altarpiece in the San Francesco Grande Church in Milan. It seems that a dispute over payment caused Leonardo to sell the first work to a private buyer, and that this version was created as a replacement when satisfactory terms were eventually agreed. Yet it was not finished when it was erected in the oratory in 1508 (as is evident when you look at the angel's hand), nor was it all Leonardo's work, some less important details (such as the haloes) having been added by a lesser artist.

As for the choice of characters, inhospitable-looking setting, and hidden meaning, all can be explained. Although there is no basis for this episode in the New Testament, it was popularly believed that the Holy Family encountered Mary's cousin, Elisabeth, and her son, John, in the wilderness at the time of the Flight into Egypt. The rocky backdrop is in turn consistent with this story, and is also a metaphor for the Immaculate Conception, or the Roman Catholic dogma that Mary, like Jesus, was born free of Original Sin. For the Virgin Mary was often referred to in devotional texts as *lapis sine manu caesus* (Latin for "a rock cleft not by human hand"), while Christ was alluded to as *mons de monte sine manu hominis excisus* ("a mountain hewn out of the mountain not by human hand"). In addition, the Old Testament refers to God as a rock and refuge (2 Samuel 22:2–3).

See also **The Virgin of the Rose Bower** (pages 35–37).

The symbolism of the palm, a frond of which is seen here behind the infant John's head, dates back to ancient times, when the tree was associated with the sun. It came to represent victory to the ancient Romans, and palm branches were strewn in Jesus's path when he entered Jerusalem on a donkey. When a palm branch appears in Christian art, it signifies saintly martyrs' victory over death, and, indeed, as a man, St. John the Baptist was beheaded on the orders of King Herod before Christ's crucifixion.

In a detail added, it is thought, by an artist who was not Leonardo, the baby John carries the reed staff, surmounted by a cross, that is one of his attributes as a grown man. "The Baptist" would later baptize Jesus in the waters of the River Jordan, along whose banks grew reeds. New Testament sources (Matthew 14:5, for example) tell us that John was considered a prophet who foretold the imminent coming of the Messiah, and who therefore must have anticipated Christ's crucifixion, which explains the presence of the cross.

The letters *ECCE A...NUS* can just be discerned winding their way down the scroll entwined around John's hands as he leans toward Jesus in greeting. These represent the Latin phrase with which John greeted Jesus then they were adults: *Ecce agnus dei*, or "Behold the Lamb of God" (John 1:29).

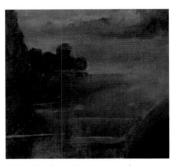

The body of water in the background may allude to the water with which John the Baptist baptized Christ (and others), and thus baptismal waters, the Christian sacrament of baptism, and initiation into Christianity. Equally, the blue sea (*mare* in Latin) may refer to Mary, as mother of Jesus and giver of life (represented by water) to the Son of God in his human incarnation.

A description contained in the Old Testament Song of Solomon (2:14), which is often applied to Mary, suits her perfectly here: "O my dove, that art in the clefts of the rock…thy countenance is comely."

The winged angel alongside Jesus is thought to represent the archangel Uriel, of Jewish tradition, who signifies the fire and wisdom of God.

Some versions of the story of this childhood meeting of John and Jesus relate that it was Uriel, rather than his mother, Elisabeth, who whisked the young John from danger and helped him to escape the Massacre of the Innocents.

Mary is often portrayed wearing a cloak of blue, the color that traditionally represents heaven, truth, faithfulness, and the waters of life.

She traditionally shelters and protects the vulnerable under her mantle's voluminous folds, and John is partly enveloped in it as she gently guides him toward her son.

In popular Christian lore, many individual flower species have special connections with the Virgin Mary, but in general, white blooms denote both her beauty and her chastity.

The Christ Child raises his hand in blessing as he acknowledges his older cousin. This hand sign symbolizes the Holy Trinity—three digits of the right hand, the thumb and first two fingers, being used to make it—and also heaven, the direction in which the two straightened fingers are pointing.

When stripped of their religious connotations, rocky caverns may denote the womb and the grave, and thus birth, death, and rebirth.

In this context, it may also be significant that after his crucifixion, Christ was laid "in a sepulchre which was hewn out of a rock" (Mark 16:46).

The Virgin of the Rose Bower

Stefan Lochner

c.1450, oil on panel, Wallraf-Richartz Museum, Cologne, Germany

When you compare German artist Stefan Lochner's portrayal of the Virgin and Child with Leonardo da Vinci's smokily *sfumato The Virgin of the Rocks* (see pages 32 to 34), the profound artistic shift that occurred during the fifty years that separate them is clear. Yet while Leonardo's trailblazing place at the forefront of Italian Renaissance art cannot be denied, Lochner is not so easily relegated to the ranks of workaday German exponents of the earlier International Gothic style. For the Cologne-based artist's use of geometry in conjuring up perspective, his delicate touch in conveying Mary's sweetness of nature, and the subtle symbolism in this meditational image (*Andachtsbild* in German) are just some of the clues that identify him as a lyrical link between the stiff Gothic and naturalistic Renaissance styles.

In *The Virgin of the Rose Bower*, Lochner has combined at least three traditional types of painting common to Marian iconography, or the ways in which Christ's mother may be represented. Firstly, Mary is depicted as the queen of heaven, as signaled by the crown whose jeweled floral motifs echo the appearance of the flowers that bloom around her. But rather than enthroning his queen, Lochner has drawn on the *Nostra Domina de Humilitate* (Latin for "Our Lady of Humility") type by depicting Mary sitting unpretentiously on the ground (albeit on a red bolster). And finally, by enclosing the mother of God within a rose bower and low walls from which flowers and fruit spill, Lochner has evoked the *hortus conclusus* ("enclosed garden") type, which alludes to Mary's simultaneous virginity and fertility, and which was inspired by the Old Testament book the Song of Solomon (4:12): "A garden inclosed [enclosed] is my sister, my spouse; a spring shut up, a fountain sealed." And that the *hortus conclusus* also signifies the Earthly Paradise is evident from the angels that surround Mary and the presence of God the Father, the Son, and the Holy Spirit.

*See also **The Virgin of the Rocks** (pages 32–34).*

The Holy Ghost is visible in the form of a white dove below a wise-looking God the Father; they are two components of the Holy Trinity.

God the Son is the third, and he is pictured as a baby perched on his mother's lap. As God the Father gazes down benevolently from on high, red-winged seraphim (one of the first hierarchy of angels) cluster around him.

A pair of angels pulls back the richly embroidered "cloth of honor" that casts a golden glow over Mary and the Christ Child to reveal this heavenly apparition.

A cross—the primary symbol of Christianity—formed by a window's mullion and transom can be seen reflected in the polished surface of the huge sapphire at the high point of Mary's crown, marking the outer edge of her radiant halo.

Not only is it said that the roses that grew in the Garden of Eden lacked thorns, but Mary, as the "new Eve," who would cancel out the sins of the first Eve, can be compared to a "rose without thorns," as well as to the "mystic rose of heaven," also being associated with the "rose of Sharon" referred to in the Song of Solomon 2:1. White roses are particularly representative of Mary's spotless purity, the Virgin having been born (as well as having given birth) as a result of Immaculate Conception, and therefore being free of the stain of Original Sin. Red roses, by contrast, evoke the blood of martyrs, including Christ's, along with charitable love. Here, white and red roses scramble up the trellis that frames Mary's figure.

Of all of the Virgin Mary's attributes, the lovely, fragrant lily, whose whiteness evokes her chastity, is most often seen alongside her. A description contained in the Song of Solomon 2:2—"As the lily among thorns, so is my love among the daughters"—is often applied to Mary.

A maiden clasping a unicorn can be discerned at the center of Mary's eye-catching piece of jewelry. Like the lustrous pearls with which it is studded, this motif is another reference to her purity, for belief in unicorns was once widespread, as was the theory that these fantastic creatures could only be caught with the help of a young virgin, whose virtuousness would attract the unicorn, which would then fall asleep in her lap. Because its horn was thought to render a snake's (i.e., Satan's) poison harmless, the unicorn became a symbol of Christ, so that the maiden and unicorn can together signify Mary and Christ.

The Christ Child holds an apple that a nearby angel has handed to him. The apple's significance relates to the fruit of the Tree of Knowledge of Good and Evil that grew in the Garden of Eden, which was eventually associated with the apple.

Because Adam and Eve's action in tasting this forbidden fruit precipitated the Fall of humankind from divine grace, the apple in the hand of Christ signals that this is the "new Adam," who will redeem believers from the Original Sin with which God cursed the descendants of Adam and Eve, and who will save them from eternal damnation.

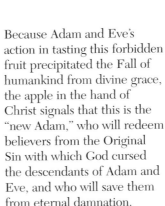

Scenes of paradise often include an angelic orchestra, for sweet music symbolizes the divine harmony of creation. This angel accompanies his fellow musicians on a portative organ.

Violets are symbolically linked to the Virgin Mary because they are regarded as unassuming little flowers that bow their heads modestly, thereby obscuring their sweet beauty. In Christian lore, the white violet turned purple—the color of mourning—when it witnessed Mary's grief at her son's crucifixion. Violets can also signify Christ's humility in being willingly born a mere man, which is why they often feature in images of the Madonna and Child.

While the strawberry's simple white flowers can, like daisies, be equated with Mary's innocence, its tripartite leaves symbolize the Holy Trinity, and its sweet, red fruit, Christ, and the blood that he shed during his Passion. According to the Roman poet Ovid, writing in his *Metamorphoses*, strawberries were among the fruits that nourished humankind during the Golden Age, which is why Christian artists have frequently included them in their representations of the Earthly Paradise.

The Coronation of the Virgin

Enguerrand Quarton

*1454, oil on panel, Musée de l'Hospice,
Villeneuve-les-Avignon, Anjou, France*

The Coronation of the Virgin Mary, belief in which had spread throughout Europe during the Middle Ages largely thanks to Jacobus de Voragine's (*c.*1229–98) book, *The Golden Legend,* is one of the most popular themes in Marian iconography. Yet it goes unmentioned in the New Testament, and can instead be traced back to later, Apocryphal texts. Although details of Mary's death ("Dormition") and ascent ("Assumption"), body and soul, into heaven, of which she was then crowned queen by her divine son Jesus, vary from source to source, it is said that she died between three and fifteen years after Jesus and was buried in either Jerusalem or Ephesus. When her tomb was subsequently opened, her corpse had disappeared, however, indicating that she had been received into heaven.

French artist Enguerrand Quarton's treatment of the subject may be one of many, but is exceptional for a number of reasons, not least its striking boldness. Commissioned by Jean de Montagnac, abbot of the Carthusian monastery of Villeneuve-les-Avignon, in the Provence region of France, the contract between patron and painter, dated April 24, 1453, survives, giving us a fascinating insight into the artist's brief. The painting was destined to hang above an altar dedicated to the divine triad of God the Father, Son, and Holy Spirit, and the first specified point was the way in which the Holy Trinity should be portrayed: "*…on doit voir la Sainte trinité, sans aucune différence entre le père et le fils; Le Saint-esprit doit avoir la forme d'une columbe…*" that is, with God the Father and God the Son appearing identical, and the Holy Spirit assuming the form of a dove. Although the Virgin Mary's appearance was left up to Quarton (as were other elements of the painting, including some of the members of the heavenly "court"), the contract went on to stipulate other "must-haves," such as representations of the cities of Rome and Jerusalem at the worldly level.

See also **The Virgin of the Rose Bower** (pages 35–37).

The host of red angels surrounding the Holy Trinity and Virgin Mary are seraphim. The blue faces of angelic cherubim can be seen within the celestial cloud that supports the Holy Trinity.

Jean de Montagnac, wearing the white habit of a Carthusian monk, kneels in prayer at the base of a cross bearing the crucified Christ, which the donor himself asked to be painted on the Mount of Olives ("*les Mont des Oliviers*"). Belief in Christ, and obedience to the teachings of the Church, may redeem his sins and eventually earn him a place in first purgatory, and then heaven, after he has departed this earth. The limestone cliffs in the distance are thought to have been inspired by those at L'Estaque, near Marseilles.

Mont Sainte-Victoire, a natural landmark near Aix-en-Provence, is believed to have served as the model for this mountain.

His brown, belted habit identifies this tonsured monk as a Franciscan.

An angel helps a former pope out of the pit that is purgatory, where his venial sins were purged following his death. Other hopefuls stand in line, enduring purgatory's purifying flames and soul-improving punishments in the hope that their patient submission will reap heavenly rewards.

St. John the Baptist is recognizable from his scruffy appearance and position at the head of a contingent of Old Testament patriarchs and prophets, who, like him, are believed to have foretold the coming of Christ.

Kings and emperors join the princes of the Church in adoring the Holy Trinity and Virgin Mary.

A servant of Satan tugs at the leg of a sinner fruitlessly trying to escape his hellish fate.

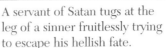

These wide-eyed innocents may have died in childhood, but because they had been baptized before they departed this world, were certain to be received into heaven rather than being dispatched to limbo.

In the distance, angelic escorts can be glimpsed carrying the souls of the blessed up to heaven.

These babies, in their underground cavern, died before they could be baptized, condemning them to spending eternity in uneventful limbo. Their closed eyes signify that the vision of God has been denied to them.

Quarton's interpretation of the Basilica of St. Peter stands in the center of the city of Rome, the seat of the pope and heart of the Roman Catholic Church. Another prominent building to the left is the Castel Sant'Angelo, which abuts a bridge over the River Tiber.

This scene (above, left) represents the episode of the burning bush, as related in the Old Testament Book of Exodus (3:2–6), when God revealed himself to Moses. The burning bush, whose woody twigs remained miraculously unconsumed by the flames, can also symbolize Mary, whose virginity remained unviolated by motherhood. To the right, the court jester, slumped on the ground on the earthly plane, signifies human folly. The church (modeled on Sainte-Croix de Jérusalem in Rome) has been depicted in cross-section so that the pious viewer may discern the figure of Christ within and link this scene with the Mass of St. Gregory the Great. According to legend, St. Gregory the Great (?540–604) prayed for a sign during Mass to convince a doubter in his congregation that the Eucharistic wine and bread really were the flesh and blood of Christ, and was rewarded by the materialization of a vision of the crucified Christ, along with the instruments of the Passion, above the altar.

The archangel Gabriel, who broke the news of her pregnancy to the Virgin Mary on the occasion of the Annunciation, stands alongside an angel who is plucking his harp and making the divine music that evokes the harmony of heaven. It is his ornate, fleur-de-lis-tipped messenger's staff, around which a scroll bearing Latin text—perhaps his message to Mary—winds, that identifies him as Gabriel.

In Quarton's imagination, Jerusalem's walls are punctuated by towers whose domes are evocative of the East, and keen-eyed scrutinizers may spot a black imp balancing on one of them.

Jerusalem may represent the "Old Law," or Judaism, while Rome may denote the "New Law," or Christianity. Indeed, it is not mere coincidence that Quarton has situated hell directly below Jerusalem, while Rome is sandwiched between angels and purgatory

This anonymous male figure represents everyman, as do others next to him (and some of them, everywoman), suggesting that a privileged position in earthly society is not a prerequisite when it comes to being welcomed into the City of God (*Civitas Dei* in Latin), as St. Augustine of Hippo (354–430) described paradise.

While the nuns are marked out as such with wimples, their long, flowing hair signals that those next to them are the female virgin saints who were martyred for their refusal to renounce their belief in Christ.

The coat of arms behind him (above) point to the man of the Church kneeling before Christ's sepulcher being Guillaume de Montjoie, the provost of a church in Aoste and a friend of Jean de Montagny, who died in 1451.

A balding, bearded, sturdy-looking St. Peter leads the apostles in witnessing the crowning of Mary as queen of heaven. Below him, their different types of headgear tell us that the blessed personages wearing tall, white miters were bishops in life; that those with low-crowned, broad-brimmed, scarlet hats were cardinals; and that the figure wearing the tiara, whose three crowns symbolize the Holy Trinity, was a pope.

Those guilty of the seven cardinal, or deadly, sins of avarice (*avaritia* in Latin), envy (*invidia*), pride (*superbia*), sloth (*acedia*), anger (*ira*), gluttony (*gula*), and lust (*luxuria*) will suffer the terrible torments of hell for eternity, which are being enthusiastically administered by the hideous minions of Satan.

Quarton's impression of the Temple, or else of the Dome of the Rock (which marks the spot where Abraham nearly sacrificed Isaac, and from which, according to Islamic tradition, Muhammad rose to heaven), dominates the city of Jerusalem, a city that de Montagnac had visited on a pilgrimage. Two men kneel in front of Mary's recently vacated tomb in the Valley of Josaphat. It may be that the man wearing chain mail and robed in red is a portrayal of Jean de Montagnac's brother, Antoine, who had predeceased him, and that his highly elaborate helmet is depicted to his right. The other person may be another likeness of Jean.

The Baptism of Christ

Piero della Francesca

1450s, egg tempera on poplar panel, National Gallery, London, England

Although the figure of Christ is positioned at the center of this painting—itself once the central panel of a polyptych—the context in which it was commissioned suggests that the most significant portrait in this baptismal scene is that of St. John the Baptist. For Italian artist Piero della Francesca painted *The Baptism of Christ* as an altarpiece for a chapel dedicated to St. John the Baptist (San Giovanni Battista in Italian) in the Camaldolese abbey situated in his Tuscan hometown of Borgo San Sepolcro (or Sansepolcro, as it is now spelled). This serene composition was therefore intended to provide a focus for the collective contemplation of the hermitlike Camaldolite monks, who spent most of their days isolated in individual cells, only gathering together to recite the prayers of the Divine Office. Given their austere way of life, it would have natural for the Camaldolites to have identified with this ascetic, desert-dwelling saint, who foretold the coming of the Messiah (Christ) and urged those who would listen to prepare themselves by repenting of their transgressions.

As his name indicates, it was St. John the Baptist who first practised baptism as a ritual way of symbolically washing away the sins of penitents in the waters of the River Jordan. And four of the New Testament Gospels—Matthew 3:13–17; Mark 1:9–11; Luke 3:21–3; and John (the Evangelist) 1:29–34—relate that he baptized his cousin, Jesus Christ, although the Gospel of St. Matthew (3:14) explains that he was initially reluctant to do so, feeling himself unworthy of the task. As "the Precursor," John "baptized with the baptism of repentance" (Acts 19:4), yet this did not constitute the sacrament of baptism that today still signifies purification, spiritual rebirth as a Christian, and acceptance into the Christian community. For that instead faithfully follows Christ's instruction to his disciples, "Go ye therefore, and teach all nations, baptizing them in the name of the Father, and of the Son, and of the Holy Ghost" (Matthew 28:19).

See also **The Virgin of the Rocks** (pages 32–34), **The Naming of John the Baptist** (pages 62–64).

Art historians have identified this tree as a walnut, and have linked it to a local legend with which the Camaldolites would have been familiar. This concerns two pilgrims, named Arcano and Egidio, who returned from Jerusalem bearing holy relics, fell asleep in the Valle di Nocea ("Valley of Walnut Trees" in Italian) on their way home, and then awoke to see the relics in the branches of a walnut tree. Unable to retrieve them, they built a shrine on the spot, around which, in time, sprang up the settlement of Borgo San Sepolcro. And in time, too, Arcano and Egidio were canonized, and were especially venerated by the citizens of the "Village of the Holy Sepulcher."

A keen experimenter with perspective, Piero employed foreshortening in depicting the dove, or Holy Ghost, so that its shape echoes that of the clouds, underlining its heavenly origin. It is from this New Testament episode that the artistic convention of using a dove to symbolize the Holy Spirit is derived, for it is told, in Luke 3:22, that as Jesus was being baptized, "the Holy Ghost descended in a bodily shape like a dove upon him, and a voice came from heaven, which said, Thou art my beloved Son; in thee I am well pleased."

Although Matthew 3:16 hints that Jesus was baptized by means of total immersion ("And Jesus, when he was baptized, went up straightaway out of the water"), Piero has depicted John trickling water from the River Jordan over his cousin's head from a dish.

The style of its buildings have led researchers to believe that the town that can be glimpsed in the distance is likely to have been inspired by Borgo San Sepolcro.

The Gospel of St. Luke (3:23) tells us that Jesus was around thirty years old at the time of his baptism, and Piero has represented him as a well-built man in the prime of life. In his *The Lives of the Artists* (1568), Giorgio Vasari states that, "Piero frequently made clay models, which he draped with wet cloths arranged in countless folds in order to sketch them and use them in various ways."

The tree stumps behind Christ allude to John's speech to the multitude of people who presented themselves for baptism, in which he told them, "now also the axe is laid unto the root of the trees: every tree therefore which bringeth not forth good fruit is hewn down, and cast into the fire" (Luke 3:9), this metaphor referring to "fruits worthy of repentance," and thus to individuals who merit God's salvation. (*See also* page 48.)

John's appearance accords with the description given in Matthew 3:4: "And the same John had his raiment of camel's hair, and a leathern girdle about his loins…" As a deeply spiritual loner and inhabitant of the wilderness, John was utterly unconcerned with sensory pleasures, dressing solely for practicality (in animal skins, the only materials to hand) and eating locusts and wild honey to keep body and soul together.

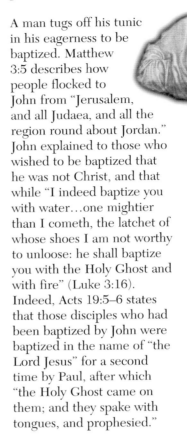

Their wings identify this trio of witnesses to Christ's baptism as angels. Some scholars have suggested that these three heavenly beings emphasize the three divine components of the Holy Trinity. Although we can see God the Son and God the Holy Spirit, God the Father appears to be unrepresented, prompting speculation that his image was portrayed in a separate panel, which was hung directly above, and in line with, the Holy Spirit and Jesus.

Alternatively, God the Father's presence may have been indicated by the golden rays—now hardly visible—that Piero painted above the dove.

A man tugs off his tunic in his eagerness to be baptized. Matthew 3:5 describes how people flocked to John from "Jerusalem, and all Judaea, and all the region round about Jordan." John explained to those who wished to be baptized that he was not Christ, and that while "I indeed baptize you with water…one mightier than I cometh, the latchet of whose shoes I am not worthy to unloose: he shall baptize you with the Holy Ghost and with fire" (Luke 3:16). Indeed, Acts 19:5–6 states that those disciples who had been baptized by John were baptized in the name of "the Lord Jesus" for a second time by Paul, after which "the Holy Ghost came on them; and they spake with tongues, and prophesied."

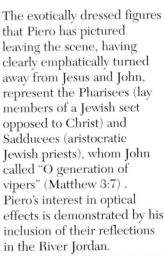

The exotically dressed figures that Piero has pictured leaving the scene, having clearly emphatically turned away from Jesus and John, represent the Pharisees (lay members of a Jewish sect opposed to Christ) and Sadducees (aristocratic Jewish priests), whom John called "O generation of vipers" (Matthew 3:7). Piero's interest in optical effects is demonstrated by his inclusion of their reflections in the River Jordan.

(Left) It appears as though one of the angels is standing ready to clothe Christ in the robe that he has slung over one shoulder.

The Agony in the Garden

Andrea Mantegna

c.1460, tempera on panel, National Gallery, London, England

It seems that the Agony in the Garden, as Christ's personal crisis following the Last Supper is called, preoccupied the nearest and dearest of Nicolosia Mantegna, née Bellini, for some years. For not only did her husband, the Paduan artist Andrea Mantegna, address it at least twice (the earliest version, dating between 1457 and 1459, can today be seen in the Musée des Beaux-Arts in Tours, France), but her brother, Giovanni Bellini (*c.*1430–1516), painted it, too, in about 1465. Moreover, it seems that the inspiration behind all of these interpretations was a drawing in the hand of Jacopo Bellini (*c.*1400–*c.*1471), Mantegna's father-in-law and Nicolosia and Giovanni's father. Of the four, the panel reproduced here, which Mantegna created in around 1460, is the most striking, its stratified rocks, swirling curves, and oppressive colors all evoking a queasily nightmarish sense of anxiety and dread that perfectly complements the tragic subject matter.

The term the "Agony in the Garden" refers to Christ's very human moment of terror at the thought of the violent death that he knew awaited him, as narrated in three of the New Testament Gospels: Matthew 26:36–46; Mark 14:32–42; and Luke 22:39–46. The evangelists tell us that after the Last Supper, Jesus led his disciples (apart from Judas, who had already set off on his mission of betrayal) to the Garden of Gethsemane, on the Mount of Olives, and asked Peter, James, and John to keep watch while he prayed. Yet the three disciples could not keep their eyes open, and Christ was repeatedly obliged to wake them. Alone, Christ struggled to come to terms with what was about to befall him, "being in an agony [Christ] prayed more earnestly: and his sweat was as it were great drops of blood falling down to the ground," according to Luke 22:44. Finally, Christ addressed God the Father with the accepting words "thy will be done" (Matthew 26:42). And it was as he roused the sleepers for the final time that the treacherous Judas approached him at the head of a hostile crowd, kissed him, and thereby sealed his fate.

See also **The Man of Sorrows in the Arms of the Virgin** (pages 49–51), **Jerusalem detail** (page 41).

Luke 22:43 relates that as Christ prayed, "there appeared an angel unto him from heaven, strengthening him." Rather than one angel, Mantegna has chosen to portray five *putti* (Italian for "boy"), who resemble the Classical, cherubic depictions of Eros/Cupid, the winged personification of divine love. They are displaying some of the Instruments of the Passion, among them the pillar of flagellation, the sponge, and the lance, the centerpiece being the cross on which Christ will be crucified. These signs to Christ that his self-sacrifice is God's will may sometimes be replaced with a chalice and communion wafer, representing the Eucharist, and visually echoing Christ's plea to God: "take away this cup from me" (Mark 14:36), by which he meant the decision of God that he should die a gruesome death.

It is surely no coincidence that the shape of the rock beneath the cloud supporting the angelic vision brings to mind an altar, which itself symbolizes a sacrificial table, at which the faithful receive the Eucharist (the bread and wine that Christ equated with his flesh and blood) in Christian churches.

Mantegna's rabbits may add a playful element to this dramatic scene, but this long-eared creature scampering up the rock also represents humankind's attempts to achieve closeness to God.

The rough steps that have been hewn out of the rock represent ascent to the divine plane.

Jesus's halo encircles a cross, mirroring the one on which his eyes are fixed, both of which emphasize his destiny.

Mantegna was an educated man, whose interest in Italy's ancient Roman past, in archaeological finds, and in buildings dating from the Classical period is evident in many of his works. In his vision of Jerusalem—depicted here as a walled city—we can, for instance, make out a circular building, probably a theater, similar to Rome's Colosseum, and next to it a sculpted column supporting a statue of a rider, another typically Roman-style edifice. His crescent-topped towers are reminiscent of later Islamic mosques, but because the crescent once symbolized Byzantium, they may simply signify an Eastern setting.

The three disciples whom Christ asked to keep watch lie only a stone's throw away from him, yet sleep has made them utterly oblivious to Christ's emotional crisis, despite his words to them: "My soul is exceedingly sorrowful" (Matthew 26:3). His white hair and beard mark out Peter, while the book that he is clutching (symbolizing his Gospel) identifies the figure on the right as John (the Evangelist), which means that the central sleeper is John's brother, James.

The arrangement of the rocks above Peter's head suggests an entrance, reinforcing the impression that Christ is kneeling on a rock similar to the stony sepulcher in which he will be entombed. It is therefore another visual reference to his impending death, but also to his resurrection.

While the dead tree from which it has split may denote sin and death (in contrast to the flourishing sapling's redemptive symbolism), because it provides a means of reaching Christ and his disciples, this bridgelike piece of timber offers the hope of spiritual salvation.

The sapling that has sprouted from the otherwise barren rock is a vigorous specimen, unlike the tree on which the vulture is perched. It symbolizes Christ's power to redeem believers' sins, and the new life that that they may hope to enjoy in heaven after their deaths, thanks to his own sacrifice.

The timber, below, may also allude to the branch from the Tree of Knowledge of Good and Evil that is said to have been used as a bridge at the time of King Solomon, and that was later incorporated into the cross on which Christ was crucified, as some believe (*see* page 174).

These white birds have been identified as pelicans, symbols of Christ himself—*nostro Pellicano,* "our pelican," as the poet Dante called him in his masterpiece *The Divine Comedy* (1306–21; *Paradiso* 25:112). This association is derived from the once prevalent, albeit erroneous, belief that pelicans nourished their young by ripping open their own breasts with their sharp beaks and selflessly feeding their offspring their flesh and blood, an assumption that has an obvious parallel with Christ's self-sacrifice and the Eucharist.

The tree stumps lining the garden path may illustrate John the Baptist's words to the Pharisees and Sadducees: "And now also the axe is laid unto the root of the trees: therefore every tree which bringeth not forth good fruit is hewn down, and cast into the fire" (Matthew 3:10). (*See also* page 44.)

Judas (significantly lacking a halo, unlike the other disciples) points the way toward Jesus as he walks at the forefront of the procession that Matthew (26:47) describes as being "a great multitude with swords and staves, from the chief priests and elders of the people."

Black birds are generally regarded as portents of doom in the lexicon of symbolism, while vultures denote death, but also purification, for they pick the bones of corpses clean of flesh that would otherwise blacken and rot in putrefaction.

The artist has secreted his signature in the rock above the disciples' heads: "OPUS ANDREAE MANTEGNA."

The Man of Sorrows in the Arms of the Virgin

Hans Memling

1475, oil on panel, National Gallery of Victoria, Melbourne, Australia

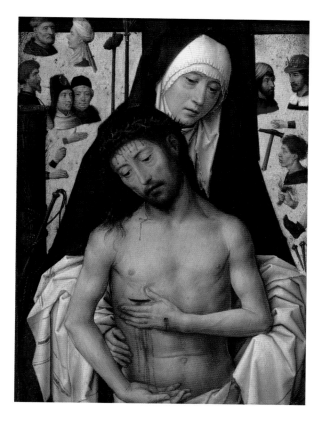

We know that by the time that he painted his poignant *The Man of the Sorrows in the Arms of the Virgin*, the German-born artist Hans Memling had established himself in Bruges, in the duchy of Burgundy. What is less certain, however, is exactly who commissioned Memling to create this devotional image, although because it is thought to be a triptych's central panel, it is likely to have been destined to hang above an altar. The Man of Sorrows (*Vir Dolorum* in Latin) was, moreover, a popular subject for altarpieces, for its elements echoed the legendary appearance of Christ to St. Gregory the Great (?540–604) and his congregation during Mass (*see* detail, page 40).

As is traditional in such representations, at least two of Christ's five bleeding wounds—one in each hand, one in each foot, and one in his side—are clearly visible in this half-length portrait, and blood from the deep scratches inflicted by the crown of thorns drips from his forehead, too. All around him are reminders to the faithful of the terrible torments that he endured during his Passion ("Passion" being derived from the Latin word *passio*, which means "suffering"), as related in all four New Testament Gospels, in the form of the faces, hands, and feet of those who contributed to his suffering, or sent him to his death, and some of the many *arma Christi* ("instruments of Christ" in Latin, and consequently "instruments of the Passion"). The most important instrument of the Passion— indeed, it has assumed such significance that it now symbolizes Christianity itself—is the cross, part of which can be seen looming darkly behind the Virgin Mary. The inclusion of Christ's weeping mother in this somber scene means that it may furthermore be classified as falling into the *La Pietà* (Italian for "Our Lady of Pity") category of Marian iconography, in which the devastated Mary supports the broken body of her son following his Deposition from the cross.

Peter, the panic-stricken disciple who denied all knowledge of Christ three times before the cock crew, is depicted here as a mature man with a characteristically short beard and haircut.

*See also **The Miracle of the Relic of the True Cross on the Rialto Bridge** (pages 174–77).*

The woman facing Peter is Caiaphas's maid, who prompted him to lie about his association with Christ when, having recognized him, she said, "And thou also wast with Jesus of Nazareth" (Mark 14:67).

The money bag around his neck identifies Judas Iscariot, the disciple who betrayed Christ for thirty pieces of silver (and we may assume that it is they that are causing his purse to bulge).

Caiaphas, the Jewish high priest who pronounced Jesus guilty of blasphemy for confirming that he was the "Son of God," is recognizable from the gold disk adorning his headdress, a symbol of priesthood (Exodus 28:36–38). The man next to him is Annas, his father-in-law, to whom Christ was first taken after his arrest, according to John 18:13, 24.

The rope that bound Christ has been wound around the pillar of Flagellation, securing to it the scourge that was used to whip him, along with a bunch of birch twigs.

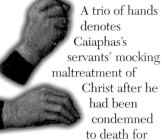

A trio of hands denotes Caiaphas's servants' mocking maltreatment of Christ after he had been condemned to death for blasphemy: "And some began to spit on him, and to cover his face, and to buffet him, and to say unto him, Prophesy: and the servants did strike him with the palms of their hands" (Mark 14:65).

Shortly before he died, a sponge was dipped in vinegar and offered to Jesus on the end of a reed as he hung in agony on the cross (Mark 15:36).

The open wound that Christ indicates with his hand was made with the lance that can be seen directly above it. The lance, or spear, was wielded by a soldier who thrust it into Christ's side to check that he was dead, causing blood and water to spurt forth (John 19:34). Tradition says that the centurion—now equated with St. Longinus—was so overawed that he converted to Christianity.

Christ's designation as the Man of Sorrows was inspired by the words contained in the Old Testament Book of Isaiah (53:3–5): "He is despised and rejected of men; a man of sorrows… But he was wounded for our transgressions, he was bruised for our iniquities…"

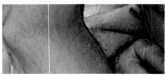

Mary cradles Christ's body in the fine linen sheet that Joseph of Arimathaea brought to serve as Christ's shroud once he had received Pontius Pilate's permission to bury him.

Memling has depicted Pontius Pilate, the Roman procurator, or governor, of Jerusalem, wearing a turban, a symbol of the East. Caiaphas sent Christ to Pontius Pilate to confirm and carry out the death penalty, and although he was reluctant to do so, he eventually gave in to the mob's wishes.

Luke 23:7–12 relates that Pilate dispatched Jesus to Herod Antipas, the tetrarch of Galilee, (pictured here wearing a crown), who, "with his men of war set him at nought, and mocked him, and arrayed him in a gorgeous robe, and sent him again to Pilate" (Luke 23:11).

In an imaginative touch, Memling has included a disembodied hand making the offensive fig, or fico, gesture, which someone may indeed have used to insult Christ.

A hammer was used to drive nails through Christ's feet and hands at the start of his crucifixion.

This rough-looking character may represent one of the soldiers who, as we can read in the Gospel of St. Mark (15:16–20), crowned Christ with thorns after his scourging (the Flagellation), dressed him in imperial purple, hit him over the head with a reed, spat on him, and paid mocking homage to him on their knees before hustling him off to be crucified.

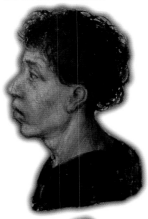

A hank of hair, which is said to have been ripped from Christ's scalp on the road to Calgary, is among the instruments of the Passion.

The swinging foot denotes the kicking that Christ no doubt received as part of the abuse that was heaped upon him.

The three nails represent those that were hammered into each of Christ's hands and through his crossed feet in order to attach his body to the cross.

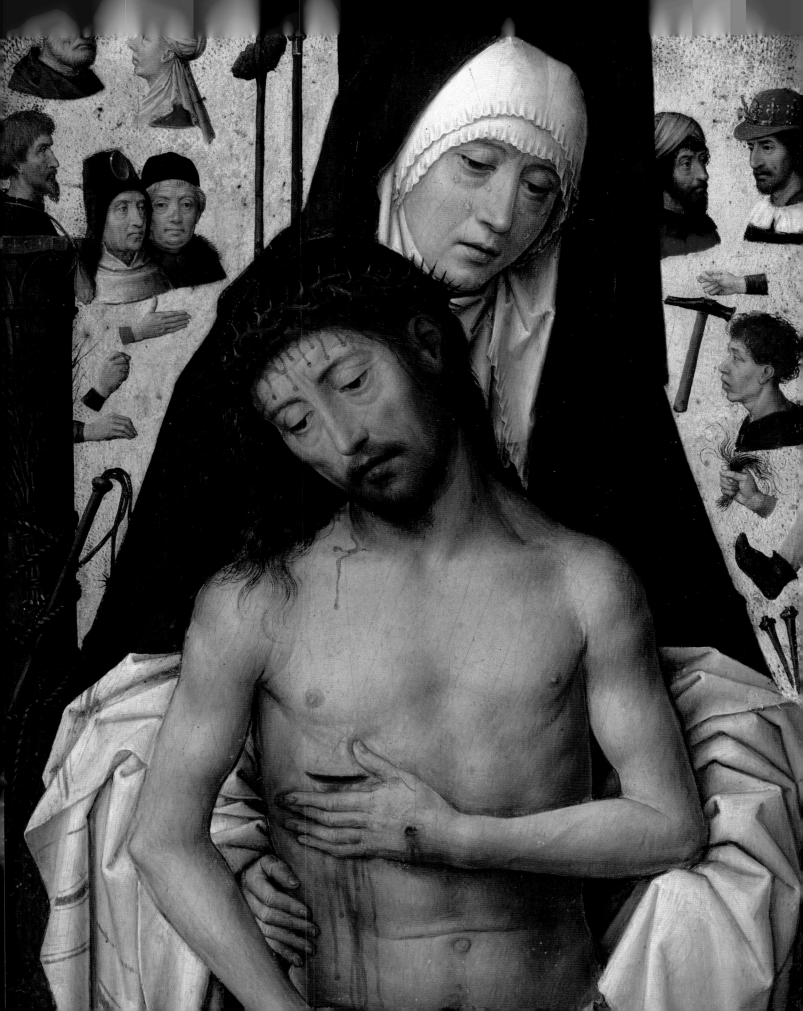

The Descent into Limbo
Master of the Osservanza

c.1440–44, tempera on panel, Fogg Art Museum, Cambridge, Massachusetts

Take one look at the squashed devil, the radiant central figure, and the array of characters gathered in the gloom, and it is not difficult to appreciate why Christ's descent into limbo, or, as it was better known during the Middle Ages, harrowing (plundering) of hell, was such a popular theme in medieval and Renaissance art. This interpretation is by the Master of Osservanza, who was active in the central Italian city of Siena during the 1430s and 1440s. Like many others, it was painted as part of a Passion cycle, and is believed to have acted as a predella (or base) panel for an unknown altarpiece.

The reason why this episode (of which no detailed mention is made in the New Testament) is considered part of Christ's Passion, rather than his Resurrection, is that Apocryphal sources state that it occurred after his entombment, but before the discovery of his empty tomb and his appearance to Mary Magdalene three days later. The fifth-century Gospel of Nicodemus II, for instance, relates that some time during those three days, Christ descended into the upper reaches of hell and dispatched Satan into its depths before raising Adam and such righteous Old Testament characters as Abraham and Moses into paradise.

In *canto* 4 of his *The Divine Comedy* (1306–21), the Italian poet Dante Alighieri described limbo as the first circle of hell (*Inferno*), where could be found "the souls of those, who although they lived virtuously and have not to suffer for great sins, nevertheless, through lack of baptism, merit not the bliss of Paradise." According to Dante, these included Abel, Noah, David, and Solomon, as well as such notable Classical thinkers as the Greek poet Homer and the philosophers Socrates and Plato. A distinction may be made between *limbus patrum* (Latin for "limbo of the fathers") and *limbus infantium* ("limbo of the infants"), where unbaptized babies and other virtuous souls reside after death. The limbo portrayed here is *limbus patrum*.

See also **Dante and his Poem the "Divine Comedy"** (page 178–81), **Christ detail** (page 136).

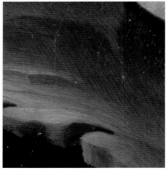

If the bowels of hell are envisaged as being at the Earth's core, limbo (whose name is derived from the Latin *limbus*, or "border") is conceived of as being situated close to the Earth's surface, just beyond hell's gates.

The red cross on the white field of the flag that Christ is carrying signals his victory over death and is known as the flag of the resurrection, or else the flag of Christ triumphant.

Christ has trampled down the door to limbo, or the gateway to hell, in the process flattening its demonic black sentry. In some representations, the demon may be replaced by Cerberus, the three-headed hound of Hades, according to Greek lore, or by the monstrous Leviathan described in the Old Testament Book of Job (41:1–34).

Christ has left his sepulcher to descend into limbo still dressed in the linen winding sheet that acted as his shroud and bearing the wounds left by the nails that were hammered through his hands and feet, and by the lance that was thrust into his side, at the crucifixion.

Not only does his halo proclaim his sanctity, but the golden glow that emanates from Christ lights up limbo's darkness, enabling those of the just who had previously been denied Christian illumination to see the source of their salvation. They have had to wait until Christ's death for the "beatific vision" of the Messiah that signifies their redemption from original sin.

Adam and Eve, the first humans, stand in the background. It was their disastrous mistake in disobeying God and succumbing to temptation that earned them their expulsion from the Garden of Eden and condemned their descendents to the terrible sentence of being born tainted with original sin.

Their flowing beards, biblical-era garments, wise countenances, and pole position at the head of a crowd of distinguished personalities suggest that this venerable pair are Old Testament figures of paramount importance, and probably the patriarch Abraham and the prophet and lawgiver Moses. Indeed, some Christian scholars equate limbo with "Abraham's bosom," where the beggar Lazarus was transported on his death (Luke 16:20–26).

John the Baptist (who had only just predeceased Christ), is portrayed wearing his characteristically scruffy, camel-hair shirt, and with unkempt hair and a long beard.

We can just discern the letters written on the scroll that he is carrying: they read *ECCE A*, which, as his indication of Christ confirms, spells out the start of the motto associated with John: *Ecce agnus ille dei, qui tollit peccatu mundi* ("Behold the Lamb of God, which taketh away the sin of the world." John 1:29).

We can identify King David by the crown that he is wearing and his kingly robes.

The book that he is holding represents the Old Testament Book of Psalms, many of which he is said to have composed himself. The New Testament Gospels of Matthew (1:1 and 1:6) and Luke (3:31) both inform us that King David was a direct ancestor of Christ.

The Adoration of the Mystic Lamb

Hubert and Jan van Eyck

1432, oil on panel,
St. Bavo Cathedral, Ghent, Belgium

Not only are there many puzzling images to decode in *The Adoration of the Mystic Lamb*, but the exact details of this painting's creation are themselves something of a conundrum. The big question mark over its attribution is due to the inscription that accompanies the Ghent Altarpiece, as the entire, twenty-scene polptych is called, which states that it was begun by Hubert van Eyck (d.1426?) and finished by Jan (his brother). To this day, scholars remain engaged in a debate that focuses on which brother painted which parts and, indeed, whether Hubert's hand can be discerned in the altarpiece at all.

The inscription otherwise clarifies rather than confuses, stating as it does the altarpiece's date of installation (1432) and the name of the man who commissioned it for a chapel in Ghent's cathedral, one Jodocus (or Joost) Vijd, a prominent citizen of the Flemish port, whose likeness, opposite that of his wife, Elisabeth Borluut, is painted on the reverse of the altarpiece and becomes visible when the polyptych is closed.

When its folded wings are opened, however, twelve images arranged in two tiers can be seen. The enthroned figure of God the Father, wearing a papal tiara, occupies the central position of the top layer, flanked by the Virgin Mary and John the Baptist (this triple arrangement being called a *deësis*, the Greek for "supplication"), angel musicians, and Adam and Eve. Directly beneath the *deësis* is *The Adoration of the Mystic Lamb*, with two panels on each side depicting the just judges and Christian soldiers on the left, and the holy hermits and pilgrim saints on the right, all converging on the already crowded scene. These figures collectively represent the different components of the Christian community of saints, or the Church triumphant, all united in their worship of Christ, symbolized here by the Lamb of God, who sacrificed his life for the redemption of humankind. The whole scene is reminiscent of the description contained in the New Testament Book of Revelation (7:9–17).

*See also **Allegory of the Old and New Testaments*** (pages 132–36).

A white dove, representing the Holy Ghost, radiates the light of divine grace. When viewed with the portrayal of God the Father in the separate panel directly above, and taking the Lamb of God directly below into account, it is evident that the three components of the Holy Trinity are in alignment at the center of the altarpiece.

In ancient Egypt, the palm tree represented the sun, and thus light and day; in ancient Rome, it signified victory, with palm branches being handed to military conquerors to carry when proceeding through the city streets in triumph. Christian artists drew on these strands of symbolism in portraying martyrs bearing palm branches, thereby signaling that they had emerged victorious from the jaws of death, due to their unshakable faith, and had been rewarded with everlasting life in heaven. Thanks to a reference in the Song of Solomon (7:7), the palm tree may also be associated with the Virgin Mary.

Popes (crowned with papal tiaras), cardinals (wearing wide-brimmed, scarlet hats), bishops (with their distinctive miters on their heads), and tonsured monks make up a group of souls that represent confessors of the faith and contemplatives.

Angels crowned with crosses surround the Lamb of God. Some display such instruments of the Passion as the cross on which Christ was crucified, his crown of thorns, the lance that lacerated his side, the vinegar-soaked sponge, and the pillar to which he was tied before being scourged.

Some of its buildings may be recognizably Flemish in style, but this is a fictious metropolis—and landscape—that represents the kingdom of heaven, heavenly Jerusalem, or the City of God (*Civitas Dei* in Latin). The City of God was described by St. Augustine of Hippo (354–430) as being inhabited by the souls of the blessed, including Christian saints and righteous Old Testament characters.

 The white lily—which represents innocence and purity—flourishes in paradise, which is envisaged as being a beautiful, heavenly garden in which all manner of exquisite flowers bloom, watered by the fountain of life.

In combination with the palm branches that they are holding (symbols of victory over death), their long, loose hair, floral wreaths, and youthful beauty identify the females in this group as virgin martyrs. St. Agnes cradles the lamb whose Latin name, *agnus*, sounds so similar to hers; St. Barbara holds aloft a model of the tower in which her pagan father imprisoned her; and St. Dorothy, or Dorothea, clutches the basket containing roses, and perhaps an apple or two, that she caused to appear on Earth as proof that paradise existed.

Its halo and golden glow identify this creature as the Lamb of God, or Christ, who, as foretold in the Old Testament Book of Isaiah (53:7), was "brought as a lamb to the slaughter." Although the young animal's characteristic innocence and gentleness are relevant, the main reason why Christ is represented as a lamb is because sheep were ritually sacrificed to God by the Jewish people to wash away sin, providing an obvious parallel with Christ's sacrifice in order to redeem the sins of humankind. The blood that spurts from the lamb's chest into the brimming chalice recalls Christ's words at the Last Supper (Mark 14:23–24), and thus makes explicit the link between the wine of the Eucharist and his blood.

Two angels swing censers, or incense burners, in front of the altar, an action that represents prayers being sent heavenward, to God.

Although this section of what may be classified as an "all saints" painting includes Old Testament prophets and patriarchs, pagan and pre-Christian personalities, which should theoretically exclude them from the Christian community, their righteousness has won them admission to paradise. The wreathed figure in white is thought to represent the Roman poet Virgil, the Italian poet Dante's guide to hell, as related in *The Divine Comedy* (1306–21).

The altar on which the lamb stands can be equated with a place of sacrifice. The bright red of the altar cloth is the color of freshly spilled blood, and thus of martyrdom. When translated from Latin, the text emblazoned across it in gold quotes John the Baptist's greeting to his cousin, as related in the New Testament Gospel of John (1:29): "Behold the Lamb of God, which taketh away the sin of the world." An abbreviated reference to John 14:6, in which Jesus states, "I am the way, the truth, and the life," can be discerned on the two vertical pieces of cloth below.

The books being reverently read at the forefront of the crowd on the left symbolize Biblical texts.

The rocks that this tonsured man has scooped up into his deacon's dalmatic identify him as St. Stephen, the first martyr, who was stoned to death.

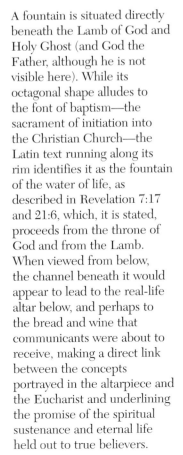

A fountain is situated directly beneath the Lamb of God and Holy Ghost (and God the Father, although he is not visible here). While its octagonal shape alludes to the font of baptism—the sacrament of initiation into the Christian Church—the Latin text running along its rim identifies it as the fountain of the water of life, as described in Revelation 7:17 and 21:6, which, it is stated, proceeds from the throne of God and from the Lamb. When viewed from below, the channel beneath it would appear to lead to the real-life altar below, and perhaps to the bread and wine that communicants were about to receive, making a direct link between the concepts portrayed in the altarpiece and the Eucharist and underlining the promise of the spiritual sustenance and eternal life held out to true believers.

Their number—twelve—and humble brown mantles identify the group of men at the head of a gathering of popes, bishops, and other Church dignatories as Christ's disciples, and thus as representatives of the New Testament and founders of the Church.

The Altarpiece of the Seven Sacraments

Rogier van der Weyden

c.1445–50, oil on panel, Koninklijk Museum voor Schone Kunsten, Antwerp, Belgium

The initial sense that we are gazing into the interior of a cathedral—induced by the Gothic rib vaulting and deepened by the convincing use of perspective—is soon dispelled when the eye settles on the crucifixion scene that dominates *The Altarpiece of the Seven Sacraments.* For Christ, of course, had died many thousands of miles away, and nearly fifteen hundred years prior to the creation of this triptych in Brussels (then part of the duchy of Burgundy) by Flemish artist Rogier van der Weyden. In fact, just as the Church—that is, the Christian religion represented by Christ—can be likened to a ship (and the central part of the cathedral in which the crucifixion is taking place is called the nave, a word derived from the Latin *navis*, "ship"), so van der Weyden has depicted a church as symbolizing the Church. It is an inspired choice of framework for this devotional painting, for church buildings provide both literal and spiritual shelter for the faithful, as well as a focus for their belief, and it is furthermore within churches that most of the sacraments are usually administered.

While Protestants consider only baptism and communion to be sacraments, Roman Catholics assert that there are seven, and because van der Weyden was painting his altarpiece for Jean Chevrot, the bishop of Tournai (or Doornik), and the Reformation was anyway around seventy years in the future, he has depicted all seven: baptism, confirmation, the Eucharist, penance, holy orders, matrimony, and extreme unction. And not only are the sacraments said to confer divine grace upon believers, they also require the mediation of an ordained minister, with the clergy collectively also being called the Church. All in all, van der Weyden's imaginary church has been represented as a spiritual haven that, through the sacraments, provides spiritual sustenance for Christians from cradle to grave. That the people that he has portrayed within his edifice (which is thought to have been modeled on Brussel's St. Gudula Cathedral) are dressed in contemporaneous Flemish fashions would have underlined the sacraments' relevance to mid-fifteenth-century viewers.

See also **Mass detail** (page 40), *Allegory of the Old and New Testaments* (pages 132–36).

The story of the sacraments, and of a Christian life, starts at the extreme left of the triptych's left-hand panel. Surrounded by its godparents, a baby is held above a font as a priest baptizes it with holy water, so washing away the original sin with which it was believed to have been born. The sacrament of baptism initiates believers into the Christian Church, and, according to traditional Catholic belief, saves the souls of those who die as babies from being consigned to limbo.

The angel that supervises proceedings is dressed in white, the color of innocence; in common with the other six angels that hover above, this heavenly figure trails a scroll whose text describes the sacrament depicted below.

Jean Chevrot himself is portrayed as the bishop administering the sacrament of confirmation by anointing the forehead of a young man with oil as a group of youngsters who have just been confirmed walk away wearing freshly tied white headbands. Like baptism, the sacrament of confirmation is considered an act of initiation into the Christian community, the crucial difference being that confirmation is the conscious desire of individuals who are old enough to know their own minds to commit themselves to Christianity. The yellow wings and robe of the angel above symbolize revealed truth or illumination, as well as the fire of the Holy Spirit.

The red wings and gown of this airborne angel denote blood and the heart, both of which have relevance to the sacrament of penance, as represented by the kneeling old man's heartfelt confession of the sins that he has committed that is being heard by the priest below. Only an ordained minister has the power to pronounce God's absolution, or forgiveness, in return for being satisfied by the contrite sinner's sincere repentance and acts of atonement.

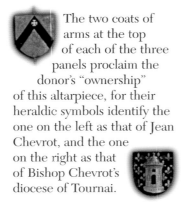

The two coats of arms at the top of each of the three panels proclaim the donor's "ownership" of this altarpiece, for their heraldic symbols identify the one on the left as that of Jean Chevrot, and the one on the right as that of Bishop Chevrot's diocese of Tournai.

Standing before the altar, under the gaze of an angel whose green gown signals hope and eternal life, a priest elevates the host (a wafer of communion bread) heavenward, prior to its consecration. That this, one of the most important sacraments—that of the Eucharist, the high point of the Catholic Mass, or communion—is portrayed as taking place in the background as Christ's broken body hangs on the cross, underlines the connection, made by Jesus himself, between his flesh and blood and the Eucharistic bread and wine, at the Last Supper, when he charged his disciples to eat and drink, ending with the words, "this do in remembrance of me" (Luke 22:19).

Van der Weyden has transported the scene of Christ's crucifixion to the Low Country, and has reproduced it at the center of his triptych. The Virgin Mary, swathed in blue, has fainted and is supported by St. John the Evangelist, while the "three Marys"—Mary, the wife of Cleophas and mother of James and Joseph; (Mary) Salome, the mother of Zebedee's children; and Mary Magdalene, who is dressed in red—give vent to their grief.

An angel who appears to have been saturated in priestly purplish-red looks down upon the ordination of a white-robed future priest as the sacrament of holy orders is administered by a bishop. Receiving this sacrament will prohibit the young man from marrying.

Those who have not entered holy orders may wed, as another young man is in the process of doing. The angel watching over the sacrament of matrimony is wearing blue, a color associated with faithfulness.

The book being so intently read is likely to be either the Bible or a missal. The dog by the reader's side symbolizes loyalty from birth (as represented, perhaps, by the dog that can be seen opposite, between the sacraments of baptism and confirmation) to death.

Van der Weyden has used artistic license in depicting a dying man in bed in a chapel. This scene illustrates the sacrament of extreme unction. The burning candle symbolizes the undimmed light of faith, and the calmness of the faces emphasizes that physical death holds no fear for true believers.

The Naming of John the Baptist

Fra Angelico

c.1430s, tempera on panel, Museo di San Marco dell'Angelico, Florence, Italy

Giorgio Vasari (1511–74) brings his chapter on Fra Angelico, in *The Lives of the Artists,* to a conclusion with the words: "In short, this friar who could never be sufficiently praised was in all he did or said most humble and modest, and in his paintings articulate and devout; the saints he painted possess more of the expression and the appearance of saints than those by any other artist." Indeed, when we look at the saintly old man concentrating single-mindedly on the act of writing, we may instinctively feel that Fra Angelico has captured the essence of this personality.

The personality in question is Zacharias, a priest whose story is told in the New Testament Book of Luke (1:5–79). The childless priest and his wife, Elisabeth, were "well stricken in years" when the archangel Gabriel appeared before Zacharias as he was burning incense in the temple and informed him that Elisabeth would not only bear a son that they should call John, but that John was destined "to make ready a people prepared for the Lord." When the astounded Zacharias questioned their ability to become parents, the angel struck him dumb "until the day that these things shall be performed, because thou believest not my words, which shall be fulfilled in their season." And so while Zacharias remained speechless, Elisabeth conceived a child, spending part of her pregnancy in the company of her cousin, the Virgin Mary, who was awaiting the birth of her own son, Jesus. When the safely delivered newborn was eight days old, he was circumcised, but when "her neighbours and her cousins" named him Zacharias, after his father, his mother corrected them, insisting that he should be called John. Baffled, because this was not a family name, they turned to Zacharias for guidance, who, as pictured here, "asked for a writing table, and wrote, saying, His name is John." As soon as he did so, "they marvelled all. And his mouth was opened immediately, and his tongue loosed, and he spake, and praised God."

See also **The Baptism of Christ** (pages 42–44).

The scene that Fra Angelico has illustrated is described in Luke 1:59–63. The importance of getting his message across has made Zacharias focus so resolutely on spelling it out that he appears oblivious to the women around him, and even to his baby son.

John, the name that the angel instructed Zacharias to call the newborn boy, means "Jehovah has been gracious," or "God has favored," in Hebrew, which is especially apt given Zachariah and Elisabeth's age and previous childlessness. John's name may also refer to his future role, as described by Zacharias: "And thou, child…shalt go before the face of the Lord…To give knowledge of salvation unto his people by the remission of their sins, Through the tender mercy of our God" (Luke 1:76–78).

There being no desk to hand, a young woman holds the pot of ink that feeds Zacharias's pen and fuels his script.

The infant John's halo, like Zacharias's, proclaims his holiness. John the Baptist—Giovanni Battista in Italian—is a patron saint of Florence (where Fra Angelico was working when he painted this panel, which was probably destined to be part of an altarpiece), making him a popular choice for Florentine works of devotional art.

"And they made signs to his father, how he would have him called" (Luke 1:62). No words are needed when the hands of the lady in blue are as expressive as these.

Swaddled tightly as he is, the baby John's unbending stance seems to prefigure his uncompromising nature as a grown man, both as an ascetic Nazirite and as the "just man and an holy" (Mark 6:20) who unhesitatingly condemned Herod Antipas's marriage to his sister-in-law, Herodias, as being unlawful, thereby incurring her undying enmity and ultimately signing his own death warrant.

Elisabeth, who is tenderly touching her miracle baby, wears a drab mantle and matronly veil appropriate to her age, in contrast to the brightly colored gowns and elaborately dressed, golden hair of some of the young women around her.

Although small blooms can be seen at Elisabeth's feet, the courtyard garden in which she stands is rather lacking in flowers, certainly in comparison with the blossoming and verdant *hortus conclusus* ("enclosed garden") in which the Virgin Mary is frequently portrayed (*see* pages 35 to 37).

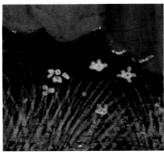

The garden's relative barrenness is emphasized by the plants and trees that Fra Angelico has depicted growing vigorously on, and outside, the garden wall, perhaps in an allusion to Elisabeth's own struggle to be fruitful until blessed by God.

The Conversion of the Magdalene
Bernardino Luini

c.1520, oil on panel, San Diego Museum of Art, California

Although comparisons can be made between the symbolism inherent in Titian's *Sacred and Profane Love* (*see* pages 102–04) and Milanese painter Bernardino Luini's *The Conversion of the Magdalene*, the message that Titian conveys is that the two women in his allegory may be different, but are nevertheless equals, like the two sides of one coin, while Luini's suggestion is that the sumptuously dressed woman on the right—the Magdalene, or Mary Magdalene—is somehow inferior to her sister on the left. In fact, Luini's Italian Catholic contemporaries would have understood this painting as representing the moment when Mary Magdalene, encouraged by her sensible sister, saw the light and turned her back on her sinful lifestyle in order to dedicate herself to Christ. They would also have known that she would eventually eclipse her sister by forging such a strong spiritual connection with Jesus that she would be the first to see the resurrected Christ. Yet while this *"Noli me tangere"* (Latin for "Touch me not") post-crucifixion scene, which is much depicted in Christian art, is described in John's Gospel (20:1–18), much of Mary Magdalene's story has no basis in the New Testament, including her conversion.

The supposed life story of Mary Magdalene, one of the most popular female saints, has been woven from many strands. She may be identified with Mary of Magdala (or "Mary called Magdalene," Luke 8:2), who was possessed by seven devils that were exorcised by Christ (Mark 16:9); with a sinner who washed Christ's feet with her tears, dried them with her hair, and anointed them with costly ointment (Luke 7:37–50); and with Mary of Bethany, the sister of Martha and Lazarus, who also anointed Christ's feet (John 12:1–8). From these strands was created a colorful picture of a "magdalen" (a reformed prostitute) whose devotion to Christ earned her near-equal footing with the male disciples. And while Mary Magdalene may symbolize the contemplative worship of God, her sister, the housewifely Martha, represents the active alternative (the source for these characterizations being Luke 10:38–42), so that in a way Luini, like Titian, has indeed portrayed the two sides of one coin.

*See also **Sacred and Profane Love** (pages 102–04).*

While her sister—whose supposed priority in life, until now, was to attract men—wears her locks long, loose, and elaborately dressed, Martha has covered her hair with a scarf, symbolizing her modesty. Yet the golden glow that the soft fabric seems to emit, due to Luini's use of the *chiaroscuro* (Italian for "light–dark") technique, lights up the picture, while Mary Magdalene's rich tresses are difficult to discern, an indication, perhaps, of Martha's spiritual illumination thanks to her belief in Christ.

Martha appears to be pointing toward heaven, exhorting her sister to devote herself to God from this moment on. By echoing her sister's gesture, Mary Magdalene is following Martha's lead, her widespread fingers suggesting that she is opening herself up to the Holy Spirit.

Martha uses her other index finger to indicate a heavy necklace that has been laid upon the table, the suggestion being that Mary Magdalene has just removed it from her neck as a sign that her days of coveting expensive jewelry with which to enhance her allure are over and done with.

While the direction in which Martha is pointing denotes the realm of the earth and material matters, that she is doing so with her left hand is significant, for the left side has long been considered evil or unlucky. The alternative meanings of *sinister*, the Latin word for "left," include "unfavorable" and "perverse," and "sinister" has been adopted into the English language to signify something threatening.

Mary Magdalene is almost always portrayed as a beautiful woman with hair flowing way past her shoulders. This is partly to signal her preconversion womanly vanity (and it is no coincidence that most of her crowning glory seems to have merged into the pitch-black background, signifying the illusory, and ultimately meaningless, importance that the narcissistic attach to their appearance), and partly an allusion to her drying Christ's feet with her hair.

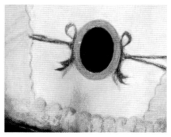

Mary Magdalene's gown, a legacy of her wanton lifestyle, is cut to show off her luminous skin and shapely shoulders and to draw admiring eyes toward her bosom. Although she has cast aside her necklace, a large jewel remains ostentatiously in place, perhaps because to remove it would reveal her bare breasts.

Sixteenth-century viewers well versed in Christian symbolism would have recognized that the container that Mary Magdalene is keeping such a firm grip on contains the expensive ointment with which she anointed Christ's feet, and which the Gospel of Mark (16:1) suggests that she took to Christ's sepulcher with the intention of anointing his corpse. Often represented in the style of a ciborium or pyx (a circular, lidded container in which the host, or communion wafer, is stored), and seemingly made of alabaster, as described in Luke 7:37, her pot of ointment is Mary Magdalene's traditional attribute. (And although this interpretation will not be found in a conventional canon of Christian symbolism, it may also be argued that, like many containers, her vessel represents the womb.)

The glowing, jewel-like colors of Mary Magdalene's silky gown outshine the drab overgarment that her sister is wearing, indicating that in her past incarnation as a scarlet woman, she was an attention-seeking lover of luxury. The unassuming and practical Martha, by contrast, clearly dresses for purposes of comfort and modesty instead. Luini has also made use of color symbolism in depicting his subjects' clothes, for while Martha's brown and terra-cotta tones convey an earthy nature, Mary Magdalene's sleeves of crimson (the hue with which she is traditionally associated) signal passion, energy, and brazenness, while green signifies hope and eternal life.

St. John the Evangelist at Patmos

Hans Memling

1479, oil on panel, Memling Museum, Bruges, Belgium

Commissioned as it was for the high altar of Bruges's Hospital of St. John (Sint-Janshospitaal), it is appropriate that this triptych's two wings are devoted to the pair of saintly Johns who, in the central panel, are pictured flanking the Virgin and Child, namely St. John the Baptist (the left-hand panel) and St. John the Evangelist (the right-hand panel, which is reproduced here). In fact, many art historians believe the altarpiece's conventional title, *The Mystical Marriage of St. Catherine Triptych*, to be a misnomer, and *The St. John Altarpiece* to be more accurate.

St. John the Evangelist, the author of the Gospel of St. John, is also believed to have been the "St. John the Divine" ("divine" being meant in the sense of "divination" rather than "godlike") who composed the Book of Revelation that concludes the New Testament. According to legend, St. John, the disciple who had been charged by Christ with looking after his mother after his death, accompanied the Virgin Mary to Ephesus before being exiled, in around 95, to the Aegean island of Patmos on the orders of the Roman emperor Domitian (51–96). Here, it is said (Revelation 1:9), he received the divinely inspired vision that he set down in Revelation, aspects of which—the Apocalyptic events described in chapters 1 to 13.2—Hans Memling has reproduced in *St. John the Evangelist at Patmos*.

St. John is pictured in the foreground of this detailed work, gazing raptly toward heaven, a book open on his lap in which he is recording the future occurrences that are being revealed to him, as instructed by "Alpha and Omega, the first and the last": "What thou seest, write in a book, and send it unto the seven churches which are in Asia" (Revelation 1:11). The unfolding revelation is indeed a riveting sight, for it gives an insight into the cataclysms that will be unleashed at the world's end, starting with the breaking of the first of the seven seals attached to a book held in God's right hand.

See also **John the Evangelist** (page 15), **disciples detail** (page 48), **lamb detail** (page 58), **crucifixion** (page 60).

Seven is a recurrent number in the Book of Revelation. John tells us that seven fiery lamps burned before the celestial throne, denoting the seven spirits of God (Revelation 4:5).

Look closely, and you may see that this gentle-looking lamb has seven horns and seven eyes, which again represent the "seven Spirits of God sent forth into all the earth" (Revelation 4:6). Also described, in Revelation 5:5, as the "Lion of the tribe of Juda, the root of David," this lamb, which appeared "as it had been slain," signifies Christ, the sacrificial Lamb of God (*Agnus Dei* in Latin).

He who called himself "Alpha and Omega" resembled "the Son of man," according to John (Revelation 1:13). Memling has chosen to remain faithful to the conventional image of Christ rather than depicting the white-haired, flame-eyed being with a sword emerging from his mouth described in Revelation 1:13–16, or he who "was to look upon like a jasper and a sardine stone [sard, or chalcedony]" (4:3), although the divine face does have a distinctly unearthly tinge.

The rainbow enclosing the heavenly throne is referred to in Revelation 4:3. Although the rainbow is an Old Testament symbol of peace and reconciliation between God and humankind, the "lightnings and thunderings" that emanate from the throne (Revelation 4:5) suggest that God's wrath is about to be unleashed.

The four beasts that John saw around the throne (Revelation 4:6–8) had six wings and many eyes, and resembled the tetramorphic vision described in Ezekiel 1:10. Each is considered to symbolize one of the four Evangelists:

Matthew (the winged man), Mark (the winged lion), Luke (the winged calf or ox), and John himself (the eagle). John is associated with the eagle because his Apocalyptic vision was inspired by God in heaven, toward which the eagle's soaring flight carries it.

Twenty-four elders dressed in white and wearing golden crowns were seated around the throne playing harps (although Memling has given them a more varied selection of musical instruments), according to John (Revelation 4:4 and 5:8). These figures have been linked with Old Testament prophets and patriarchs.

John tells us how he "saw a strong angel proclaiming with a loud voice, Who is worthy to open the book, and to loose the seals thereof?" (Revelation 5:2).

Some of the sights that manifested themselves when the Lamb broke the seventh seal can be discerned around the edge of the rainbow enclosing God's court. These include the seven angels who were given seven trumpets and the angel who stood at a golden altar and used a golden censer to offer prayers to God (Revelation 8:2–6).

The opening of the first four seals brought four horses and riders, collectively known as the four horsemen of the Apocalypse, galloping into view (Revelation 6:1–8). The first rider wore a crown, wielded a bow, and sat astride a white horse; he may represent the Church, or else Christ, the all-conquering hero. The second, bearing a sword and riding a red horse, signifies war.

A black horse carried the third rider, denoting famine, who carried a pair of scales.

Death, John explains to us (Revelation 6:8), rides a pale horse and is closely followed by Hell, which Memling has portrayed as the fire-breathing, all-consuming head of a ferocious creature.

When the second angel blew his trumpet, it caused "a great mountain burning with fire" to be cast into the sea," whereupon "the third part of the ships were destroyed' (Revelation 8:8–9).

"The moon became as blood" (Revelation 6:12) after the sixth seal was broken, followed by a third of the lunar surface darkening after the fourth angel sounded his trumpet (Revelation 8:13).

John's vision of a pregnant woman, "clothed with the sun, and the moon under her feet, and upon her head a crown of twelve stars" (Revelation 12:1), has been interpreted as representing the Virgin Mary, an association that Memling has emphasized by cloaking her in Mary's traditional color—blue—and enveloping her in an aureole, or body halo. Rather than being devoured by the seven-headed red dragon whose tail "drew the third part of the stars of heaven, and did cast them to the earth" (Revelation 12:3–4), the "man child" (that is, Jesus) that she then delivered was carried safely to God's throne.

After a third of humankind had been killed, a mighty angel descended from heaven in a cloud, a rainbow above his head and a book in his hand. His feet, John relates, were "as pillars of fire," and while he balanced his right foot upon the sea, he planted his left foot on earth. The "seven thunders" that "uttered their voices," echoing his booming cry, can be seen as smoky explosions to his right (Revelation 10:1–3). John himself is visible as a small, red-robed figure standing in line with the angel's left hand.

The sounding of the fifth angelic trumpet heralded the falling of a star, along with a key, into a bottomless pit, sending out smoke, and also locusts with the face of men, whose winged bodies looked like warhorses, and whose tails resembled those of scorpions (Revelation 9:3–11). Their leader, the "angel of the bottomless pit," was named Abaddon, or Apollyon.

Here, the dragon confers his power and authority upon the seven-headed, leopardlike beast named blasphemy (Revelation 13:1–2). Both monstrous creatures' seven heads may be equated with the seven deadly sins.

Ranged along the shore are the four angels of death, whose cavalry of lion-headed, serpent-tailed horses slaughtered a third of humankind with fire, smoke, and brimstone (Revelation 9:19).

The sounding of the third trumpet prompted a fallen star named Wormwood to poison a third of the rivers and springs—that is, drinking water, represented here by a well—on earth (Revelation 8:10–11).

No one was safe from God's wrath, John explains in Revelation 15–17, be it "the kings of the earth, and the great men, and the rich men, and the chief captains, and the mighty men, and every bondman [slave], and every free men," who "hid themselves in the dens and in the rocks of the mountains."

After informing us that "there was a war in heaven: Michael and his angels fought against the dragon," John goes on to tell us that "that old serpent, called the Devil, and Satan" was overcome, along with his "angels" (Revelation 12:7–9).

After Satan had been defeated by the archangel Michael's army, he attacked the woman, who had fled to the wilderness after giving birth. She, however, was able to escape with the help of a pair of wings and the assistance of the earth, which "swallowed up the flood which the dragon cast out of his mouth" (Revelation 12:13–16).

The Conversion of St. Paul

Michelangelo Buonarroti

1542–50, fresco, Cappella Paolina, Vatican, Vatican City, Italy

Strictly speaking, the title of Michelangelo's fresco should really be *The Conversion of Saul*, for this was the name by which St. Paul was known when he experienced his Damascene conversion. That said, Michelangelo's fresco homes in on the exact moment when the Pharisee Saul literally saw the light of God, setting him, as the Christian Paul, on the path to preaching the Christian message to the Gentiles, a path that would end with him dying alongside St. Peter in Rome. It should also be remembered that Michelangelo created this image for the private chapel (the Cappella Paolina) of Pope Paul III (1468–1549), who had been born Alessandro Farnese, but had chosen to be known by Paul's name on his election to the papal throne in 1534.

Although other sources have enabled scholars to piece together his life story, the circumstances of Saul's conversion are described in the New Testament, in the Acts of the Apostles 9:1–9. It seems that Saul of Tarsus, a city in Asia Minor, was born in around AD 5, the son of a Jewish father who had Roman citizenship. Saul grew up into a Pharisee who zealously rooted out and persecuted Christians for their faith, and it was such a mission that saw him bound for the synagogues of Damascus, armed with letters of authority from the high priest at the Temple in Jerusalem, and "breathing out threatenings and slaughter against the disciples of the Lord" (Acts 9:1). As he neared Damascus, however, "there shined round him a light from heaven," and he heard a voice saying, "Saul, Saul, why persecutest thou me?" (Acts 9:3–4). After learning that the voice was that of Jesus, the "trembling and astonished" Saul rose, and, having been struck blind, was led by his companions to Damascus. Three days later, a God-sent disciple named Ananias visited Saul and laid his hands on him, "And immediately there fell from his eyes as it had been scales: and he received sight forthwith, and arose, and was baptized" (Acts 9:18).

See also **Humanizing Holiness** (pages 12–13), **The Seven Deadly Sins** (page 100).

Surrounded by awestruck ethereal beings, God, who identifies himself as Jesus to Saul/Paul, hurls a bolt of lightning down to earth.

The brightness of the yellow ray of light and his billowing red robe contribute to the dynamic energy with which Michelangelo has imbued this divine personage.

Acts 9:7 tells us that "the men who journeyed with him [Saul/Paul] stood speechless, hearing a voice, but seeing no man."

That Jerusalem was under Roman rule at the time of his conversion is signaled by the armored skirt that one of Saul/Paul's martial companions is wearing, which is recognizably in the style of the uniform worn by Roman legionaries.

Saul/Paul shields his eyes from the beam of concentrated light emanating from the heavens, but it is too late: he has been temporarily blinded by its radiance. Michelangelo has depicted Saul/Paul—who, scholars estimate, would have been around thirty when this event took place in about AD 35—as an older man, perhaps partly in reflection of his relative maturity at the time of his conversion, and partly to suggest his later role as a founding father of the Christian Church. In addition, Michelangelo was sixty-seven years of age when he began painting this fresco, while Pope Paul II was seventy-four, so that portraying the saint as a graybeard would have made it easy for both artist and patron to identify with the saintly figure.

The hilt of a sword is visible by Saul/Paul's side. Although it does not look out of place amid the armor of his military escort, this weapon is one of Paul's traditional attributes because it was the instrument of his martyrdom. For Paul met his death on, it is said, the orders of the Emperor Nero when he was beheaded with a sword in Rome in around AD 66. (As horrible an end as it was, decapitation was regarded as a more honorable way for a Roman citizen like Paul to die than crucifixion, the method of execution to which St. Peter was condemned.)

It may be no coincidence that the upturned helmet that this soldier has slung over the shield on his back may, at first sight, resemble an owl, for medieval and Renaissance artists often used this nocturnal bird as a symbol for those—especially Jews—who did not believe in Christ and who therefore chose to remain spiritually unenlightened, or in the darkness. This interpretation is reinforced by the soldier's face, which Michelangelo has depicted as turning away from the divine light radiated by God.

The bolting horse at the center of Michelangelo's fresco indicates the startling suddenness, and disconcerting unearthliness, of the manifestation of the divine presence overhead. Michelangelo's contemporaries would, moreover, have recognized the riderless horse and its unseated mount as a symbolic reference to pride (*superbia* in Latin), one of the seven deadly sins, coming to a fall. And it is significant in this context that after his humbling before God and his Damascene conversion, Saul (whose name means "asked of God" in Hebrew) chose to give himself a Christian name that was derived from *paulus*, the Latin word for "small."

Such is the confusion on the road to Damascus, with those on the ground heading in every possible direction in their panic, that it is difficult to tell whether the oriental-looking city depicted here is Damascus (the capital of Syria, and, some believe, the oldest inhabited city in the world) or Jerusalem, the city from which Saul/Paul and his arrest party had set out.

St. Philip Exorcizing the Demon from the Temple of Mars

Filippino Lippi

c.1497–1502, fresco, Santa Maria Novella, Florence, Italy

Although he was one of Christ's original twelve disciples, not much is known about Philip, nor has he ever been a particularly popular saint, which begs the question why Filippo Strozzi (1428–91), an ally of Lorenzo de' Medici (1449–92), should have commissioned Filippino Lippi, in 1487, to depict scenes of Philip's life on the walls of the chapel that he had bought in Florence's Santa Maria Novella church. The obvious answer lies in their shared name, Filippo being the Italian version of Philip. There may also have been a connection between this scene, which depicts St. Philip as an agent of Christ vanquishing the forces of paganism or heresy, as represented by Mars—the Roman god of war whose Greek equivalent was Ares—and the situation in Florence after Strozzi's death. For by the time that Lippi had completed his frescoes in 1502, Florence was reeling from a period of turbulent political and religious conflict heralded by Lorenzo's death and focused on the divisive figure of Girolamo Savonarola (1452–98), whose uncompromising preaching had led to the overthrow of the Medici family and the establishment of the Republic of Florence in 1494. Four years later, the rabble-rousing Dominican friar was tried and executed for heresy.

According to Jacobus de Voragine's thirteenth-century compendium *The Golden Legend*, St. Philip traveled to Hierapolis, a city in Phrygia, after Christ's death, where this early Christian missionary was ordered to bow down before an effigy of Mars. As he stood defiantly in the temple, gripping his cross firmly as he refused to comply with his captors' demands, a dragon emerged from within the statue and immediately polluted the air around it with its noxious breath. Philip then confronted the demonic creature with his cross, causing it to turn and scurry away. His demonstration of Christ's superior strength condemned Philip to death by crucifixion, however, his death being portrayed by Lippi in a lunette above *St. Philip Exorcizing the Demon from the Temple of Mars*.

See also **Popular Saints** (pages 13–16).

Massed weapons and armor, the symbols of the Roman god of war, adorn his temple (which itself resembles a triumphal arch, reflecting Lippi's interest in the architecture of ancient Rome). They make a fearsome show of military might, but this bristling display contrasts dramatically with the solitary, unarmed figure of Philip, stressing that the peaceful message and methods of Christianity will prevail, even against heavily stacked, heretical odds.

The hazy, heavenly vision of a man holding aloft a cross represents Christ himself, the divine source of Philip's demon-exorcizing power.

Mars appears disconcertingly lifelike as he brandishes his weapon, which appears to be a broken lance, perhaps a reference to his impotence before one of Christ's chosen representatives.

A beady-eyed bird clings to the pedestal that supports and elevates the figure of Mars. This is a woodpecker, a bird that was sacred to Mars on account of its fearlessness and its ability to destroy trees by pecking at their trunks with its powerful beak. A woodpecker was also said to have helped feed Romulus and Remus while they were being nurtured by their lupine foster-mother. Lippi may, moreover, have known that a woodpecker perched on a wooden pillar was once considered to act as an oracle of Mars at the god's temple in Tiora. Renaissance artists sometimes included the woodpecker in their works to symbolize both Satan and those who promoted heretical beliefs, who were supposedly working to destabilize Christianity.

A wolf can be seen by Mars's side. This creature was an attribute of the Roman war god, partly on account of its predatory habits, and partly because a she-wolf was said to have suckled Romulus (the legendary founder of the city of Rome) and his brother Remus, Mars's sons by Ilia, or Rhea Silvia. In the symbolism of Christianity, because it threatens sheep, and flocks are associated with Christian believers, the wolf denotes the devil and heresy.

Phrygia was situated in western-central Asia Minor, an area that is now Turkish. The crescent moon on the military standards that are flying in this martial shrine appeared on the flags of both the Byzantine and Ottoman empires, whose capital was Constantinople, or the modern Istanbul.

Bystanders cover their noses in an attempt to block out the terrible, fatal stench carried by the dragon's breath. Such gestures may have been a familiar sight on the streets of Florence, where outbreaks of the plague (spread, it was believed, through the air) still regularly caused people to sicken and die.

His exotic headdress and dark skin signal that this man is an inhabitant of a foreign land far to the east of Rome.

Some versions of this tale state that it was the priest's son that succumbed to the dreadful, demonic fumes, others, that it was the priest himself, the offspring of a king, or else two Roman soldiers. It is also often said that Philip revived the poisoned victim.

In accordance with the age-old tradition of the devil and his Satanic servants being depicted as snakes and dragons, Lippi has envisaged the demon that inhabited the temple of Mars as one of these mythical, fire-breathing beasts and guardians of treasure. Some interpretations of the legend assert that Mars and the dragon were one and the same.

Philip's gesture mirrors that of Christ in heaven. It is from this legendary episode in his life that Philip derives his attribute of a cross, before which the dragon shrank and fled. The base of his cross rests alongside the spot at the base of the idol from which the demon emerged at the start of the exorcism process.

His religious-looking regalia identifies a bearded elder as a priest of Mars.

The Martyrdom of St. Sebastian Luca Signorelli

1498, oil on panel, Pinacoteca Comunale, Città di Castello, Italy

Gruesome depictions of the terrible torments that many saintly martyrs endured before death finally released them from their suffering were familiar sights in Renaissance-era cathedrals, churches, and chapels across Europe, for the steadfastness with which they clung to their faith while enduring unspeakable pain made them the ultimate role models for pious Christians. Yet despite dying a martyr, paintings of St. Sebastian being pierced by arrows—such as this work, which was created by Italian artist Luca Signorelli for the church of San Domenico in Città di Castello—are not concerned with his violent death, even if the inevitability of that is implicit.

Although St. Sebastian's life story can be traced back to a fifth-century source, that it became widely known during the Middle Ages is partly due to the popularity of *The Golden Legend*, a collection of saintly accounts gathered by Jacobus de Voragine during the thirteenth century. A citizen of the northern Italian town of Milan, Sebastian, it is said, was a commander of the Praetorian Guard (whose members acted as the Roman emperors' bodyguards) and a covert Christian when the virulently anti-Christian Diocletian and Maximian were the joint emperors of Rome (between 286 and 305). Unaware of his faith, both emperors thought highly of Sebastian, that is, until they received reports of him strengthening the resolve of twins Marcellianus and Marcus to be executed rather than renounce Christianity, whereupon Diocletian ordered that Sebastian be tied to a tree and used as a target by the imperial archers. De Voragine tells us that the archers then "hit him with so many arrows that he looked like a hedgehog, and they left him there for dead." Yet Sebastian survived, returned to Diocletian to berate him for his treatment of Christians, and was then clubbed to death in punishment. His corpse was flung into Rome's main sewer, the Cloaca Maxima, but was later retrieved by St. Lucina and interred in a catacomb beneath the Via Appia, or Appian Way.

So why were these "target-practice" scenes so prevalent? Partly because artists relished the challenge of portraying a good-looking, unclothed, upright male figure, but, more importantly, for purposes of protection against the plague.

See also **Piety in the Age of the Plague** (page 11).

Signorelli has used a foreshortening technique for his rendition of God the Father, who appears to be bending forward and looking directly into the suffering Sebastian's eyes, thereby giving him the strength to survive his ordeal.

Surrounding the figure of God is an aureole, or a body-enclosing halo, which signifies sanctity, divine light, and separation from the Earthly plane. Cohesion and connection between the divine and Earthly realms is, however, indicated by the triangular composition of the picture's crucial elements, with God at the apex and the archers forming the base.

One might expect Sebastian's features to be contorted with agony as arrows are shot into his flesh, but God's divine gaze has clearly not only empowered him, enabling him to disregard his physical pain, but has filled Sebastian with ecstasy.

A triumphal arch is just one of the Classical edifices that sets this scene in ancient Rome, for this traumatic event in Sebastian's life is said to have taken place on the Palatine Hill (and he is considered the third most important of Rome's patron saints after Peter and Paul). Signorelli no doubt reproduced these monumental, if crumbling, relics of Rome's imperial might as they appeared to him when he was living in Rome and working on the Sistine Chapel during the 1480s. There may be another reason why he depicted them in ruins, however, and that is to signal that by the time of Sebastian's martyrdom, the rise of Christianity had long since put paid to Rome's pagan pantheon, relegating it to ancient history.

One of the primary explanations for St. Sebastian's popularity in medieval and Renaissance Europe, when contagious diseases decimated populations with horrifying frequency, is due to his renowned ability to protect people against the plague (or Black Death), then the most deadly, and feared, illness of all. This belief arose from his survival of the onslaught of arrows (all of which apparently missed his vital organs), for since antiquity, arrows had symbolized solar rays, the main means by which the bow-carrying Roman sun god, Apollo, supposedly infected those who had displeased him with serious sicknesses. Because, the reasoning went, Sebastian was clearly immune to the deadly effects of arrows, invoking him at those times when plague threatened communities, would, God willing, elicit his aid in either warding off or overcoming this airborne infection.

Signorelli was notable for his interest in human anatomy, and especially in ways of replicating human musculature in paint, as is evident from his inclusion of two nearly naked archers.

This dynamic figure is aiming a longbow at St. Sebastian.

The smartly dressed archer who is absorbed in reloading his crossbow looks far more like an Italian courtier than a Roman soldier.

It is likely that Signorelli devoted time and attention to this central character's clothing, for according to Giorgio Vasari, who knew Signorelli as a child, "Luca…lived splendidly and enjoyed dressing well" (*The Lives of the Artists*).

Some versions of the legend of St. Sebastian relate that a young woman named Irene, the widow of St. Castulus (another of Christianity's martyrs) took him home and nursed him back to health after he was left for dead. Irene is often depicted in a Benedictine nun's dark-colored habit, as here.

A powerful archer directs his crossbow at his immobilized living target.

Although longbows were faster to reload, crossbows dispatched arrows with greater velocity at close range, causing deeper penetration. Developed by the Romans, both weapons were still in use on the battlefield at the time that this panel was painted.

Either Sebastian, or another victim of Diocletian's zero-tolerance policy toward Christians, is hustled through streets that were probably modeled on those of the Umbrian town of Città di Castello, by soldiers whose helmets, uniforms, and horses' trappings appear more fifteenth than third century in style. This would have underlined the relevance of Sebastian's story—and potentially efficacious, epidemic-quelling powers of intercession between God and humankind—to contemporary viewers. The letters "S.P."—the first two letters of the Roman legions' abbreviated Latin motto, *Senatus Populusque Romanus*, "the Senate and the People of Rome," can just be discerned on the red standard.

Although research has shown that Pisanello based some of the birds and beasts that populate his painting on images that he found in pattern books, as well as in the International

Gothic illuminated manuscripts of the Netherlandish Limbourg brothers (all of whom died of the plague in 1416), many were inspired by his own observations.

Some have symbolic significance, including the pelican, which represents Christ's self-sacrifice.

The Vision of St. Eustace

Antonio Pisanello

c.1438–42, egg tempera on wood, National Gallery, London, England

Hunter saints, foremost among whom can be counted St. Eustace (or Eustachius) and St. Hubert, had an especially devoted following in France, Germany, and northern Italy, all countries within whose boundaries can be found dark, mysterious forests harboring all manner of creatures, including deer. And it may have been northern Europe's pagan heritage that caused these woodlands to be regarded as somehow sacred spots, while the stag's noble bearing, magnificent, treelike antlers, and status as the huntsman's quarry and provider of coveted venison all contributed to its symbolic association with Christ, who was similarly hunted down and killed, and who furthermore made an explicit link between his flesh and food. *The Vision of St. Eustace*, by Antonio Pisanello, a native of northern Italy, captures and conveys the sense of magical mysticism that cast such a potent spell over pious Christians during the medieval and Renaissance period. It also obviously gave the artist a welcome opportunity to juxtapose courtly artifice and natural forms.

St. Eustace's tale was popularized by Jacobus de Voragine's thirteenth-century work *The Golden Legend*, which informed its readers that despite being the Roman emperor Trajan's military commander-in-chief and "an idol worshipper," Placidus, as he was called before the fateful confrontation depicted by Pisanello, was a charitable man. While out hunting deer one day, he gave chase to a handsome stag, pursuing it to the top of a rocky outcrop, where it stopped and turned. As their gazes locked, Placidus's attention was drawn to a radiant cross, bearing the body of the crucified Christ, that could be seen shining between the stag's antlers. Then Christ spoke to Placidus through the stag's mouth, explaining that his good deeds had caused Christ to assume the form of a stag in order to lure and win over the pagan huntsman. And so it was that Placidus converted to Christianity, an action that would set him, following his baptism as Eustace by the bishop of Rome, on a trial-strewn path to martyrdom, which is said to have occurred in 118.

*See also **Portrait of a Knight*** (pages 167–69).

The pure-white swan (an unlikely forest-dweller) may allude to the Virgin Mary's spotless beauty and chastity, and also to martyrdom, for this otherwise mute waterbird was believed to sing—beautifully—when it was at the point of death.

The Golden Legend relates that Placidus and his fellow hunters came across a herd of deer, gentle creatures that may be compared to the defenseless and peace-loving followers of Christ.

The horn slung around his waist identifies the rider as a huntsman, and thus as Placidus.

Although it is not known who commissioned this painting from Pisanello, it is likely that his patron enjoyed hunting. That hunting was a noble pursuit is evident from the rider's rich garments and his horse's expensive-looking trappings, all of which are highlighted in gold.

This is the first of the huntsman's nine dogs to spot the Christ–stag, the others apparently still being deeply absorbed in picking up scents.

In International Gothic and Renaissance art, a scroll (known in Italian as a *cartellino*, or "label") like this usually bears a word or two of text pertinent to the image, rather like an annotation on a diagram. It is not known why Pisanello has left this otherwise incongruous element in his forest scene empty.

Because stags were once thought to detest snakes, and to trample them to death, they were likened to Christ, who symbolically crushes Satan underfoot.

Symbolically speaking, Christ's crucifix and the stag's antlers have much in common. Both may be equated with the tree of life, for instance, for while the wood of the cross on which Christ died was said to have been provided by the Tree of the Knowledge of Good and Evil that grew in the Garden of Eden (see pages 174 to 177), and his death gave believers the chance of enjoying eternal life, antlers both regenerate and resemble branches. In addition, the golden glow of the crucifix may signify spiritual illumination, or Christianity, in a densely wooded place of darkness, or heathenism.

The chasm that separates the hunter and stag may denote the gulf between pagans and Christians, but also the threshold that the huntsman is about to cross, leaving his life as Placidus in the past and moving forward, toward Christ, as Eustace.

The fleet-footed greyhound in pursuit of a fleeing hare may be an archetypal image of hunting, hunter, and hunted, but may furthermore have Christian connotations in that the hare, like the rabbit, may denote lust (on account of its tendency to breed prolifically) put to flight by the faithful servant of Christ (the greyhound, which, in common with all dogs, represents fidelity and obedience).

Since hunted almost to extinction, bears could still be found in northern European woods during the fifteenth century. Although they generally denoted danger and the Devil, they could have positive significance in Christian art, too. For it was believed that cubs were born blobs, and that they only assumed bearlike form when their mother literally licked them into shape, a notion that caused the newborn cubs to be likened to pagans, and the mother bear to the mother Church, which converts, guides, and sustains.

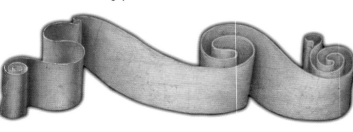

The Vision of St. Augustine

Vittore Carpaccio

1502–8, oil on canvas, Scuola di San Giorgio degli Schiavoni, Venice, Italy

Books, books, books—everywhere you look in *The Vision of St. Augustine*, you see books, be they piled higgledy-piggledy on the desk, propped up against the wall, ranged along shelves, or balanced on a revolving book stand. And it is this library of books that is the key to identifying the subject. For books symbolize learning and authorship, which, when the other clues in the painting are taken into consideration, point toward a theologian who was also a bishop, and thus to St. Augustine. Indeed, St. Augustine (354–430) was not only appointed bishop of Hippo (in his native Numidia, today, the North African nation of Algeria) following his baptism in 386, but wrote such hugely influential works as *De Civitate Dei* ("Of the City of God"). His intellectual and literary contribution to the Christian canon earned St. Augustine his status as one of the "fathers of the Church," or "Latin doctors" (that is, learned theologians of the early Roman Catholic Church), the others being St. Ambrose (339–97), St. Jerome (*c.*341–420), and St. Gregory the Great (*c.*540–604). And while St. Ambrose was largely responsible for Augustine's decision to dedicate himself to Christianity, Jerome and Augustine were correspondents, and the artist has depicted Augustine at the very moment that Jerome is said to have informed him of his death.

The Vision of St. Augustine is the last in a cycle of paintings focusing on the lives of St. George and St. Jerome that Vittore Carpaccio created for the Venetian Scuolo di San Giorgio degli Schiavoni (the School, or Confraternity, of St. George of the Slavs), and the combination of this paymaster and the elegant, Renaissance-era *studiolo* ("study" in Italian) setting point to another subject: Cardinal John Bessarion (1403–72). In 1468, four years after he had favored the confraternity by granting indulgences on the feast days of its patron saints (George, Jerome, and Tryphon), this Byzantine-born scholar and cleric presented his personal collection of eight hundred manuscripts to Venice's Senate, actions that caused him to be remembered with gratitude.

See also **Popular Saints** (pages 13–16), **The Neoplatonist Philosophy** (pages 96–97).

A statuette of Aphrodite/Venus, the Greco–Roman goddess of love, stands on a shelf amid other ornaments. This representation of a pagan deity would be a strange object to include in a faithful representation of a saintly, fourth- or fifth-century scholar's personal space, except that Carpaccio has used artistic license and has followed prevailing artistic fashion in depicting St. Augustine in a sixteenth-century humanist's *studiolo* crammed with thought-provoking ancient and contemporary curiosities and treasures. Indeed, the Renaissance period was notable for educated men's interest in the Classical world, and particularly in the theories of Greek philosophers like Plato (*c.*427–348 BC).

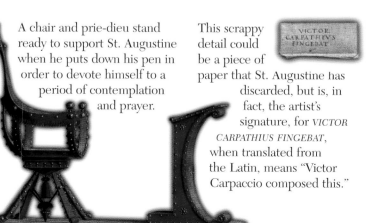

A chair and prie-dieu stand ready to support St. Augustine when he puts down his pen in order to devote himself to a period of contemplation and prayer.

This scrappy detail could be a piece of paper that St. Augustine has discarded, but is, in fact, the artist's signature, for *VICTOR CARPATHIUS FINGEBAT*, when translated from the Latin, means "Victor Carpaccio composed this."

VICTOR
CARPATHIVS
PINGEBAT

St. Augustine's Maltese dog pricks up its ears and stares toward the window with button-like eyes in response to the golden light and resonant sound that has interrupted the quiet scratching of his master's pen. This charming element injects a little life into the otherwise still scene, but in the Christian context, it may also be significant that dogs symbolize faithfulness and vigilance.

Its six red wings classify this angel as one of the seraphim, which, according to the Old Testament Book of Isaiah (6:1–2), stand above the throne of God. Its presence may denote divine inspiration.

A large bronze figure of the resurrected Christ occupies a prominent position at the center of the painting. The flag of the resurrection (or of Christ triumphant, as it is alternatively called) stands out on account of its eye-catching red cross on a white field. This is also the flag of St. George, the primary patron saint of the Scuola di San Giorgio degli Schiavone.

Carpaccio may have modeled St. Augustine's rapt features on Cardinal John Bessarion's face. His white cassock denotes a man of the Church.

The distinctive shape of a miter and the curved crook of a pastoral staff (which is sometimes called a crozier) signal that the *studiolo*'s occupant is a bishop.

The shell on the edge of St. Augustine's desk may have been included to hint at travel to exotic shores, but may also refer to the tale that tells that Augustine was wandering along a beach one day, pondering the mysteries of the Holy Trinity, when he came across a small boy scooping sea water into a hole in the sand. When Augustine commented that this exercise was futile, for the sea could never be "emptied" and the hole could never be filled, for the water would always seep through the sand, the Christ Child (for it was he) retorted that it was no more futile than Augustine's deliberations.

The occupant of the *studiolo* may pick up his bell simply to summon a servant, but Carpaccio may have depicted one on his desk as a reminder of the Sanctus bell that, in Roman Catholic churches, is rung to denote the presence of Christ during mass.

His pen poised in mid-air, St. Augustine gazes intently out of the window by his desk. According to legend, he was in the middle of writing to St. Jerome when a dazzling light lit up his window and Jerome's voice announced that he had died and gone to heaven.

Researchers have ascertained that this oval seal corresponds to one used by Cardinal Bessarion, and it may be that the document to which it is attached was intended to represent the very one received by the confraternity granting it indulgences—which supposedly reduced the time that Christians spent being punished in purgatory after they had died—on the days dedicated to their patron saints.

The sand-filled hourglass is a timepiece that measures the passing of time, and can therefore represent ageing and the inevitability of the death that awaits us all when the sands of our time on earth have run out.

Apart from giving the artist a chance to demonstrate his skill, the armillary sphere (a model of the planets' relative positions) that hangs by St. Augustine's desk is evidence of an intellectual interest in astronomy, as are the quadrant and astrolabes that can be seen strung up alongside the window in the opposite corner. Renaissance gentlemen were expected to make a study of this sphere of celestial science in order to reconcile it with their understanding of the Christian heaven.

The notes on the musical scores that Carpaccio has painted facing the viewer are so large that their tunes may be followed.

Representing music in this way may signify St. Augustine's study of music; the divine music that is said to pervade heaven (and art historians assert that one of these pieces of music is a hymn); a cultured person's accomplishment as a musician; and Venice's status as Europe's leading publisher of printed music at that time.

The Meditation of St. Jerome

Quentin Massys

Date unknown, oil on panel, private collection

Like St. Augustine (*see* pages 83 to 86), St. Jerome (*c*.341–420) was greatly esteemed by those who valued extreme expressions of piety, learning, and multilingualism, which, due to the influence of humanism, meant that his body of admirers grew ever larger during the Renaissance. Indeed, Jerome (who is also known as Hieronymus and Geronimo) not only spent much of his long—and well-documented—life immersed in books, but also put his considerable learning and knowledge of Greek, Latin, and Hebrew to selfless use by revising and translating the Old and New Testaments into Latin to create the "Vulgate" version of the Bible at the behest of Pope Damasus (*c*.304–84). It is largely this monumental achievement that caused St. Jerome to be counted among the four "Latin doctors," or "fathers of the Church," and he may consequently often be depicted in the company of St. Ambrose (339–97), St. Augustine (354–430), and St. Gregory the Great (*c*.540–604).

Quentin Massys elected to portray St. Jerome alone, however, as a scholar in his study—again, a popular humanist theme, according to whose conventions the study appeared as an idealized Renaissance haven of erudition rather than a sparely furnished monkish cell—also cunningly incorporating a scene illustrating another of his aspects into the backdrop. For according to *The Golden Legend*, a collection of saintly biographies compiled by Jacobus de Voragine in the thirteenth century, the Dalmatian-born Jerome had developed such an appetite for the (Latin) works of the Roman author Cicero (106–43 BC) when studying in Rome, that he dreamed of being accused by God of being a follower of Cicero, rather than of Christ. The repentant Jerome subsequently spent around four years alone in the Syrian desert, where he was tormented by "the fires of lust" stoked by visions of "bevies of young girls," and continually beat himself in penance and disgust. After working for Damasus in Rome between 382 and 384, he retired to a monastery in Bethlehem, where he spent the rest of his life studying and writing.

See also **Popular Saints** (pages 13–16), **The Neoplatonist Philosophy** (pages 96–97).

The scene in the background depicts an episode in St. Jerome's past: his years spent as an anchorite in the Middle Eastern desert (which, in Massy's vision, resembles the verdant countryside of Western Europe's Low Countries). Although *The Golden Legend* reports that Jerome beat his breast when beset by lustful thoughts, "until the Lord brought me peace again," the rock that he holds in his hand is an artistic invention, while the lion's presence, rather than being a documented fact, is similarly a fanciful inclusion based on it being one of St. Jerome's traditional attributes. (That said, although a lion did play a part in Jerome's life story, it may also symbolize his leonine personal qualities, such as courage and strength.) The book (which probably represents his Bible), crucifix, and the cardinal's hat and robe that feature in the foreground are likewise all echoed here.

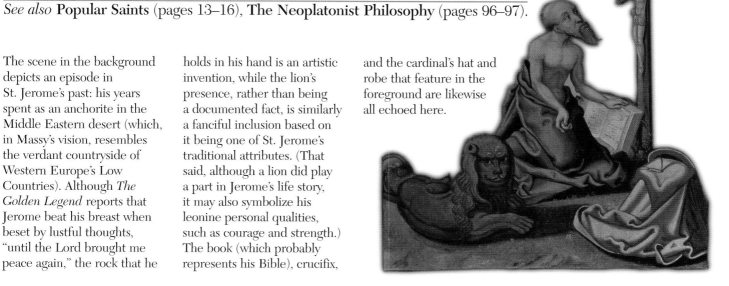

As writing instruments, this old-fashioned pen and inkhorn signify a writer, author, and correspondent. Not only was St. Jerome all three, but his renown is based on the written material that he left on his death, works that are still studied by religious scholars nearly sixteen centuries later.

Although the position of cardinal of the Roman Catholic Church did not exist during St. Jerome's lifetime, the services that he rendered to Pope Damasus caused him to be regarded as such by later generations. That is why a red, wide-brimmed, shallow-crowned cardinal's hat like this can usually be seen with Jerome in artistic representations of the saint.

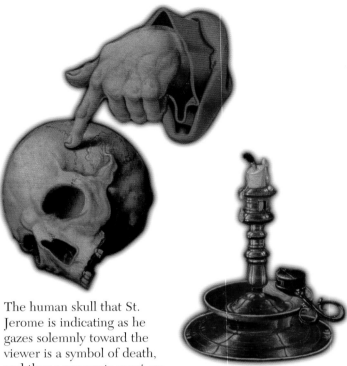

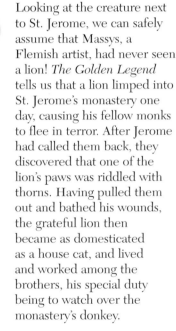

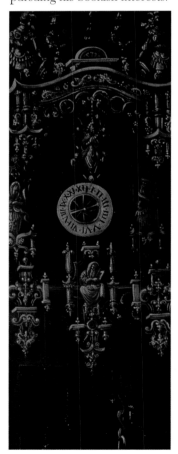

The human skull that St. Jerome is indicating as he gazes solemnly toward the viewer is a symbol of death, and thus a *memento mori*, or a reminder that death is the only certainty in life, that our days are numbered, and that believing in Christ may ensure our souls' eternal survival in heaven after we have departed this world. As a hermit saint who spent much time meditating alone on Christianity's mysteries, Jerome is often pictured with a skull, the implication being that death was central to his contemplations.

The Latin text that curves around the niche that encloses a crucifix is drawn from the meditations on the stations of the cross: *Adoramus te, Christe, et benedicimus tibi. Quia per sanctam crucem tuam redemisti mundum* ("We adore you, O Christ, and we praise you. Because by your holy cross you have redeemed the world").

In the days before electricity, people read by candlelight—then the only way of illuminating dim interiors—which is why this candlestick may occupy such a prominent position on St. Jerome's desk. Yet the stubby candle that it holds is the remnant of a far larger one that has burned away over time, and it may therefore represent Jerome, whose youthful vigor has diminished over the years, and whose time, and usefulness, on Earth are clearly drawing to an end.

Looking at the creature next to St. Jerome, we can safely assume that Massys, a Flemish artist, had never seen a lion! *The Golden Legend* tells us that a lion limped into St. Jerome's monastery one day, causing his fellow monks to flee in terror. After Jerome had called them back, they discovered that one of the lion's paws was riddled with thorns. Having pulled them out and bathed his wounds, the grateful lion then became as domesticated as a house cat, and lived and worked among the brothers, his special duty being to watch over the monastery's donkey.

A burning candle, symbolizing divine light and the presence of God, as well as ardent faith, burns in front of the crucifix that is the focal point of St. Jerome's private devotions.

Eyeglasses, or spectacles, denote a reader whose advanced age, and years spent poring over text, have caused his eyesight to fail, so that artificial help is required if he is to continue pursuing his bookish interests.

Like the candle on the desk, the handsome, ornately gilded, Renaissance-era wall clock (right) reflects the passing of time, and thus the inevitability of death.

The Legend of St. Ursula

Master of the Thalheimer Altarpiece

c.1530, oil on panel, private collection

Although there is so little evidence supporting the existence of St. Ursula that her feast (October 21) was removed from the Roman Catholic calendar in 1969, her remarkable tale—and explicit connection with many European places—earned her a devoted following.

The bare bones on which the story of St. Ursula and her companions was based before being imaginatively embroidered over the course of several centuries is a Latin inscription, dating back to around 400, in the St. Ursula Church in the German Rhineland city of Köln (Cologne), explaining that this once ruined basilica had been restored to honor the virgins who had been martyred there. And it was partly thanks to the discovery, during the first half of the twelfth century, of a great number of human bones in the vicinity (many of which now decorate the church, with others having dispersed throughout Europe as holy relics), and partly due to the reported visions of a German nun, Elizabeth of Schönau (*c.*1129–1165), that the fantastic account of St. Ursula and the eleven thousand virgins evolved. This was then popularized by Jacobus de Voragine's thirteenth-century compendium of saintly anecdotes, *The Golden Legend*.

According to this account, the lovely Ursula, who lived during the third or fourth century, was the Christian daughter of a British king (or else the king of Brittany). She agreed to be betrothed to Conon, a pagan prince of Anglia, on condition that he be baptized; that she be provided with ten virgins as companions, and that they each be supplied with a thousand more virgins, as well as a fleet of ships; and that the marriage should be delayed for three years. To her surprise, these conditions were agreed, and Ursula and her chaste ladies set off on a pilgrimage, which took them along the River Rhine to Cologne, and then to the Swiss city of Basel (Basle), where they disembarked before continuing overland to Rome, in Italy. On their return to Cologne, all were slaughtered by an army of Huns for being Christian—all, that is, except Ursula, after whom the chief Hun lusted. But when she rejected his advances, she, too, was killed, with a single arrow.

See also **Popular Saints** (pages 13–16), **resurrected Christ detail** (page 136).

Although it does not resemble the twin-spired edifice that towers over the city of Cologne today, this riverbank church represents the Kölner Dom, or Cologne Cathedral, whose erection began in 1248.

It was raised not far from the Rhine, on ground that had once supported a fourth-century Roman temple. By the time that the Master of the Thalheimer Altarpiece painted his homage to St. Ursula, only the choir, the nave, and part of the southern tower had been completed.

A fresh complexion, youthful figure, and beautiful long hair are all hallmarks of a virginal young woman in Renaissance art. The Ursuline Order, which was established in 1535, in Italy, by St. Angela Merici (1474–1540), is dedicated to educating young girls, and is named for Ursula in tribute to the protective role she played in relation to her virgin companions.

While her bejeweled crown signals Ursula's royal status on earth, her halo symbolizes her spiritual saintliness.

So serene and accepting is Ursula's expression that it is only when the viewer's gaze drifts downward that one becomes aware of the arrow buried deep in her chest. This instrument of her martyrdom is one of Ursula's traditional attributes. Artistic license has been taken advantage of in this depiction, for written accounts assert that Ursula was the last of her party to die, not the first, and that she was murdered on dry land, not aboard her ship.

His triple-crowned tiara marks out the man behind Ursula as a pope. According to *The Golden Legend*, this is Cyriacus (or Ciriacus), who received Ursula on her arrival in Rome, and, some say, also her betrothed, Conon, whom the pope baptized, and who was known thereafter by his Christian name, Etherius (or Aetherius). When still in Rome, Cyriacus had dreamed that he would be martyred alongside Ursula and her companions, prompting him to resign his office and join them as they set sail for Cologne. His abdication so outraged the cardinals ("who thought he was mad to relinquish the glory of the pontificate in order to chase off after some silly women") that they erased his name from the list of popes.

Because she made a pilgrimage to Rome—the papal headquarters ever since St. Peter established the bishopric of Rome—Ursula is often depicted with a pilgrim's staff. This grand version is surmounted by a cross (so that it resembles an archbishop's processional staff or crozier) and flies the flag of the Resurrection, or of Christ triumphant, which, in Christian art, represents victory over death and may therefore denote martyrdom.

The Golden Legend refers to one of Ursula's traveling companions as "Vincent, a cardinal priest," whom the artist has portrayed here wearing a cardinal's red hat and robes.

The ragged hose of the boatman look out of place alongside his passengers' expensive-looking garments and regalia. The moneybag tied to his waist, and his easy stance as he grips his vessel's tiller, suggest that he has been hired for his navigational skill and familiarity with the Rhine. Both would have been prerequisites when sailing from the mouth of the river (in the North Sea, at Rotterdam) through the Low Countries, France, Germany, and Austria, to Basel, in Switzerland (the farthest point that can be reached by sea-going ships), and back again, for many perilous stretches of water punctuate this 820-mile-long river, including the Lorelei, a lowering rock a few miles south of Cologne that is supposedly the home of a singing siren and the marker of many a watery grave.

ALLUSION AND ALLEGORY

The work of art is the exaggeration of an idea.

André Gide, *Journals* (1896)

Above: The Venus of Urbino *(1538), by Titian, portrays the Classical goddess of love as a contemporary, overtly sensual young woman.* ***Top:*** *A detail from Jacopo del Sellaio's* The Story of Cupid and Psyche: Part I, *c.1473 (see pages 109–111).*

Given the humanist interest in the literature, art, and philosophy of Classical antiquity, its lust for learning, and its appetite for intellectual experimentation, as well as the growing desire of Renaissance-era rulers to be seen as shining examples of erudition and civilization, it was, perhaps, inevitable that the art of this age should have branched out from the primarily pious focus of the Middle Ages to venture increasingly into the "pagan" past.

During the fifteenth century—significantly longer than a millennium since their stories and images were first recorded with styluses and chisels—many of the celebrated mythical and historical personalities of the ancient Greco–Roman worlds were once again being portrayed in both narrative and allegorical paintings. Yet although artists' themes were expanding beyond the sober confines of the Bible, other Christian texts, and hagiographies of the saints, providing mouth-watering opportunities to tackle such juicy subjects as sensual seductions, hybrid beings, and the curvaceous or muscular naked bodies whose prototypes were Classical statues, painters continued to follow certain medieval conventions, such as the inclusion of traditional attributes with which to facilitate the identification of the personalities depicted with them (an eagle, for instance, usually appearing alongside Jupiter).

There was, moreover, almost always a moralizing element underpinning such paintings, sometimes in accordance with a medieval tradition of comparing and contrasting the Old and New Testament—or Judaism and Christianity—using symbolic messages in such a way that Judaism invariably appeared wanting in comparison to Christianity (see also *Allegory of the Old and New Testaments*, pages 132 to 136). In this way, Venus, the Roman goddess of love (who corresponds to the Greek Aphrodite, but who, like other characters from Classical mythology, was invariably known by the Roman name with which scholars were familiar from Latin texts), could symbolize the deadly sin of Lust. Equally, crumbling Roman ruins, though true to life, could represent the decay of the old pagan order, which could never endure because it was built on false foundations, symbolically speaking, in contrast to an everlasting, incorruptible world founded on rock-solid Christian principles (see, for example, *The Martyrdom of St. Sebastian*, pages 77 to 79). Gradually, however, these pagan personalities and constructs began to be regarded more neutrally as the jaundiced

Above: The center panel from Hieronymous Bosch's triptych The Last Judgment, c.1482. *Below: Lorenzo Lotto's* A Lady as Lucretia (1530), *featuring a message on a piece of paper lying on the table, may be read as a moral statement.*

view of the Church was tempered by a more philosophical mindset, one in which they, like many Old Testament characters, were considered aspects of the universal truth, or what we might today call archetypes, which was believed to have been divinely inspired.

Thus it was that a whole new category of characters was added to the vocabulary of art, many of them quickly progressing to become vehicles for the personification of such abstract qualities as reason (Apollo and Minerva, for instance), war (Mars), strength (Hercules), and music (Orpheus). Yet, as in medieval times, not all of the personifications that appeared in Renaissance art were intended to be recognizable individuals, with the Four Cardinal Virtues, for example, typically being portrayed as women whose only distinguishing features were their attributes (see *Minerva Chasing the Vices from the Garden of Virtue*, pages 127 to 131).

All in all, while color, composition, gestures, and expressions could together convey the gist of an artwork's meaning, if the viewer was to appreciate its true significance—maybe as a moral allegory rather than a narrative painting or a straightforward illustration of a literary tale—it was vital that he or she was familiar with a growing range of symbolic attributes, and with the literary sources from which they were drawn. And while members of the intellectual elite of the Renaissance period delighted in pitting their wits against pictorial puzzles, many of its artists relished building up elegant, and often beautiful, allegories piece by piece, whose depths of meaning could only be truly appreciated by those who were well versed in the language of symbolism, allusion, and philosophy.

CLASSICAL ALLUSIONS AND ALLEGORIES

One of the ways in which Renaissance artists and those good Christians who commissioned work from them sought to validate their growing focus on the larger-than-life divine characters whose adventures they had read about in such Latin-language works as *The Aeneid*, by the poet Virgil (70–19 BC), and *The Metamorphoses*, by Ovid (43 BC–AD 17), was to claim parallels with Christianity, as had also been done with the Old Testament, the justifying theory being that many pre-Christian writers had unwittingly been inspired by the Christian God. And a contemporary interpretation of *The Metamorphoses* called "The Moralized Ovid," continuing the tradition of the "Moralized Bible" and the earlier, visual *Biblia Pauperum* ("Bible of the Poor"), which juxtaposed images from the Old and New Testament, did just that. Thus while the Old Testament David, the shepherd boy who was anointed king of Israel by the prophet Samuel, could be considered a precursor, or "type," of Christ, so, too, it was reasoned, could Orpheus, who, like Christ, descended into the underworld and returned from it unscathed (see *Orpheus and Eurydice*, pages 118 to 121, and *The Descent into Limbo*, pages 52 to 54). Similarly, Danaë, the young woman who was impregnated by Jupiter in the form of a golden shower, later giving birth to the hero Perseus, was considered a precursor of the Virgin Mary, the mother of Jesus, as was Juno, who, like Mary, was accorded the status of queen of heaven. In this way, Classical personalities and myths could be regarded as allegories of Christian characters and "truths."

It was the humanist interest in all things human, and admiration of the extraordinarily realistic achievements of the sculptors of antiquity, that caused the human body to be scrutinized and portrayed by artists—especially through the medium of

Above: Giovanni Boccaccio. Below: The first scene from Botticelli's series of paintings (c.1483) based on the story of Nastagio degli Onesti, a knight in a novella of Boccaccio's Decameron.

Classical mythology—with an intensity and frequency that had not been seen for centuries. Yet nudity was not unknown in Christian art, for Adam and Eve were invariably depicted naked (apart from a strategically placed fig leaf), although it would admittedly take time for the symbolism associated with the unclothed female body to shift from the sin and shame represented by Eve to the admirable quality of Truth, having been filtered through the catalyst of the beautiful, shameless, inviting Venus (see *Sacred and Profane Love*, pages 102 to 104).

THE NEOPLATONIST PHILOSOPHY

One of the most important sources for scholars, artists, and writers who were interested in Classical mythology was *De genealogiis deorum gentilium* (*Genealogies of the Pagan Gods*), by the Italian poet and writer Giovanni Boccaccio (1313–75). Boccaccio, whose works influenced and inspired many prominent Renaissance painters (see *The Wedding Feast*, pages 140 to 143), argued that the Classical myths incorporated universal truths that were not at odds with Christianity, an essentially Stoic view that was shared by many Renaissance thinkers who had immersed themselves in the teachings of ancient Greek philosophers, most notably the Neoplatonists.

As their name, which means "the new Platonists," indicates, the Florentine-based Neoplatonists were enthused by the philosophy of Plato (*c*.427–348 BC), or rather by that devised by Plotinus (?205–?270 AD), a Roman Neoplatonist who popularized a fusion of Platonic, Pythagorean, and Aristotelian theories. Having been inspired by George Gemistus Plethon (1355–1452), the Byzantine author of *On the Differences between Aristotelian and Platonic Philosophies* (1439), a central figure of the "Platonic Academy" founded in Florence by Cosimo de' Medici some time after 1439 was Marsilio Ficino (1433–99), who translated Plato's body of work from Greek into Latin. In doing so, Ficino concluded that the Platonic theory of Ideas, namely that objects that we perceive with our senses are manifestations of ideal, uncorrupted universal forms or ideas that exist on a higher realm, was not incompatible with Christianity.

What especially fired the imagination of artists within the Neoplatonic circle like Sandro Botticelli (see *Primavera*, pages 122 to 126) were consequently the idealizing allegorical possibilities inherent in portraying figures of Classical mythology, as well as the challenge of depicting ideals of physical beauty, as embodied by Leonardo da Vinci's *Vitruvian Man* (1490), whose "ideal" proportions were derived from guidelines presented by the Roman architect Vitruvius, in the first century BC, in his influential treatise on architecture, *De architectura*. And so sensuous depictions of Mars succumbing to Venus's physical charms came to symbolize War tamed by Love, and therefore peace, with similar combinations of Roman gods and goddesses alluding in pictorial form to the interaction of the intangible qualities that they represented.

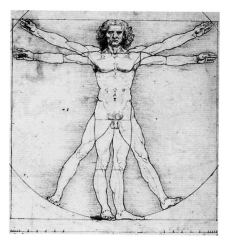 

Above, left: Leonardo da Vinci's iconic Vitruvian Man *(1490) demonstrates the great artist's mastery of geometry and anatomy, as well as drawing.* **Above, right:** *Titian's late, allegorical masterpiece* The Flaying of Marsyus *(1575–76) is laden with symbolic content.*

CLASSICAL FIGURES IN RENAISSANCE ART

Many figures drawn from Greco–Roman mythology have near-nudity in common in Renaissance art. Other ways in which it is possible to identify Classical deities and personalities (which, following the convention of Renaissance times, are listed under their Roman, rather than their Greek, names) include noting their physical characteristics and symbolic attributes. Those of some of the most popular Classical figures are listed below.

Jupiter (Zeus) *Appearance:* an older, authoritative-looking, bearded man, sometimes with a crown and scepter. *Attributes:* an eagle; thunderbolts or lightning; an oak tree or leaves; a bull; a swan; a cloud; a shower of gold. See *Allegory*, pages 147 to 149.

Juno (Hera) *Appearance:* a mature, imperious-looking woman, perhaps with a crown and scepter. *Attributes:* a peacock; a girdle; a cow; a cornucopia; a pomegranate; a lily; a cuckoo.

Neptune (Poseidon) *Appearance:* an older man with long hair and a flowing white beard. *Attributes:* water, especially seas and oceans; a trident; a horse; hippocampi (seahorses); dolphins; seashells; mermen; mermaids.

Mars (Ares) *Appearance:* an athletic-looking man in his prime, perhaps dressed as a warrior and wearing a helmet. *Attributes:* armor; weapons; a wolf; a woodpecker. See *St. Philip Exorcizing the Demon From the Temple of Mars*, pages 74 to 76.

Venus (Aphrodite) *Appearance:* a beautiful woman in her prime, often naked, with long hair. *Attributes:* a mirror; a necklace; a girdle; a scallop shell; white doves; white swans; a swallow; a rabbit; red roses; pearls; myrtle; an apple, sometimes golden; a quince; violets; Cupid; *putti* or cherubs; the Three Graces; Flora; a turtle; a dolphin; a torch; a heart. See *Sacred and Profane Love*, pages 102 to 104; *Primavera*, pages 122 to 126; *Minerva Chasing the Vices from the Garden of Virtue*, pages 127 to 131.

Vulcan (Hephaestos) *Appearance:* a small, sinewy man, with a strong torso and weak-looking legs. *Attributes:* a hammer and anvil; pincers; fire; a forge; a crutch; dogs.

Ceres (Demeter) *Appearance:* a mature woman, sometimes crowned with ears of corn. *Attributes:* a cornucopia; ears or sheaves of corn; a sickle; a cow; a pig; poppies; a torch.

Apollo (Apollon) *Appearance:* a young, clean-shaven man with golden hair, sometimes emitting a radiant glow; sometimes crowned with a laurel wreath. *Attributes:* the sun; a golden chariot pulled by four horses; a bow and arrow or quiver; a lyre or musical instrument; the nine Muses; a snake; a tripod; sheep; a crook; a laurel tree; a swan; a globe; a wolf. See *The Story of Cupid and Psyche*, pages 105 to 107; *School of Athens*, pages 162 to 166.

Above: Zephyr (or Zephyrus), god of the west wind, seen here in Botticelli's The Birth of Venus *(1485–86), was a herald of spring.*

Diana (Artemis) *Appearance:* a young, serious, athletic-looking woman. *Attributes:* lovely nymphs; a crescent moon; a bow and arrow or quiver; a javelin; a shield; hunting dogs; a stag; a bear. See *Minerva Chasing the Vices from the Garden of Virtue*, pages 127 to 131.

Mercury (Hermes) *Appearance:* a young, clean-shaven man wearing winged sandals and a winged hat (the petasus). *Attributes:* a snake-entwined staff (the caduceus); a moneybag; a ram. See *Primavera*, pages 122 to 126.

Minerva (Athena) *Appearance*: a young woman dressed as a warrior, often wearing a helmet with plumes (a panache) and a breastplate. *Attributes*: a shield (or breastplate) bearing the Gorgon's head; a cloak fringed with snakes (the Aegis); a spear; an owl; books; an olive tree. See *Minerva Chasing the Vices from the Garden of Virtue*, pages 127 to 131; *School of Athens*, pages 162 to 166.

Juventas (Hebe) *Appearance:* a young woman, often wearing a sleeveless gown. *Attributes:* a cup; a jug or pitcher.

Cupid (Eros) *Appearance:* either a cherubic, winged child or a handsome young man; sometimes blindfolded. *Attributes:* a bow and arrow, or arrows, or a quiver; Venus; a torch; a globe; a bee or honeycomb; cherubs or *putti*. See *The Story of Cupid and Psyche*, pages 105 to 107; *Sacred and Profane Love*, pages 102 to 104; *Primavera*, pages 122 to 126.

The Three Graces (Gratiae or Charites) *Appearance:* three lovely young women, hands entwined, dancing in a circle. *Attributes:* apples; dice; myrtle; roses. See *Primavera*, pages 122 to 126.

Zephyr (Zephyrus) *Appearance:* a bluish or greenish disembodied face, with a puffing mouth, sometimes winged; a flying figure, sometimes with wings. *Attributes:* a young female in his arms (Flora). See *Primavera*, pages 122 to 126; *The Story of Cupid and Psyche*, pages 105 to 107.

Bacchus (Dionysus) *Appearance:* a young man, sometimes half-naked, wearing an animal skin or crowned with vine leaves and grapes. *Attributes:* vines; grapes; a wine glass; the thyrsus staff; ivy; satyrs; goats; a bull; tigers; leopards.

Hercules (Herakles) *Appearance*: a baby; a powerfully built man, with curly hair and a short beard, sometimes wearing a lion skin. *Attributes:* snakes; a club; a lion; the Hydra; a stag; a boar; the Stymphalian birds; a bull; horses; a belt; cattle; golden apples; Cerberus; a bow and arrows or a quiver; a distaff; two women, respectively representing Virtue and Vice.

Jason *Appearance:* a young man with blond hair, wearing a leopard skin, or dressed as a soldier. *Attributes:* a ship (the *Argo*); other young men (the Argonauts); the Golden Fleece. See *The Argo*, pages 115 to 117.

Orpheus *Appearance:* a young, clean-shaven man, sometimes crowned with laurels. *Attributes:* a lyre or viol; wild animals and birds. See *Orpheus and Eurydice*, pages 119 to 121.

THE PERSONIFICATION OF IDEAS, IDEALS, AND INIQUITIES

Although the symbolic expression, through personification, of Christian virtues promoted by the Church, the vices that it deplored, the general vagaries of fortune that tested the faithful with its arbitrary ups and downs, and other such facts of life had long been popular, the humanist focus on humankind resulted in all manner of qualities and concepts—positive, neutral, and negative—being portrayed as a person or people.

Classical mythology was now supplying a rich cast of characters, and these were increasingly being joined by literary figures, and even historical personalities, in taking the place of the anonymous women who often performed the personification function by default, who could be said to be mere clotheshorses to which to attach attributes. Plato, the proposer of the Four Cardinal Virtues (Prudence, Justice, Fortitude, and Temperance, which, he asserted, the citizens of the ideal republic should possess), was, for instance, portrayed in Raphael's *School of Athens* (see pages 162 to 166), at the center of an illustrious group of the age of antiquity's most important thinkers, many of whom were soon being used to personify the subjects that collectively formed the Seven Liberal Arts. It should again be stressed, however, that none but the most highly educated individuals of Renaissance society would have recognized them.

POPULAR PERSONIFICATIONS IN RENAISSANCE ART

Renaissance artists often personified the characteristics that they considered it either desirable or undesirable for a person to possess, the most significant of which were the Four Cardinal Virtues, the Three Theological Virtues, the Seven Deadly Sins, and the Seven Liberal Arts (outlined below). In such instances, note that it is a figure's attributes that are usually more important conveyors of the qualities that they symbolize than his or her appearance.

Note, too, that many more qualities, conditions, subjects, virtues, and vices were commonly portrayed, including Abundance, Chastity, Concord, Constancy, Cruelty, Deceit, Despair, Discord, Fame, Fidelity, History, Hospitality, Humility, Ignorance, Innocence, Melancholy, Obedience, Patience, Peace, Philosophy, Poverty, Vanity, Vigilance, Victory, and Wisdom, to name but a few. See *Minerva Chasing the Vices from the Garden of Virtue*, pages 127 to 131.

Collective personifications include the Ages of Man (typically Infancy, Childhood, Youth, Maturity, and Old Age), the Ages of the World (Gold, Silver, Bronze, and Iron), Day and Night, the Four Elements (Water, Earth, Fire, and Air), the Twelve Months, the Four Parts of the World (Europe, Africa, Asia, and America), the Four Seasons (Spring, Summer, Fall, and Winter), the Five Senses (Hearing, Sight, Smell, Touch, Taste), and the Four Temperaments (Phlegmatic, Sanguine, Choleric, and Melancholic).

Aspects of Human Life Personified

Fortune, Death, Folly, and Truth are just four important aspects of human life that were frequently personified by Renaissance artists.

Fortune (*Fortuna*) *Appearance:* a blindfolded woman, sometimes balancing on a globe, sometimes winged. *Attributes:* a wheel; a rudder; a sail; a ship; a dolphin; a shell; a cornucopia; dice; a bridle. See *The Wheel of Fortune*, pages 144 to 146.

Death (*Mors*) *Appearance:* a skeleton, sometimes shrouded in a hooded black cloak; a skull. *Attributes:* a scythe; an hourglass; a toad.

Folly (*Stultitia*) *Appearance:* a court jester or an obviously idiotic person. *Attributes:* donkey's ears; a cap with earlike projections or feathers, decorated with bells; a staff with a grotesque head on top; a striped outfit; an ape. See *The Ship of Fools*, pages 137 to 139; *The Coronation of the Virgin*, pages 38 to 41.

Truth (*Veritas*) *Appearance:* a naked woman. *Attributes:* a mirror; the sun; a peach to which one leaf is attached; a globe; a laurel wreath. See *Sacred and Profane Love*, pages 102 to 104.

The Four Cardinal Virtues

The Four Cardinal Virtues, which are also called the "natural" virtues, were first specified by the Greek philosopher Plato (?427–?347 BC), in *The Republic*, as being the most important moral qualities that humankind is inherently capable of displaying.

Prudence (*Prudentia*)

Appearance: a young woman, often with two or three heads. *Attributes:* a mirror; a snake; a book; compasses; a stag. See *Minerva Chasing the Vices from the Garden of Virtue*, pages 127 to 131.

Below: Hans Baldung's The Three Ages of Woman and Death, *1510.*

Justice (*Justitia*) *Appearance:* a young woman, sometimes blindfolded. *Attributes:* a sword; scales; fasces; a globe; compasses; a set-square; a lion. See *Minerva Chasing the Vices from the Garden of Virtue*, pages 127 to 131.

Fortitude (*Fortitudo*) *Appearance:* a young woman, sometimes wearing a lion's skin or a helmet and armor. *Attributes:* a pillar, sometimes broken; a club; a lion; a shield; a spear; a sword. See *Minerva Chasing the Vices from the Garden of Virtue*, pages 127 to 131.

Temperance (*Temperantia*) *Appearance:* a young woman. *Attributes:* one or two jugs or pitchers; a sheathed sword; a bridle. See *Minerva Chasing the Vices from the Garden of Virtue*, pages 127 to 131.

Left: An armor-clad woman personifying courage is the subject of Botticelli's early painting Fortitudo *(1470).*

The Three Theological Virtues
Although the Church approved of the Four Cardinal Virtues, it regarded the Three Theological Virtues as being special gifts of God to humankind. These are listed in the New Testament book, 1 Corinthians 13:13: "And now abideth faith, hope, charity, these three; but the greatest of these is charity."

Charity (*Caritas*) *Appearance:* a gentle-looking woman, sometimes breastfeeding children. *Attributes:* a flaming heart; a flaming vase; a torch; a candle; children; a cornucopia; fruit; moneybags; a pelican feeding its offspring.

The Seven Deadly Sins

According to the teachings of the Church, committing any of the Seven Deadly Sins put one in danger of spending eternity in hell, while being guilty of other vices would, it was believed, certainly increase time spent in purgatory. In art, each deadly sin was sometimes pictured in opposition to an appropriate virtue. See *The Coronation of the Virgin*, pages 38 to 41; *Dante and his Poem the "Divine Comedy,"* pages 178 to 181.

Lust (*Luxuria* or *Libido*) *Appearance:* a naked woman whose genitals are being devoured by toads and snakes; Venus; satyrs. *Attributes:* a pig or boar; a donkey; a cock; a goat; a hare; a rabbit; a dove; an ape; a mirror; a toad. See *Minerva Chasing the Vices from the Garden of Virtue*, pages 127 to 131; *The Ship of Fools*, pages 137 to 139.

Gluttony (*Gula*) *Appearance:* an obese person, grossly overeating and drinking too much. *Attributes:* vine leaves; food and drink; a pig or boar; a bear; a wolf; a hedgehog. See *The Ship of Fools*, pages 137 to 139.

Avarice (*Avaritia*) or Greed *Appearance:* Someone carrying or stockpiling valuable objects, sometimes blindfolded. *Attributes:* A purse or moneybags; coins; golden balls; luxury items; a

harpy, sometimes grasping golden balls in its claws. See *Minerva Chasing the Vices from the Garden of Virtue*, pages 127 to 131; *The Moneylender and his Wife*, pages 150 to 153.

Sloth (*Acedia*) *Appearance:* someone dozing or lazing around. *Attributes:* an ass; an ox; a pig.

Wrath (*Ira*) or Anger *Appearance:* someone inflicting violence on another or ripping his or her clothes. *Attributes:* a lion; a sword or dagger.

Envy (*Invidia*) *Appearance:* a sour-faced, scrawny woman, sometimes eating snakes or her own heart or intestines. *Attributes:* a snake; a dog.

Pride (*Superbia*) *Appearance:* a woman looking in mirror; a man falling from a horse. *Attributes:* a peacock; an eagle; a lion; Satan's face in a mirror. See *The Conversion of St. Paul*, pages 71 to 73.

Above: *A musical instrument, scroll, scorpion, and set-square are among the clues to the subjects of Botticelli's* A Young Man Being Introduced to the Seven Liberal Arts *(1484–86).*

Faith (*Fides*) *Appearance:* a dignified-looking woman, sometimes wearing a helmet, with her hand on her heart. *Attributes:* a cross; a book; a candle; a chalice; a baptismal font; a cube.

Hope (*Spes*) *Appearance:* a young woman, sometimes with wings, with her hands together in prayer. *Attributes:* an anchor; a ship; a crown; flowers; a crow.

The Seven Liberal Arts

It was considered essential for privileged young men to have a thorough grounding in the Seven Liberal Arts in Renaissance times. The seven subjects were divided into two groups, with grammar, rhetoric, and logic being collectively given the Latin name *trivium* ("the three roads"), and astronomy, geometry, arithmetic, and music being categorized as the *quadrivium* ("the four roads"). These subjects could be personified by venerable, wise-looking figures drawn from the history of human thought or as women, with each art being distinguished by fitting attributes. An eighth figure may represent Philosophy, who was considered the "mother" of the Seven Liberal Arts. See also *School of Athens*, pages 162 to 166; *The Ambassadors*, pages 200 to 203.

Grammar (*Grammatica*) *Appearance:* a man with the features of Priscian or Donatus; a woman watering plants; a woman teaching pupils. *Attributes:* a scroll or book; writing instruments; fruit; a whip or rod; a drinking fountain; a door.

Rhetoric (*Rhetorica*) *Appearance:* a man with the features of Cicero; a woman. *Attributes:* a scroll or book; a sword; a shield; a globe.

Logic (*Dialectice*) or Dialectics *Appearance:* a man with the features of Aristotle; a woman; two older men talking. *Attributes:* a flowering branch or flowers; a scorpion; a snake or snakes; a lizard; scales; a scroll or book.

Astronomy (*Astrologia*) *Appearance:* a man with the features of Ptolemy; a woman. *Attributes:* compasses; a (celestial) globe; an astrolabe or a sextant; an armillary sphere.

Geometry (*Geometria*) *Appearance:* a man with the features of Euclid; a woman. *Attributes:* a ruler; a set-square; compasses; scientific instruments; a terrestrial globe.

Arithmetic (*Arithmetica*) *Appearance:* a man with the features of Pythagoras; a woman. *Attributes:* an abacus; a ruler; a scroll or book covered in mathematical calculations.

Music (*Musica*) *Appearance:* a man with the features of Pythagoras or Tubal-cain; a woman; Orpheus. *Attributes:* a scroll or book covered in musical notation; musical instruments, especially the lute; a swan.

Sacred and Profane Love

Titian

c.1515, oil on canvas, Galleria Borghese, Rome, Italy

It is only relatively recently that *Sacred and Profane Love* has been generally accepted as the title of Titian's painting of a clothed and naked woman posed before such recognizably Renaissance elements as a Classically inspired frieze and realistically rendered landscape. This scholarly consensus in turn suggests that the Venetian artist's intriguing image has an allegorical, rather than a straightforward, meaning.

Dictionary definitions of "sacred" and "profane" conjure up a black-and-white picture of diametrically opposed extremes of love that is rather at odds with Titian's pastoral of harmonious hues. More apt adjectives are, perhaps, "celestial" and "terrestrial," which were first used by the Greek philosopher Plato (*c*.427–348 BC) in his dialogue *Symposium* in connection with the Greco–Roman goddess of love Aphrodite/Venus. According to his dualistic concept, Venus had two aspects, depending on the manner of her birth: as the child born of Zeus/Jupiter and the Titan Dione, she was Aphrodite Pandemos ("Aphrodite of All People" in Greek) or Venus Vulgaris ("Common Venus" or "Earthly Venus" in Latin), the goddess of terrestrial, earthly, or profane love; as the daughter of Uranus and sea foam, she was Aphrodite Urania ("Aphrodite of Uranus"), or Venus Coelestis ("Celestial Venus"), the embodiment of celestial, spiritual, or sacred love. Neoplatonic theories

refined by such Italian Renaissance scholars as Marsilio Ficino (1433–99) did much to popularize the concept of this union of opposites (*concordia oppositorum*), and *Sacred and Profane Love* was painted in this spirit.

Decoding the symbolic messages that can be seen this painting when taking its alternative title, *Venus with the Bride*, as a starting point leads the viewer to a similar conclusion, namely, that although they may assume different forms, all aspects of love spring from the same source and are beautiful. And the knowledge that this painting was commissioned to celebrate the wedding, in 1514, of Nicolò Aurelio, a Venetian dignitary, to Laura Bagarotto, a widow, gives this interpretation added poignancy.

See also **rose detail** (page 36), **The Neoplatonist Philosophy** (pages 96–97).

In earlier times, the castle was regarded as the counterpart of the church in making an architectural statement, in this case, in proclaiming secular, or earthly, power. The suggestion is therefore that after her marriage to the king of the castle, the bride will reign as queen of hearts.

Rabbits were considered sacred to Aphrodite/Venus in her earthly aspect because they breed prolifically. Their inclusion here thus signals sensuality and the hope and expectation that the fruits of earthly love will be numerous children.

Her fine clothes identify the lady on the left as Profane Love (or Earthly Venus), for impressive appearances, as well as the flaunting of wealth, are important on earth.

 The beautiful embodiment of earthly love is wearing a crown of myrtle, just as brides did in ancient Roman times. This plant was linked with Aphrodite/Venus because it smells sweet, bears fruit, and is evergreen, all of which can be said to characterize ideal, everlasting love, which is why the myrtle came to represent the perfect marriage.

Artistic convention decreed that the female personification of earthly love should be depicted with a bowl of jewels, the flashy beauty of these costly gems mined from the earth hinting that the value with which mortals invest them is primarily based on their material worth, a consideration that only has significance on earth.

The unifying presence of Eros/Cupid, the son of Aphrodite/Venus and personification of love, at the center of this painting confirms that love is its central theme. He is dipping his hand into a curious structure filled with water (a symbol of life), which may be a sarcophagus or a well. Whichever it is, tomb or fount, the message is the same: love renews and sustains life.

The horse that is depicted being led across the frieze signifies the human body, or our "animal passions." The coat of arms that adorns the frieze is that of the bridegroom, Nicolò Aurelio. Beneath it, a spout feeds a plant the waters of love.

Her nudity (and preserved modesty) tell us that Profane Love's twin sister is Sacred Love (or Celestial Venus), for the naked truth is nothing to be ashamed of, while a pure and innocent mind will not be sullied by impure thoughts. Although both Profane and Sacred Love are equally beautiful, Neoplatonists believed that Profane Love should nevertheless aspire to the virtues embodied by Sacred Love.

 The rose is a symbol of Aphrodite/Venus, and while the color red signifies her carnal, or earthly, aspect, and white, her spiritual spotlessness, this bloom's shade of pink and position alongside Profane Love hint at an impending marriage.

The vaselike lamp that Sacred Love is holding burns with the fire of religious zeal, the flame that also represents divinity, spiritual enlightenment, and hope. It seems as though it is causing clouds, which may be obscuring heavenly truths, to disperse around it.

Rabbits are hunted here, suggesting that there is no room for lust in Sacred Love's world.

To the right, a flock of sheep, representing faithful believers in Christian iconography, graze contentedly.

The church steeple pointing heavenward in the background emphasizes that Sacred Love's half of the painting is concerned with spiritual matters.

The Story of Cupid and Psyche: Part I Jacopo del Sellaio

c.1473, tempera and gold on panel, Fitzwilliam Museum, University of Cambridge, England

The story of Cupid and Psyche was an ideal subject with which to decorate a costly Italian wedding *cassone*, or wooden storage chest. The dramatic ups and downs of this bitter-sweet love affair were first related by the Roman writer Lucius Apuleius in his second-century book *The Golden Ass*, and were repopularized over a thousand years later through the works of the Italian scholar Giovanni Boccaccio (1313–75), notably *De genealogiis deorum gentilium* ("Of the Genealogies of the Pagan Gods").

In brief, it is told that having been born to Apollo and a mortal queen, Psyche grew up into a beauty whose loveliness rivaled that of Venus (Aphrodite in Greece), the Roman goddess of love. So jealous was the goddess that she charged her son, Cupid/Eros, with causing Psyche to make a disastrous love match. Her plan misfired, however, when Cupid became besotted with Psyche, prompting him to have Zephyr carry her to safety when abandoned by her parents. Having spied, and entered, an enchanted castle, Psyche enjoyed idyllic nights with Cupid, happy to comply with his wish that she never see his face on pain of parting until her envious sisters sowed the seeds of doubt in her mind. Lighting an oil lamp, she gazed at the sleeping Cupid and was ecstatic when she saw him to be handsome beyond her wildest dreams. He, however, awakened by a drop of hot oil falling on his skin, flew into a fury and fled.

This is the first part of the story, as depicted by del Sellaio. A second panel portrays Psyche's despair and Venus-inflicted trials and tribulations before Jupiter/Zeus eventually intervened and she and Cupid were married and lived happily ever after. Psyche means "soul" in Greek, so read allegorically (and Platonically), her story describes the rational soul that suffers in search of divine love (represented by Cupid), and whose perseverance is ultimately rewarded with fulfillment and the gift of Voluptas ("Pleasure" in Latin), as Cupid and Psyche's daughter was called.

See also **Classical Figures in Renaissance Art** (page 97–98).

His blazing red garments and the golden sun rays that emanate from his body identify the sun god Apollo *in flagrante*, in the act of begetting his daughter, Psyche. Her mother is Endelechia, who, because she is a queen, is wearing a crown.

Del Sellaio tells Psyche's story in continuous-narrative form, rather like a comic strip. The baby Psyche is about to be swaddled in a cloth of white, the color (which denotes innocence and purity) that she wears throughout this painting. Her carers are her two elder sisters, who wear the same outfits throughout this pictorial narrative.

Del Sellaio's temple of Apollo follows the convention set by Renaissance artists in depicting pagan places of worship, that is, as a colonnade-supported dome. The golden statue of Apollo appears to show him playing a lyre, indicating his role as the god of light, reason, culture, divine inspiration, and divination.

Now of marriageable age and poised to leave her childhood behind her, the beautiful Psyche stands, eyes modestly downcast, at the door of her family home. A host of eligible suitors have come to pay court to her. (This scene would have struck a chord of recognition with the young bride for whose *cassone* this painting was destined.)

Cupid is transfixed by the sight of Psyche. Paralyzed by the spell that her beauty has cast on him, he is unable to fire his arrow of infatuation at her, for to comply with his mother's demands would mean that Psyche would fall in love with someone else.

Zephyr purses his lips, puffs out his cheeks, and blows in Psyche's direction until he is blue in the face.

The king of Miletus and his queen follow solemnly in the footsteps of their daughter, while Psyche trips along ahead, unaware that the oracle, or sibyl, that they consulted at Apollo's temple prophesied that their daughter was destined to make a disastrous choice of husband and instructed them to take her to a mountaintop.

Her family have bid Psyche farewell (a scene that is played out in the central foreground) and have left her alone, on top of a mountain. She could die of exposure, or else throw herself into the depths below, or be abducted by a lust-crazed demon, but Cupid has enlisted the aid of Zephyr (also known as Zephyrus or Zephyros), the west wind.

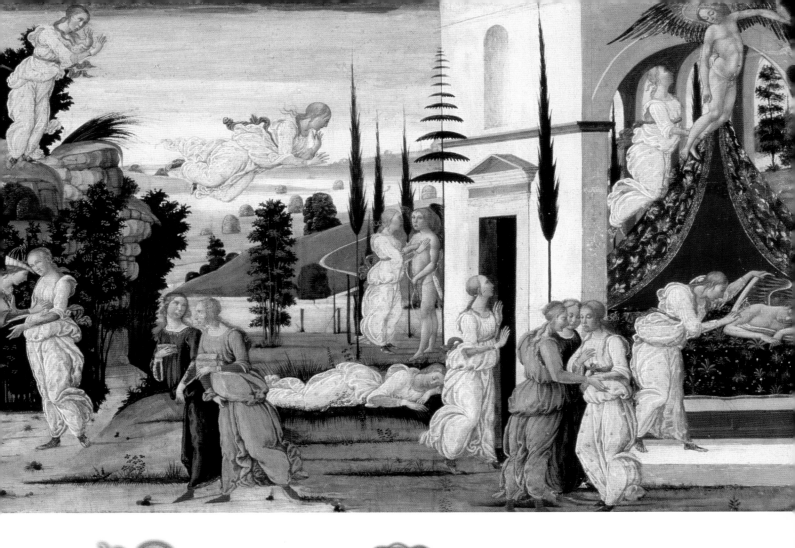

Supported by the warm, sweet-smelling breath of the west wind, Psyche wafts gently to earth.

Having fallen into a deep sleep, Psyche awakes to see the white walls of a fairy-tale castle gleaming before her. (Psyche's action in entering Cupid's castle of love would have had a real-life parallel in the life of the young Florentine woman whose bedchamber this depiction would grace, for she, too, would similarly soon pass through the doorway of her future husband's home.)

Worried that her sisters believe her to be dead, and longing for some company during the daytime, Psyche begs Cupid to allow her to invite her siblings to her fantastic new home.

Although pretending to be delighted by her good fortune, Psyche's sisters are consumed with jealousy. On learning that she knows nothing about her nocturnal lover, they urge her to look at his face, if only to satisfy herself that he is not a monster.

Mischief made, Psyche's sisters leave, laden with the jewels and other treasures that their trusting young sibling has pressed on them.

Having crept out of bed and lit a lamp in the dead of night, Psyche peers intently at her sleeping lover.

As Cupid rockets into air, fueled by anger and berating Psyche for her disobedience, she clutches desperately at his ankle in a vain attempt to prevent him from leaving her. (A male-dominated society prevailed in fifteenth-century Florence, so was this a subtle warning to the young Florentine bride-to-be, a lesson in how not to behave?)

Charon Crossing the River Styx

Joachim Patenier

1515–24, oil on panel, Prado, Madrid, Spain

On seeing Joachim Patenier's work while on a visit to Antwerp in 1521, the German artist Albrecht Dürer described him as a "good landscape painter." Indeed, not only has history proved Patenier (or Patinir) to have been an innovative influence in this respect on the Flemish painters that followed, but the satisfaction that he gained from depicting naturalistic details amid sweeping vistas is evident in his work.

What is also clear is that Patenier drew on many sources in creating his highly original visions. *Charon Crossing the River Styx*, for example, is based on ancient Greek tales of the afterlife, Charon being the ferryman who transported the souls of the dead along the River Styx before depositing them in the dark realm of Hades, lord of the dead. According to later Classical belief, Hades's domain consisted of two distinctly different regions: Elysium (or the Elysian Fields, which was also known as the Island of the Blessed), which was populated with worthy souls (and is equated with Christianity's earthly paradise, or heaven), and Tartarus, where the souls of the wicked endured eternal punishment (and which corresponds to hell). These three fundamental elements—Elysium, Charon powering his boat down the River Styx, and Tartarus—can all be convincingly discerned in the three vertical planes into which Patenier has divided his painting. Yet look closer, and you'll spot Christian angels escorting the righteous souls around the pagan Greek Elysian Fields, as well as grasses and marsh plants that could only have thrived in the boggy lowlands of northern Europe. They may have been added almost as an afterthought, perhaps to enliven and give meaning to the landscape that had primarily absorbed his attention, but Patenier's idiosyncratic inclusions add both native charm and symbolic depth to a subject that may otherwise have seemed somewhat alien to all but the most highly educated of Antwerp's Christian merchant–citizens.

See also **Dante and His Poem The "Divine Comedy"** (pages 178–181).

The bright sky of Elysium contrasts vividly with the smoke-darkened atmosphere that casts a sooty shadow over Tartarus, emphasizing that Elysium is the home of the good, while the black of heart will spend eternity in Tarturus.

In Christian eyes, peacocks represent immortality and heaven (but to the Greeks, centuries earlier, these strutting birds were the companions of the proud Hera, their pantheon's divine first lady).

The fountain symbolizes eternally renewed life, while the body of water that it supplies may be that referred to in the New Testament's Book of Revelation (22:1): "a pure river of water of life, clear as crystal, proceeding out of the throne of God." Or it may be the fount that is said to give rise to the four rivers that flow through Christianity's earthly paradise. Alternatively, the watercourse may be either the River Eridanus, which was said to nurture the Elysian Fields, or the River Lethe, which had the power to impart forgetfulness.

The unmistakable silhouette of a snow-white unicorn can be seen in Elysium. This fabulous beast's Christian connotations (of spiritual purity and Christ as the savior of humankind) are probably more pertinent in this context than its ancient Greek symbolism (it was an attribute of the virgin huntress and moon goddess Artemis).

Deer are Christian symbols of both Christ and resurrection. Psalm 42:1 furthermore explicitly links them, and their thirst for water, with love for God: "As the hart [deer] panteth after the water brooks, so panteth my soul after thee, O God."

Patenier no doubt included swans in his earthly paradise on account of their whiteness, beauty, grace, and distinctive profile. Both the Classical and Christian lexicon of symbolism equate the swan with light, and therefore goodness, and because it was said only to sing (its "swan song") before it dies, it was considered sacred to Apollo, the Greco–Roman god of music, and the musical Muses, and was associated with both the Virgin Mary and Christian martyrs.

Charon propels a wraithlike soul toward the gates that lead to Tartarus. Greek literature describes the gray-bearded ferryman as being a dirty, scruffy, and ill-tempered character, who insisted on being paid for his services (which is why, in ancient Greece, a silver coin was placed under the tongues of the newly deceased).

Ancient Greeks spoke with dread of the dragon-tailed, three-headed Cerberus, the ferocious hellhound that guarded the gates to Hades's shadowy realm to ensure that no one ever escaped it.

Classical lore tells of the souls of those who had been neither good nor bad when alive being left to spend eternity wandering in fields of asphodels (which scholars believe to denote narcissi), which Patenier may have portrayed in the foreground, on both the left and right banks of the Styx. This may explain why flowers, fruiting trees, birds, and apelike creatures are depicted among green groves on terrible Tartarus's side of the river.

The fires of Tartarus and hideous scenes being played out there are reminiscent of the *Inferno* (Hell) described by the visionary Florentine poet Dante in *The Divine Comedy* (1306–21), and the hellfire and demons with which Christian authorities threaten the sinful.

A Satyr Mourning Over a Nymph

Piero di Cosimo

c.1495, oil on panel, National Gallery, London, England

Its shape, and the wooden panel on which it is painted, suggest that this enigmatic image was commissioned from Italian artist Piero di Cosimo to be incorporated into the furnishings of a wealthy home.

No one knows for sure, but it is possible that the dead beauty at the center of this painting represents Procris, the wife of Cephalus, whose sad story was first told by the Roman poet Ovid in his *Metamorphoses* (Book VII: 692–865), and which was revived and tweaked by Italian writer Niccolò da Correggio (1450–1508) in his popular play *Cefalo* (1486). On their marriage, lovebirds Cephalus and Procris had promised that they would always be faithful to one another, as Cephalus indeed remained when Aurora carried him off. Miffed, the spurned Roman goddess of the dawn sent him back to his beloved Procris, having sowed the seeds of doubt in his mind and altered his appearance so that his wife did not recognize him. In his guise as a rich stranger, Cephalus offered Procris a fortune for a night of passion, and when she hesitated, identified himself. So mortified was Procris that she fled to join the nymphs of Diana, the Roman moon, virgin, and huntress goddess. Eventually she returned, bearing peace offerings: a javelin that always hit its target and returned to the thrower of its own accord and a hunting dog that ran faster than any other. After an ecstatic reunion, Procris soon suspected that her husband was having an affair and shadowed him while he was out hunting. Hearing a rustle, he hurled his javelin in its direction, and was devastated when his wife collapsed before him, mortally wounded.

And the lesson of this allegory? That wives should always trust their husbands and be true to them!

See also Popular Personifications in Renaissance Art (page 99), Cerberus detail (page 111).

Satyrs, or fauns, the followers of Dionysus, or Bacchus, the Greco–Roman god of wine, and Pan, or Faunus, the deity of flocks, pastures, and forests, feature regularly in Classical mythology, and are described as having a goat's body (and tail) from the waist down, and a man's torso, arms, and head, albeit with pointed, hairy ears and a pair of horns.

Symbols of uncouth masculinity, these lecherous beings enjoy nothing more than getting drunk and trying to force themselves upon nubile nymphs.

Not only is this satyr showing uncharacteristic sensitivity in tenderly touching the dead nymph, he does not appear in Ovid's version of the Cephalus and Procris's story either.

That said, a faun plays a crucial role in *Cefalo*: having fallen in love with Procris, he encourages her to believe that Cephalus is cheating on her in the hope that she will transfer her affection from her husband to him.

In Classical belief, nymphs, who assumed the form of lovely young women and had the power to foresee the future, were actually feminine nature spirits who inhabited bodies of water, woods, hills, and valleys. As the chaste attendants of Diana, they spent much time hunting and bathing alongside her. Although Ovid tells us that Cephalus's javelin pierced Procris's breast, and Piero di Cosimo has depicted an entry wound in her throat,

the absence of the murder weapon hints that it has flown back to its owner, just as his spear would have boomeranged back to Cephalus.

The dogs scampering along the sandy shore are most likely Cephalus's hunting dogs, for such working canines, and especially packs of them, were often depicted accompanying mythical hunters (the divine Diana included). But their presence on the beach may be sending a more profound message, for while shifting sands signify impermanence, as well as the merging of the earthly and watery realms (symbolically speaking, the coming-together of two worlds), dogs acted as psychopomps in guiding the souls of the dead to the underworld or afterlife in Classical belief.

Reinforcing the suggestion that the dogs on the shore may be waiting to escort the soul of the dead nymph to the afterlife, a path in line with her feet winds from the meadow to the water (which may be an estuary of Oceanus, the river that the ancients envisaged flowing around the world and linking up with the four rivers of the underworld, including the Styx).

In Piero di Cosimo's era, Italians were Christians, not pagans, and his contemporaries would have regarded this pelican as being a profound Christian symbol of sacrifice and salvation. The pelican feeds its young by poking regurgitated food from its distensible pouch down their throats with its beak, from which the misunderstanding arose that it was pecking open its breast in order to nourish its offspring with its own flesh. It consequently became a symbol of Christ, in the context of his self-sacrifice, as well as of piety, devotion to family, and the virtue of Charity.

Their wings and ability to fly heavenward have caused birds to be equated with the soul departing the body after death.

In *Metamorphoses*, Cephalus reveals the name of the dog that he received from Procris, and ultimately from Diana: Laelaps. The melancholy way in which the dog is gazing mutely at the dead girl suggests that he is mourning her demise, that he had a connection with her in life, and that this is therefore Laelaps. Piero di Cosimo has also skillfully demonstrated why Renaissance artists often portrayed a dog as the attribute of Melancholy, the personification of one of the four temperaments. A dog may also denote loyalty and faithfulness, particularly in marriage.

The wildflowers that are bright spots on the grassy ground on which the dead nymph lies suggest the ephemeral nature of life, and the poignancy inherent in the beauty that is cut down in full flower.

The Argo Lorenzo Costa

1484–90, oil on panel,
Museo Civico, Padua, Italy

Tales of epic journeys, or quests, have enduring fascination, with the most famous, *The Odyssey*, which was set down by the Ionian poet Homer in the ninth century BC, now even giving its name to any long, action-packed voyage. And the events that occurred on another famous expedition of Classical literature, that of Jason and the Argonauts, were recorded by the poet Apollonius of Rhodes in his four-volume *Argonautica*, which dates from the third century BC, and also feature in the Roman poet Ovid's *Metamorphoses* (Book VII) three centuries later.

According to these ancient writers, Jason's father was Aeson, a king of Iolcus, in Thessaly, who had been deposed by his half-brother, Pelias. Pelias had sent Jason away as a boy, and when he returned as a man, his uncle agreed to cede the throne in return for the Golden Fleece that a dragon guarded in Colchis, on the Black Sea. Jason and his companions accordingly set off in the *Argo*, and after many heroic exploits, returned to Iolcus with their prize. It is a scene from this tale that Italian artist Lorenzo Costa has depicted.

The reason why such adventures have appealed to generation after generation is partly because the dramatic details of the unfolding narrative, the cliff-hangers, the impossible challenges that the heroes face, and the ingenious solutions that they come up with, all make for an enthralling story. A more profound explanation lies in their symbolic significance, however, for such voyages have allegorical parallels with the journey through life, and because most are journeys into the unknown, or uncharted territory, with entering a different plane or phase, be it by transcending a mundane mindset or by passing from this world into the next, that is, the afterlife. Some are journeys of no return, but when the purpose is the retrieval of a precious object against all odds, these usually signify the hard-won attainment of life-changing knowledge. All in all, epics like these prepare and instruct as much as entertain.

See also **Orpheus and Eurydice** (pages 118–21).

The two ornate columns that somewhat incongruously frame each side of Costa's painting represent the Pillars of Hercules, or the two promontories (the Rock of Gibraltar and Jebel Musa, or Mount Hacho) that stand at the eastern end of the Strait of Gibraltar, one on the European side, and the other, on the African side. They were named for Hercules because he was said to have forced apart the mountain into which Mount Calpe and Mount Abyla, to give them their ancient names, were once fused around the time that he was engaged on his tenth labor. The Pillars of Hercules were believed to mark the end of the known world when the Argonauts' story was composed.

Although Costa has transformed the *Argo* into a fifteenth-century carrack, it is more accurately envisaged as a galley, for the Argonauts, sitting in pairs, each wielded an oar. This sturdy vessel was built by the shipbuilder Argus, following instructions from Athena (the wise Greek goddess of martial arts and crafts whose Roman counterpart was Minerva), and it may be that his creation was named after him. Its name may also have been derived from the Greek for "speedy sailing," and, indeed, it was said to have been the largest and fastest ship ever built (and, some say, the first, too).

A band of around fifty heroes accompanied Jason on his quest. Called the Argonauts because they sailed on the *Argo*, they included such illustrious names as Heracles (Hercules), Castor and Polydeuces (Pollox), and Theseus. Most were warriors, as is indicated here by the weapons and shields of some. Others had different skills, however, such as Orpheus, who sang and played the lyre like no other, and who was excused rowing duty in exchange for distracting the others with his enchanting music.

According to some descriptions of the *Argo*, its mast contained a piece of oak from the forest of Dodona, whose trees were sacred to Zeus (Jupiter), which had the power of prophesy, as well as of speech. Others say that it was incorporated into the prow. Wherever it was lodged, all of the sources agree that it often gave Jason crucial insights into the future, and therefore sound advice. (Given that the society in which Costa lived and worked was devoutly Christian, the cross that the mainmast forms may have had additional significance.)

Jason is the only one of the Argonauts who is not dressed as a fifteenth-century Italian nobleman. This is because the Classical sources explicitly state that an oracle instructed him to wear a leopard skin; they also inform us that he had blond, shoulder-length hair.

One of the perilous obstacles that the Argonauts faced was the Symplegades (Greek for "Clashing Rocks"), or the Cyanean ("Steel Blue") Rocks, on either side of the Bosphorus, which, whenever any vessel tried to sail through the channel between them, sprang together to crush it. Having rid him of the Harpies, the grateful King Phineus advised the Argonauts that as they neared the rocks, they should send a dove (a bird that was sacred to Aphrodite/Venus) ahead of them. This they did, and the rocks duly moved together, trapping the bird's tail feathers. As the rocks separated in preparation for springing together again, the oarsmen rowed furiously and Athena gave the already fast-moving ship an almighty push, though the passage and into the Black Sea. The rocky trap closed a second later, and from that moment on, the Clashing Rocks were unified, never to clash again. That the two rocks have become stuck together to form a bridge is emphasized here by the riders that canter over the water that can be seen below them. The *Argo*'s ordeal is behind it, as is confirmed by the direction in which its sails are billowing.

Orpheus and Eurydice

Titian

1511, oil on canvas, Galleria dell' Accademia Carrara, Bergamo, Italy

Titian may have portrayed a tale from Classical mythology in *Orpheus and Eurydice*, yet once its symbolism has been decoded, it becomes evident that at the heart of his image lies a profound preoccupation with an issue that is central to Christianity: the fate of the soul after death.

We have mainly the Roman poets Ovid and Virgil to thank for passing down the tragic story of Orpheus and Eurydice (in their *Metamorphoses*, Book X, and *Georgics*, Book IV, respectively). Between them, they relate that although it was a love match, the marriage of Orpheus and Eurydice, a lovely young nymph, had seemed doomed from the start, and that shortly after their wedding, Eurydice was killed by a snake bite. Refusing to accept that she was lost to him forever, Orpheus traveled to Tartarus, the realm of the dead, to plead for Eurydice's release. There, the sweet, plaintive song and enchanting music created by this extraordinary poet and musician enraptured all who heard it, and melted the hearts of Pluto and Proserpine (the rulers of the underworld whose counterparts were the Greek Hades and Persephone). Agreeing that Eurydice could return to the world of the living, they warned that if he was to have his heart's desire, Orpheus must not look back until they reached it. Orpheus complied, but just as safety was in sight, temptation overcame him, and he turned to check that Eurydice was following him. And indeed she was, but on seeing his face as he turned, she died a second death and fell back into the underworld's dark depths.

Himself a devotee of the Greek god Dionysus (who had successfully rescued his mother, Semele, from Hades), it is said that Orpheus brought back secrets from the underworld that became the basis of Orphism, a mystery religion that spread across Greece from the sixth century BC. Scholars believe that many fundamentally Dionysian and Orphic beliefs—not least in a heroic descent into the underworld and the immortality of the human soul—were incorporated into Christianity.

*See also **Charon Crossing the River Styx** (pages 108–11), **The Argo** (pages 115–17).*

Eurydice was fleeing the amorous advances of the beekeeper Aristaeus when she stumbled over a snake and was fatally bitten on the ankle. In this context, the snake (which Titian has depicted as resembling a dragon, perhaps to underline its power to do harm) may simply represent a "snake in the grass," or a deceitful, malicious individual.

But because snakes shed their old skins and emerge apparently renewed, they have long been associated with rebirth, and may thus be equated with the soul that, upon the death of the body that housed it in life, is liberated from its earthly ties.

The church spire that is silhouetted against the sky in the distance emphasizes that this section of the painting is concerned with events on earth. And because it is unmistakably a Christian edifice, Titian may be subtly making a connection between Christians' worship of God in life, and the resulting salvation of their souls in the afterlife.

The shadowy figures of the dead can be discerned at the entrance to the subterranean realm where they are destined to spend eternity.

The wheels alongside the mouth of Tartarus may simply power the furnaces that are said to make hell, Christianity's underworld equivalent, so infernally hot. Alternatively, Titian may have sketchily portrayed the snake-infested or fire-engulfed wheel to which Ixion, a Lapith king, was bound for all eternity as a punishment for having lusted after Juno (or Hera, the supreme goddess of the Greco–Roman pantheon).

Both Ovid and Virgil report that when Orpheus sang in the underworld, Ixion's wheel came to an awed standstill.

Orpheus, who was believed to be the son of Calliope, the Muse of epic poetry, and either the lyre-playing sun god Apollo or King Oegrus, appears to have slung his lyre over his shoulder as he speeds across

the gloomy Valley of Avernus toward the land of the living. His mistake in looking back teaches us that even the most transcendentally talented and blessed in life may be brought down by their own human weakness. If the lesson is that disobeying divine commands and giving into irresistible temptation has catastrophic consequences, Orpheus's tale has a parallel with that of Adam and Eve and the Fall of humankind. From this point on it would all be downhill for Orpheus, who, after a period of agonized mourning for Eurydice, and for what might have been, would eventually be ripped to pieces by frenzied Maenads.

Titian has pictured Eurydice (whose white gown identifies her as the same figure as that in the foreground left) stopping in her tracks as her husband turns his head to gaze at her. Her body is clearly beginning to respond to the invisible force that is tugging her back to Tartarus for once and for all.

Primavera

Sandro Botticelli

c.1478, tempera on panel, Galleria degli Uffizi, Florence, Italy

One of the most famous works of Renaissance art, *Primavera* (the Italian word for "spring") is also one of the most puzzled over, for many have sought a deeper level of meaning than an initial identification of this image as a Classically inspired allegory of the season of spring would suggest. In fact, there may be at least two, both of which hinge on the central figure of Venus—the Roman goddess of love and beauty whose Greek counterpart was Aphrodite—who raises her hand as though welcoming the viewer into her realm.

The first possible additional explanation is that *Primavera* is an allegory of young love and sexual awakening, for spring is the time of year when the natural world starts to spring to life, the birds and bees pair off, and single young men and women's thoughts traditionally turn to courtship and marriage. Indeed, it is believed that this painting was commissioned to be hung at the Medici villa at Castello, outside Florence, to commemorate the marriage, in 1482, of Lorenzo di Pierfrancesco de' Medici (1463–1503) to Semiramide Appiani, daughter of the ruler of Piombino.

The second is that although *Primavera* depicts a pagan scene peopled with Greco–Roman deities, it is, in fact, a Neoplatonist celebration of such ideal Christian virtues as spiritual love, liberality, and charity, qualities to which humans should aspire in the hope of being rewarded, through God's grace, with a life that resembles heaven on earth. That said, if this was the intended message, it was more likely to have been aimed not at the future bridegroom, but at the bride-to-be, who is almost certainly represented by the middle Grace, whose head has been turned by the handsome Mercury (Hermes), the messenger of the Greco-Roman gods and guide and protector of those undertaking the potentially perilous journey between this world and the next. Equally, however, the hidden meaning may again simply allude to the marital joys into which the innocent young bride is about to be initiated.

See also **Sacred and Profane Love** (pages 102–04), **The Medici Family** (pages 159–60).

As the son of Maia, Mercury is associated with the springtime month of May. Here he uses his caduceus to disperse the clouds that must never be allowed to cast a shadow over this enchanted garden, or to obscure divine love's glorious beauty. Botticelli has used artistic license in depicting the snakes (symbols of healing and harmony) that usually entwine themselves around the caduceus as dragons. As the staff carried by heralds, the caduceus denotes peace, as well as a link between the lower and higher realms, or earth and heaven.

His helmet and sword signify Mercury's readiness to protect the gentle occupants of this heavenly haven from interlopers intent on causing harm. They also imply masculine maturity and strength. Mercury's winged boots symbolize his fleetness of foot, as well as his ability to fly from one plane of existence to another.

That the trees in this orange grove bear delicate blossoms at the same time as juicy fruits demonstrates the magical power of love. Being both white and fragrant, orange blossoms represent chastity and beauty, while the oranges that, once fertilized, they produce symbolize fecundity and plenty (i.e., a large family of children), which is why brides traditionally wore orange blossom in their hair.

Oranges may be equated with the golden apples of Classical mythology, notably those that grew in the garden of the Hesperides, and consequently often denote paradise. Their presence in this painting may also refer to the Medici bridegroom, partly through a verbal pun on his family name, the orange sometimes being called *malus medicus* (Latin for "medicinal apple") in Renaissance times, and partly through a visual allusion to the red balls adorning a golden shield that comprised the Medici coat of arms.

In Greco–Roman mythology, the three Graces (*Gratiae*, as they were known in ancient Rome, or Charites, as the Greeks called them) were the lovely attendants of Venus/Aphrodite.

In both Classical and Renaissance times, they were typically portrayed dancing, holding each other's hands as they described a delicate circle. Along with gracefulness and loveliness, they represent the giving, receiving, and returning of a grace, be it a gift, a benefit, or God's grace, and consequently liberality. According to artistic convention, one Grace is depicted with her back to the viewer; symbolically, this denotes that giving away something beneficial will cause it to be returned twice over (as signified by the two Graces facing the viewer). The Greeks named the individual Graces Aglaia, Euphrosyne, and Thalia, but they were given alternative appellations in Renaissance Italy,

such as Chastity (*Castitas*), Beauty (*Pulchritudo*), and Love (*Amor*) or Sensuality (*Voluptas*). Here, Love (or Sensuality) and Beauty

may be pictured gently encouraging Chastity's growing desire for Mercury.

Lustrous pearls are attributes of the sea-born Venus (and by extension, the Graces).

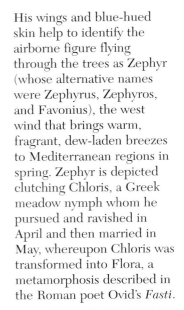

Venus's cherubic son, Cupid (also known as Amor, or Eros), the personification of love, wears a blindfold, for love is blind. Tautening his bowstring, he aims his flaming arrow at the central Grace; when it strikes its target, she will be inflamed with burning desire for Mercury.

In depicting her wearing a *gamurra*, the fashionable dress of the day, Botticelli has made Venus appear pregnant, the ideal body image for even unmarried women to aspire to, for it hinted at their ability to bear many children. Both Venus and Mercury's red drapery signify sexual maturity.

The halolike semicircle of blue sky that frames Venus's head creates a subtle link with those female Christian figures that are equated with divine love, especially the Virgin Mary. The shape of the leaves silhouetted against the sky identifies them as myrtle, an evergreen plant that was sacred to Venus and that graced the heads of Roman brides and grooms, for it represented desire, fertility, and eternity, and thus everlasting marital love.

Spring's influence has not yet touched the trees that bow before the irresistible force of Zephyr's passion, for the creative union of Zephyr and Chloris has not yet taken place. These trees have been identified as laurels, and may be a pun on the Latin version of Lorenzo's name— Laurentius —for their own Latin name is *Laurus*.

Botticelli portrays the erstwhile Chloris as having blossomed into Flora, making the connection explicit through the flowers that spill from the nymph's mouth to decorate the dress of her new incarnation, whose exquisite garb resembles that of a Florentine bride. Garlanded with blooms, the goddess of flowers and spring gathers up her gown to form an apron with which to hold the roses that she scatters at Venus's feet.

His wings and blue-hued skin help to identify the airborne figure flying through the trees as Zephyr (whose alternative names were Zephyrus, Zephyros, and Favonius), the west wind that brings warm, fragrant, dew-laden breezes to Mediterranean regions in spring. Zephyr is depicted clutching Chloris, a Greek meadow nymph whom he pursued and ravished in April and then married in May, whereupon Chloris was transformed into Flora, a metamorphosis described in the Roman poet Ovid's *Fasti*.

Roses were considered sacred to Venus and represented love, beauty, and flowering femininity.

Minerva Chasing the Vices from the Garden of Virtue

Andrea Mantegna

1499–1502, oil on canvas, Musée du Louvre, Paris, France

Although some of the characters in this action-packed scene are recognizably figures drawn from Greco–Roman mythology, their juxtaposition on the canvas does not correspond to any specific Classical story. That each of these figures represents an archetypal figure or quality, and that the remainder appear to be grotesque figments of the artist's imagination, point to this painting being an allegorical image.

Decoding the symbolic messages hidden within this canvas, translating the text that can be discerned at various points, and then attempting to form a clear picture of the painting's message from all of these clues must have been a delightfully absorbing task for Isabella d'Este (1474–1539), who commissioned this work from Mantegna for her *studiolo*, or study, in the ducal palace in Mantua. The daughter of Ercole d'Este, the duke of Ferrara, and, from 1490, the wife of Francesco II, the Gonzaga duke of Mantua, Isabella was a remarkable woman, and not just on account of her high social status, although this admittedly equipped her with the education, spending power, and interest in the arts that made her one of the leading patrons—male or female—of her age. In creating this thought-provoking allegory for her perusal, Mantegna (a favored painter at the Gonzaga court), guided by the court poet Paride da Ceresara, paid tribute to Isabella's learning, strong-mindedness, and moral rectitude by comparing her to the Greco–Roman goddess Athena/Minerva in her martial aspect of Pallas. Not only was Mantegna explicitly likening the influential lady with the Classical epitome of wisdom and the defender of just causes, but he was clearly suggesting that this pure, noble, and vigorous personage would wage active war on such interloping vices as Avarice, Ignorance, and Idleness, be it within her own mind or at her court, for the enclosed garden may represent any area over which Isabella ruled supreme, be it metaphorically or literally.

See also **The Neoplatonist Philosophy** (pages 96–98), **The Este Family** (page 159).

The hybrid tree–woman is reminiscent of Daphne, who, in Greek myth, was the daughter of the River Ladon. Daphne had sworn to remain chaste, but caught Apollo's lustful eye. Losing ground as she fled from the sun god, she cried out to her father to save her from violation, whereupon she was transformed into a laurel tree. Here representing *Virtus Deserta* (Latin for "Deserted Virtue"), the arms of this arboreal personification of Chastity are portrayed as olive, rather than laurel, branches, for the olive was sacred to Athena/Minerva and symbolized such positive qualities as prosperity, knowledge, and peace.

A legend is spelled out in three different languages and scripts: in Latin (top), Greek (middle), and Hebrew (bottom). Many influential Biblical and Classical secular and philosophical texts were written in these ancient tongues, which is why they were valued by humanist scholars, and therefore also by Isabella.

Translated into English, the message scrolling around the tree–woman reads: "Come, divine companions of the virtues, who are returning to us from the heavens, and drive these repulsive, monstrous vices from our home."

Athena/Minerva charges into action wearing her characteristic accouterments of war: a helmet from which a flamboyant panache flares; a breastplate decorated with the gorgoneion (the snake-haired head of the Gorgon Medusa); a shield (the *aegis*); and a spear.

Athena/Minerva's spearhead lies on the ground, evidence of the force with which she has launched her attack on the vices. Scholars believe that this detail is also a reference to the broken lance presented to Isabella by her husband after the Battle of Fornovo, suggesting that she had been his inspiration on the battlefield.

The Latin inscription that can be discerned behind the armless figure is *OTIA SI TOLLAS PERIERE CUPIDINIS ARCUS*, which is taken from the Roman poet Ovid's work *Remedy for Love*, and means: "If you destroy idleness, Cupid's bows will perish."

The Latin word *OTIUM*, which can be seen parallel with the armless figure's navel, identifies it as being the vice of Idleness, and, indeed, no hands equals no work. Idleness is being led by a vice whose name winds around her forearm, which needs no translating: *INERTIA*.

The airborne members of a swarm of *amoretti* (literally, "little loves" in Italian) look at Athena/Minerva with consternation. These cupids—love personified—typically attend Aphrodite/Venus, the Greco–Roman goddess of carnal, or profane, love. Their butterfly wings may be a reference to Psyche, Cupid's wife, whose name means "butterfly" in Greek.

A second group of *amoretti* have owlish faces. The owl, signifying wisdom, is an attribute of Athena/Minerva, so it is unclear whether they are on the side of this goddess or that of their traditional mistress, Aphrodite/Venus.

The offspring that the dismayed fleeing female figure clutches have inherited their mother's cloven hooves and furry legs, although their ears are not yet as pointed as hers. Their physical features suggest that the family members are related to the satyrs, and that they therefore have a rampant animal nature from the waist downward.

The one-breasted, simian character represents vanity, stupidity, and the "monkey" that lust makes of humankind. The Latin words for "malice," "fraud," and "undying hatred" are inscribed on some of the pouches and ribbons that hang off this creature's body, suggesting that it spreads these vices—and others—wherever it goes.

White roses signify chastity.

Her bow and quiver full of arrows (which respectively symbolize the crescent moon and the shafts of light that it radiates) identify the woman in blue as Artemis/Diana, the virgin Greco–Roman goddess of the moon and hunting who was famously protective of her chastity. The green-robed woman sprinting alongside her, sheathed sword in hand, may be the personification of the virtuous Chastity, whose mortal enemy is Lust.

Lemons and oranges represent fruitfulness and plenty, demonstrating that sweet rewards are the result of taming nature and cultivating an orderly garden—in other words, of keeping tight control of one's baser instincts and desires.

Her beauty and brazen nudity identify the woman being carried away on the centaur's back as the goddess Aphrodite/Venus, who adores and encourages indolence and the pleasures of the flesh.

Idyllic landscapes populated by naked people denote the innocence of the mythical Golden Age, a time of harmony and plenty, before humankind was corrupted.

Their myrtle wreaths, which were worn by bridal couples in ancient Roman times, hint at newlyweds, a suggestion that is underlined by the burning hymeneal torches (signifying the flames of conjugal passion) held by the *amoretto* next to this cowed-looking pair. Had the vices started to corrupt them?

Like the centaur (a human–horse hybrid) alongside him, the satyr (a human–goat fusion) symbolizes the merging of the human power of rational thought with violent animal instincts, which all too often prevail. Both mythical creatures therefore symbolize brute sexuality, unbridled libidinousness, and licentiousness. The boar or pig behind the satyr similarly represents the vice of Lust.

When translated from the Latin, the message fluttering from the wall on the side of the garden that has been taken over by the vices reads: "And you, O divine ones, help me, mother of the Virtues." Isabella would have understood that this cry for help came from Prudence, the fourth, and original, cardinal virtue, who has been imprisoned by this brick structure.

Their headbands give their names: INGRATITUDO, IGNIORANCIA, and AVARICIA, in other words, the vices of Ingratitude, Ignorance, and Avarice (or Greed, a deadly sin). Ignorance is represented as being too obese to walk, her unseeing eyes associating her with Ploutos, the blind Greek bestower of wealth, while her crown both links her with a character with a similar name, Pluto, the Greco–Roman ruler of the underworld, and signals "Ignorance rules."

Having been pushed out of their garden by the vices, three of the cardinal, or natural, virtues observe the unfolding mêlée from the vantage point of a cloud, on which they will descend once it is safe to do so. Originally named (in his work *The Republic*) by the Greek philosopher Plato (*c*.427–348 BC) as the qualities that ideal citizens should possess, Prudence, Justice, Fortitude, and Temperance were later confirmed as cardinal virtues by the Church fathers, who explained that they could be acquired by adhering to the Gospels.

Mantegna has depicted his trio of virtues bearing their traditional attributes. Justice holds her sword of authority and the scales that signify her impartiality. Fortitude demonstrates her strength by shouldering a pillar similar to that which the

Old Testament strongman Samson pulled down, burying the Philistines in rubble, as well as a club that links her with the Greco–Roman hero Herakles/Hercules, who, like her, wore a lion's pelt draped around his shoulders. Her two pitchers—one containing water, and the other, wine—enable us to recognize Temperance, who represents moderation in all things, including alcoholic intake.

Allegory of the Old and New Testaments

Hans Holbein the Younger

c.1533–35, oil on panel, National Gallery of Scotland, Edinburgh, Scotland

As the painter of the Dutch humanist Desiderius Erasmus (*c.*1466–1536), and later of Henry VIII (1491–1547), the English king who rejected papal supremacy in 1533, the German-born artist Hans Holbein must have been well versed in the Protestant principles of Martin Luther (1483–1546), the prime mover behind the Reformation. Indeed, although it is packed with conventional Christian imagery, the message conveyed by his *Allegory of the Old and New Testaments* (or *Laws*) underscores the Lutheran assertion that the salvation of Christian souls can be achieved by faith alone (*sola fidei* in Latin).

Even without an understanding of Latin—the language in which its various characters and scenes are annotated—the viewer can see that this is a painting of two halves, and one that resembles an open book, with the central tree acting as its spine. Holbein's use of color suggests that everything on the shadowy, left-hand side is negative, or bad, while all that can be discerned on the brighter, right-hand side is positive, or good. It is almost as though Holbein has illustrated a list of pros and cons. But what do these pros and cons focus on? The answer lies at the center of the image, in the confused-looking naked man (*HOMO*), who represents everyman, or humankind, and in the Latin text beneath him: *MISER EGO HOMO, QUIS ME ERIPIET EX HOC CORPORE MORTI OB NOXIO? RO. 7.* This is a reference to verse 7:24 of the New Testament Book of Romans, which reads: "O wretched man that I am! Who shall deliver me from the body of this death?" The answer, as Holbein has depicted on the right-hand side of the panel, headed *GRATIA* ("grace"), is contained in the New Testament: through the grace of God, only belief in Jesus Christ can secure eternal salvation. By contrast, those who adhere to Mosaic law (*LEX*) (i.e., Jews), as laid down in the Old Testament—highlights from which can be seen on the left-hand side—are condemning themselves to death and damnation.

See also **The Reformation** (page 17), *Abraham and Melchizedek* (pages 23 to 25).

After leading the Israelites from Egypt, Moses—the Old Testament's most important leader—ascended Mount Sinai, where he received the law (the "Old Law") from God, as described in the Old Testament book of Exodus (24:12): "And the Lord said unto Moses, Come up to me into the mount, and be there: and I will give thee tables of stone, and a law, and commandments which I have written; that thou mayest teach them."

The law, and particularly the Ten Commandments (the Decalogue), are consequently usually represented in art as two adjacent, inscribed slabs of stone.

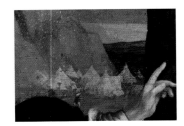

While *en route* from Egypt to the Promised Land, the Israelites lived in tents.

Having punished the Israelites for their complaints by inflicting a plague of fiery serpents upon them, God relented in the face of their repentance. Following God's instructions, Moses "made a serpent of brass, and put it on a pole, and it came to pass, that if a serpent had bitten any man, when he beheld the serpent of brass, he lived" (Numbers 21:9). The legend above the brazen serpent reads *MYSTERIUM JUSTIFICATIONIS* ("the mystery of justification").

The story begins with a serpent precipitating the Fall of humankind from paradise by tempting Eve to take a bite from the forbidden fruit of the Tree of the Knowledge of Good and Evil (Genesis 3). God curses them for their disobedience and banishes Adam and Eve from the Garden of Eden.

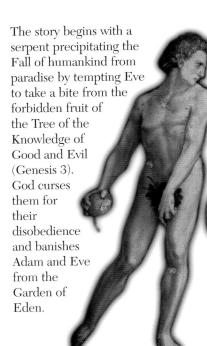

MYSTERIVM IVSTIFICATIONIS

LEX

GRATIA

MYSTERIVM IVSTIFICATIONIS

IVSTIFICATIO NOSTRA

AGNVS DEI

PECCATVM

HOMO

VICTORIA NOSTRA

MORS

MISER EGO HOMO, QVIS ME ERIPIET EX HOC CORPORE MORTI OB NOXIO. RO. 7

ESAYAS PROPHETA
ECCE VIRGO CONCIPIET ET PARIET FILIVM. ISA. 7

IOANNES BAPTISTA.
ECCE AGNVS ILLE DEI, QVI TOLLIT PECCATV̄ MVDI. IO. 1

PECCATVM

The descendants of the first man and woman would henceforth be born with Original Sin, and with no hope of redemption, or consequently of eternal life. *PECCATUM*— "sin"—has been written above the heads of the serpent and Eve.

The combination of the skeleton, coffin, and label *MORS* ("death") hammer home the message that death awaits all humans.

MORS

The tree that divides the painting may be equated with the *axis mundi*, or the world axis that links the underworld, terrestrial world, and heavenly world, as well as with the tree of life. In the latter context, it is particularly significant that

while the foliage on the left-hand, "Old Law," side of the tree has withered and died away, that on the side dedicated to the "New Law" is green and flourishing, suggesting that belief in Christ is a powerful source of spiritual sustenance and life.

The old man exhorting the miserable wretch to turn to the light (in the process also directing viewers' eyes to the next chapter in the scriptural story) is the Old Testament prophet Isaiah (*ESAYAS PROPHETA*), whose link with the New Testament, or "New Law," is summarized in the prophetic words traced below: *ECCE VIRGO CONCIPIET ET PARIET FILIUM. ISA. 7*. These are taken from Isaiah 7:14, "Behold, a virgin shall conceive, and bear a son…"

Everyman appears to be in an agony of confusion as to whether to arraign himself on the side of the Old Law (Judaism) or the New Law (Christianity). Both Isaiah and John the Baptist are pointing him toward Christianity.

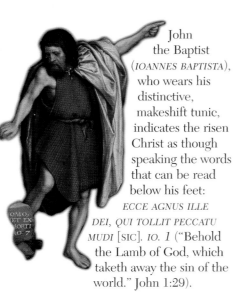

John the Baptist (*IOANNES BAPTISTA*), who wears his distinctive, makeshift tunic, indicates the risen Christ as though speaking the words that can be read below his feet: *ECCE AGNUS ILLE DEI, QUI TOLLIT PECCATU MUDI* [SIC]. *IO. 1* ("Behold the Lamb of God, which taketh away the sin of the world." John 1:29).

GRATIA

IVSTIFICATIO NOSTRA

INRI

AGNVS DEI

HOMO

MISER EGO HOMO,
QVIS ME ERIPIET EX
HOC CORPORE MORTI
OB NOXIO · RO 7

VICTORIA
NOSTRA

IOANNES BAPTISTA

M · ISA · 7   ECCE AGNVS ILLE DEI, QVI TOLLIT PECCATV MVDI. IO. I

The resurrected Christ climbs out of the tomb, clothed in a mantle whose blood-red color represents life. The flag of the resurrection, whose design is based, it is said, on the cross that the Roman emperor Constantine the Great (*c.*280–337) dreamed of seeing in the sky, as the words "*In hoc signo vinces*" ("With this sign shall you conquer") resonated in his mind, the night before his victory at the battle of the Milvian Bridge, flies triumphantly from the cross that he bears. This has crushed the dragonlike demon (representing evil and Satan) that had previously prevailed over death, signifying that Christ has won the ultimate victory. The words VICTORIA NOSTRA ("our victory") proclaim that his victory was won on behalf of Christian believers, for it is written in Romans 10:9, "That if thou shalt confess with thy mouth the Lord Jesus, and shalt believe in thine heart that God hath raiseth him from the dead, thou shalt be saved."

His halo, and the words above it—*AGNUS DEI*, "Lamb of God"—single out Jesus Christ at the head of a group of his disciples. He is gesturing toward his crucified self, indicating that this is his fate, and that his death will be crucial to his followers' faith.

The crucified Christ is depicted opposite the *tau* cross that bears Moses's brazen serpent, emphasizing the words contained in the Gospel of St. John (3:14–15): "And as Moses lifted up the serpent in the wilderness, even so must the Son of man be lifted up: That whosoever believeth in him should not perish, but have eternal life." Above the "INRI" sign that identifies "Jesus of Nazareth, King of the Jews" (*Iesu Nazarenus Rex Iudaeorum* in Latin) are the words *JUSTIFICATIO NOSTRA* ("Our justification"), which refers to the Protestant belief in justification by faith.

As related in the Gospel of Saint Luke (2:8–11), an angel appears before shepherds watching their flock to inform them of the birth of "a Saviour, which is Christ the Lord."

In an interesting artistic variation on traditional Annunciation scenes, Holbein has portrayed the Virgin Mary kneeling on a hilltop, surrounded by a heavenly host of cherubic angels, and bathed in a pool of brilliant light (in stark contrast to the fiery red cloud that envelopes Moses on the opposite side) as an angel bearing a *tau* cross reminiscent of that supporting the brazen snake informs her of her pregnancy.

The Ship of Fools

Hieronymus Bosch

c.1500, oil on panel, Musée du Louvre, Paris, France

When the Netherlandish artist Hieronymus Bosch painted *The Ship of Fools*, Martin Luther (1483–1546), the German cleric, initiator of the Reformation, and founder of Protestantism, had still to nail his inflammatory ninety-five theses attacking the papal-approved sale of indulgencies to the door of the Schlosskirche ("Castle Church") in Wittenberg. Although that would not happen until 1517, criticism of certain sleazy practices and abuses of power within the Roman Catholic Church had already become increasingly prevalent in northern Europe, albeit in allegorical, rather than overt, form.

Bosch's painting is based on one such satirical work, namely *Das Narrenschiff* (German for "*Ship of Fools*"), by the German satirical writer Sebastian Brant (1457–1521), which, due in part to its biting woodcut illustrations, was widely disseminated and translated following its publication in 1494. The framework for this allegorical poem concerning human folly is a ship bound for the fictitious destination of Narragonia—a fool's paradise that has been equated with the equally fictitious Land of Cockaigne, where peasants could eat and drink themselves senseless, among other pleasurable activities, without lifting a finger or paying a price for their self-indulgence. The ship of fools' passengers come from every walk of life, but all have folly in common, ranging from simple stupidity, through a predilection for engaging in such vices as avarice, to deliberate dishonesty and shameless corruption. And without a captain or navigator, the ship sails aimlessly on, with the scenes on board becoming ever more chaotic.

The ship of fools was a clever choice of literary vehicle with which covertly to criticize clerical shortcomings, for while the Church could be symbolized by a boat, there was a long tradition of fools who uttered uncomfortable truths being allowed to go unpunished. What better subject for a painter who not only relished the grotesque, but was also a devout Christian and committed member of the Brotherhood of the Holy Virgin of laymen in his hometown of s'Hertogenbosch (Bois-le-Duc)?

See also **The Reformation** (page 17), **Popular Personifications in Renaissance Art** (page 99–101).

Although the owl often represents wisdom, in this Christian context it is likely to signify heresy, for being a bird that hunts at night, it may symbolize the spiritually unenlightened, or those (such as the Jews) who do not recognize Christ as their savior. Its association with darkness also links it to Satan, evil, death (and Bosch may have painted its face to convey a death's head, or skull), and, referring to the mindset that accepts such symbolic parallels, superstition.

The foliage that flourishes at the top of the mast suggests that the mast is, in fact a tree, in which case it may symbolize both the tree of life (and consequently life itself) and the *axis mundi* (Latin for "world axis"), or the axis around which the world revolves.

The crescent moon at the top of the banner (*see* previous page) represents many sacred figures and concepts, including such goddesses as the Greco–Roman Artemis/Diana. In this instance, however, it probably signifies Islam, which, like Judaism, Christians of Bosch's time considered to be a heretical belief system.

The plucked chicken that has been skewered on the ship's trunklike mast ready for roasting is reminiscent of old European fairground games in which young men were invited to climb a greasy pole in order to seize the prize impaled on the top, which was often a succulent hunk of meat. Few succeeded, but their undignified attempts caused much merriment. Alternatively, it may symbolize gluttony—a deadly sin whose Latin name is *gula*—as may the spoon that is being used as an oar (indeed, a now separate part of this painting is called *Allegory of Gluttony and Lust*).

This passenger's outfit identifies him as a professional fool, or court jester, and the personification of folly or foolishness. Sewn to his cap is a pair of mock donkey's ears (a symbol of stupidity), while his staff—called a bauble, or marotte—is his scepter of office. During the Middle Ages, and well into the sixteenth century, such fools were regarded as the polar opposite of the rulers around whose courts they capered, and thus the perpetuators of such ancient, world-turned-upside-down, "lord of misrule" traditions as the Saturnalia of ancient Rome.

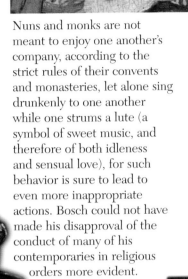

The boat's rudder is operated by a man who has clearly had too much to drink, indicating that the vessel is going around in circles and will never make headway.

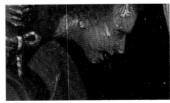

Nuns and monks are not meant to enjoy one another's company, according to the strict rules of their convents and monasteries, let alone sing drunkenly to one another while one strums a lute (a symbol of sweet music, and therefore of both idleness and sensual love), for such behavior is sure to lead to even more inappropriate actions. Bosch could not have made his disapproval of the conduct of many of his contemporaries in religious orders more evident.

The upturned pitcher signifies that the ship's company has made significant inroads into its supply of alcohol, stored in the barrel behind the monk.

Cherries represent sweet rewards and, in Christian art, paradise, but because they are sexually suggestive fruits, they may alternatively hint at lust (*libido* or *luxuria*, one of the Seven Deadly Sins) and sexual licentiousness.

Scholars believe that the object dangling in front of the nun and monk's open mouths—clearly part of a drinking game—is a pancake, and because pancakes are traditionally cooked and eaten the day before Ash Wednesday as a way of using up eggs and milk before Lent, that it signifies the wasteful luxury of overindulging in rich food.

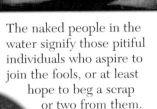

The naked people in the water signify those pitiful individuals who aspire to join the fools, or at least hope to beg a scrap or two from them.

Drawing inspiration, perhaps, from Noah's ark, early Christians likened the Church to a ship that carries the faithful safely across the sometimes turbulent waters of life to the "other side," or the afterlife. In art, this association is often underlined by the shape of the cross that may be formed by the mast and yard.

The Wedding Feast

Sandro Botticelli

1483, oil on canvas, private collection

In his chapter on Botticelli, Giorgio Vasari, author of *The Lives of the Artists* (1568), informs us: "for the Pucci home, he illustrated Boccaccio's novella of Nastagio degli Onesti, in four paintings with tiny figures, which are most lovely and delightful." The novella to which Vasari refers can be read in *The Decameron* (1351–53), by Italian writer Giovanni Boccaccio (1313–75), and is the eighth tale told on the fifth day of the ten days of story-telling that give the book its Greek name.

Boccaccio relates that Nastagio degli Onesti, a young man who has just proposed marriage, but was turned down, has sought solitude in a forest when a panic-stricken young woman rushes past him. A mounted, sword-brandishing knight is in hot pursuit (as illustrated in Botticelli's first painting). To Nastagio's horror, the woman falls, whereupon the knight cuts out her heart and throws it to his hunting dogs to devour (this gruesome scene is depicted in the second painting). But then she gets to her feet and runs off, the dogs and knight hard on her heels, and Nastagio surmises that this is a phantom hunt. His hunch is later confirmed: this scenario is fated to be repeated for eternity because after the woman refused to give the knight her heart in life, he vowed to steal it by force. Nastagio, drawing a parallel between his lady love and the fate of the nay-saying ghost, invites her family to dine with him in the forest, and the third painting in the series conveys the company's revulsion when the same shocking scene is played out before them. The formerly disinterested object of his desire quickly draws her own conclusion and agrees to marry Nastagio, the feast being portrayed in the fourth painting.

The quartet of paintings was commissioned by either Antonio Pucci or Lorenzo de' Medici to mark the marriage of Giannozzo Pucci, Antonio's son and Lorenzo's godson, to Lucrezia Bini in 1483. Had Lucrezia initially rejected Giannozzo's advances, or was she being warned never to do so?

See also ***The Journey of the Magi to Bethlehem*** (pages 29–31).

The trees that decorate each of the columns in the foreground are laurels (*Laurus nobilis*), which, because they are evergreen, represent immortality and victory. Not only that, but laurels were the personal emblem, or *impresa*, of Lorenzo de' Medici, whose Christian name equates to Laurentius in Latin, which sounds similar to *Laurus*. Lorenzo's laurel was often depicted with the Latin motto *Ita ut virtus*, which means "So is virtue."

The rings that hang like pendants from the bottom of each tree are reminiscent of another Medici *impresa*: a diamond ring, which was sometimes paired with the Latin word *semper* ("always") in a symbolic proclamation of the Medicis' adamantine strength, which would, it was thus promised, endure forever.

The coat of arms surmounting the left-hand column is that of the Pucci family, and features the head of a moor wearing a white bandana.

The positioning of the Medici coat of arms in such a prominent spot at the top of the central column both honors Lorenzo de' Medici, then the ruler of Florence, and indicates that he played an influential part in uniting the bride and groom, or rather their families, in marriage. The six red balls on the Medici coat of arms may represent oranges (the orange was sometimes known as *malus medicus*, Latin for "medicinal apple"), pills, or coins (reflecting the Medici dynasty's history as doctors and bankers).

The right to incorporate three fleur-de-lis (the heraldic symbol of France) on a blue field into its coat of arms was granted to the Medici family by King Louis XI of France (1423–83) in 1465.

The inclusion of the Pucci moor's head on the left-hand side of the coat of arms at the top of the right-hand pillar suggests that this impalement, heraldically speaking, is designed to celebrate a new dynastic link, and that the coat of arms on the right is that of the bride's Bini family.

The woman in maidenly white being offered a dish is the bride.

Many of the ladies are using two-pronged forks, then new-fangled utensils that were still uncommon, even among the rich.

The Roman arch at the back of the painting signals victory, triumph, and a noble heritage dating back to antiquity, all of which any dynasty with pretensions to glory would have been delighted to be associated with. It also serves to direct the viewer's eye toward the vanishing point, as do the columns that delineate this *al fresco* dining area.

A magnificent display of elaborately decorated *maiolica* (tin-glazed earthenware) dominates the central foreground. The size, quality, and quantity of the pieces signal the host's wealth and good taste.

No doubt reflecting the usual practice of the times, the women and men are shown dining at separate tables.

His contemporaries would have recognized Antonio Pucci's face among the wedding guests—many also familiar-looking. The handsome young groom wears pink.

The Wheel of Fortune

Artist unknown, French school

1503, tempera on panel, Bibliothèque Nationale, Paris, France

In his prologue to *The Lives of the Artists* (1568), Giorgio Vasari used the wheel of Fortune as an analogy for the fall of the Roman Empire, stating that "…after carrying men to the top of her wheel, either for amusement or out of regret, Fortune usually returns them to the bottom…" and going on to observe that this also explains "the progress of art's rebirth and the state of perfection to which it has again ascended in our own times…" The notion of the constantly turning wheel symbolizing the eternal passage of time, as well as the cycle of existence, is thousands of years old, and has its origin in the daily passage of the sun across the sky. The allegorical figure of Fortune dates back to Classical times, however, and is based on a fusion of the Greek goddess Tyche and her Roman counterpart, Fortuna, with a sprinkling of the Greek concept of *kairos*, or the opportune moment, thrown into the mix.

Tyche was envisaged mainly as an unpredictable controller of human fate, and was thus often depicted wielding a rudder or balancing precariously on an unstable globe, sometimes also carrying a cornucopia from which she distributed blessings. Fortuna was initially regarded as more of a Lady Bountiful type, but as the centuries passed, was increasingly associated with the fickleness of fate, with respect to nations, as well as to individual destinies. In this aspect, "Dame Fortune" (or "Lady Luck"), as Fortuna, or Fortune, was often called, was accorded many of Tyche's marine attributes, among them the rudder, and later the sail (signifying the unpredictability of the wind). And it was the Roman writer Boethius (*c*.480–*c*.524), who, in *De consolatione philosophiae* ("*The Consolation of Philosophy*"), described the function of Fortune's wheel as being to raise up the fallen and cast down the proud, thereby providing the visual metaphor that would prove so popular a thousand years after the Roman consul's own dramatic fall from grace and execution.

See also **Popular Personifications in Renaissance Art** (page 99).

In this painting of two halves, those whom fortune has favored are bathed in bright light, while those who have experienced sudden misfortune are cast into in dark shadow.

Dame Fortune has five sets of hands, enabling her simultaneously to give and take. With her right hand, she presses a bag of coins upon a lucky recipient, while snatching a purse from a well-to-do man with her left.

A king is crowned on the side of the chosen few, at the exact moment that another is unceremoniously demoted to the ranks of the lowly.

No one is immune from the vagaries of fortune, even the pope, as Dame Fortune demonstrates by pulling off one papal tiara on one side of the painting and patting another firmly in place on the other.

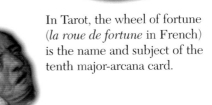

In Tarot, the wheel of fortune (*la roue de fortune* in French) is the name and subject of the tenth major-arcana card.

Dame Fortune selects a new emperor by placing a jewel-encrusted crown on his head, at the same time deposing his predecessor by tugging off his own costly symbol of imperial authority.

Crowned figures, signifying absolute temporal or spiritual authority, are often portrayed at the apex of the wheel of Fortune, symbolizing the pinnacle of achievement on earth. Where four figures can be seen on each of the circle's four quarters, these are often accompanied by the Latin legends *regnabo* ("I will reign") in the west; *regno* ("I am reigning") in the north; *regnavi* ("I have reigned") in the east; and "*sum sine regno*" ("I am without a reign") in the south.

Even if her skirt were not labeled with the word "*PROSPERITE*" (French for "prosperity"), it would still be clear that this sleek, richly dressed woman personifies prosperity.

Golden-haired "*JOYE*" ("joy") turns the wheel that will indeed bring joy to those on an upward trajectory, culminating in the ecstasy that comes from being on top of the world. That feeling will be fleeting, however, for the relentlessly turning wheel will all too soon fling them into the depths of darkness and despair.

Hard-earned muscles straining, the ragged, hungry-looking "*ADVERSITE*" ("adversity") demonstrates how pride can come before a fall as she pulls an erstwhile ruler roughly back down to earth.

As is traditional, Dame Fortune wears a blindfold, signifying her lack of awareness of those whose fate she controls, and thus her impartiality—and unpredictability. The artist has painted one half of her face white, and the other, black, to emphasize her power to consign individuals from one extreme to another in life.

The black-clad "*DOLEUR*" ("suffering" in French), aided by "*CRAINTE*" ("fear"), grabs a hapless individual whose world has been turned upside down.

Dame Fortune stabs a man in the neck with a dagger held in her fifth left hand, while, in cruel contrast, its counterpart on the right gently caresses a fortunate individual upon whom Lady Luck has smiled.

Allegory   Filippino Lippi

c.1485–90, oil on panel, Galleria degli Uffizi, Florence, Italy

No one knows exactly what the Florence-based artist Filippino Lippi's enigmatic *Allegory* signifies. Over the centuries, art historians have attempted to solve the puzzle by deconstructing each symbolic element of this painting before attempting to reassemble the pieces to form a clearer picture. Ultimately, however, they have been left with as foggy a view as the Florentine cityscape in the background.

Two main theories regarding *Allegory's* possible meaning prevail. The first is that it refers to the fate of the Trojan priest Laocoön and his sons. This was related by the Roman poet Virgil in Book II of his epic poem *The Aeneid* (30–19 BC): having offended her by advising his fellow Trojans to reject the wooden horse left for them by the deceitful Greeks, the Greco–Roman goddess Athena/Minerva retaliated by sending two sea serpents to crush Laocoön and his two sons to death. Yet this Classical-focused explanation does not explain the apparent presence of Zeus/Jupiter, who played no part in the trio's demise. If you accept that the supreme god of the Olympic pantheon symbolizes the Judeo–Christian God, and that the setting and clothes have relevance to the society in which Lippi lived, however, another explanation presents itself. For it may be that *Allegory* represents the political and religious strife—instigated by the Dominican friar Girolamo Savonarola (1452–98)—that was threatening to tear Florence apart at this time (and, indeed, the Medici rulers would be ousted and a republic established in 1494). And a third suggestion is that the snakes signify the plague that was still rife and deadly in fifteenth-century Europe, an outbreak of which, in contemporary belief, may have been visited on Florence as a punishment from God.

All of these theories have merit, but equally, maybe Lippi was simply indulging in an artistic fantasy or was sending a barbed message to a certain disloyal family member whose name has been obscured by the mists of time.

See also **St. Philip Exorcizing the Demon from the Temple of Mars** (pages 74–76).

Prominent amid the towers and spires of Florence is the great dome of the city's cathedral (whose formal name is the Basilica di Santa Maria del Fiore, but which is informally known as the Duomo), which was erected by architect Filippo Brunelleschi between 1420 and 1436 in accordance with his groundbreaking design.

The Latin text that winds its way across the center of the painting, linking the two men in sober black, reads: *NULLA DETERIOR PESTIS Q FAMILIARIS INIMICUS*. This may be translated as "No plague is worse than an enemy in the family," a sentiment that is emphasized by the striking physical—family—resemblance between the two men. (But note that it may well be that the two are actually one and the same.)

An ermine, whose white coat signifies purity, can be seen alongside one of the stricken men. Does it refer to his spotless character? And if so, is the suggestion either that he is the injured party in a tale of family treachery, or that disease is no respecter of virtue?

With his flowing gray hair and beard, and robe the color of lifeblood, the imposing, wise-looking father figure who observes the young man's distress with apparent detachment conforms to traditional representations of the God of Christianity. Yet look closer, and you'll see that his scepter comprises zigzagging arrows, in other words, thunderbolts, the attributes of Zeus/Jupiter, ruler of the skies and the supreme god of the Greco–Roman pantheon. Either way, these deadly weapons signify the power to smite down from on high those who have caused offense on Earth. The golden wings that can be discerned at hand level may be those of Zeus/Jupiter's companion eagles, or may simply denote airborne flight.

Snakes, which have positive, as well as negative, symbolic associations, were once believed to spread disease.

The notion that dishonesty, betrayal, and their effects inspired this allegorical painting is boosted by the depiction of two "snakes in the grass," whose forked tongues symbolize the ability to speak deceitful words, and who denote the unseen threat that rises up and attacks without warning.

The leaves and fruits silhouetted against the sky identify this tree as an olive, which symbolizes peace and plenty in both Christian and Greco–Roman belief. In the context of Laocoön, it may be significant that the olive tree was sacred to Athena/Minerva, and in that of Christianity, it is notable that it denotes a sign of God's reconciliation with humankind.

Some scholars have proposed an alternative interpretation: "Nothing is worse than the plague, which is the enemy of friends," referring to the contagiousness of this dire disease.

They can also denote divine punishment, for the Old Testament (Numbers 21:6) tells us that God sent a plague of venomous "fiery serpents" to attack the Israelites for their lack of trust in him. In Christian tradition, the tale of the serpent that tempted Eve in the Garden of Eden, leading to the Fall of humankind, caused snakes to be equated with Satan, evil, deception, heresy, envy, temptation, and the spreading of sin.

That poisonous words and actions lead to hard times, and even death, is hinted at by the bare branches of the lifeless-looking shrubs in the foreground.

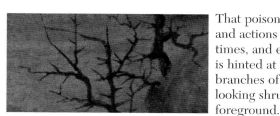

The Moneylender and His Wife — Quentin Massys

1514, oil on panel, Musée du Louvre, Paris, France

Although all acknowledge *The Moneylender and his Wife* to be a valuable visual record of the Antwerp office of an early sixteenth-century financier, art historians are divided into two opposing camps when it comes to interpreting this work. For while some believe that it is simply an early example of the type of genre painting that became hugely popular in Holland a century later, others insist that the symbolism inherent in many of the objects surrounding the central couple transform it into an allegory.

This division of opinion hinges on how moneylending, or usury, was regarded in northern Europe at the time that Massys (also known as Metsys) added this image to his oeuvre. Those who believe this painting to be a generic portrait argue that the moneylender is pictured engaging in an everyday transaction, the likes of which played a crucial part in oiling the wheels of business in a busy hub of commerce like Antwerp (then, as now, a major European port).

Those who champion an allegorical interpretation, by contrast, point to the incongruous presence of certain objects within the moneylender's place of business, as well as to the close proximity of his wife, whose own housekeeping duties would have kept her busy behind the scenes. It is possible, of course, that Massys had been commissioned to create a double portrait, and that the inclusion of the prominently placed prayer book served both to highlight the lady's piety and showcase the artist's abilities. Given, however, the Roman Catholic Church's condemnation of usury, or of lending money at exorbitant rates of interest, at this time, it is possible that Massys was subtly commenting on the moneylender's avarice (*avaritia* in Latin), one of the seven deadly sins. After all, according to the New Testament, "For the love of money is the root of all evil: which while some coveted after, they have erred from the faith" (1 Timothy 6:10).

See also **Dante and his Poem the "Divine Comedy"** (pages 178–81).

The costly, gold-embellished, crystal vessel on the table may have been given to the moneylender in exchange for cash. Yet its presence may also have an allegorical explanation, for this may be either a ciborium, a lidded container in which the Host is kept, or else a chalice. In either case, it represents the Eucharist, the body and blood of Christ, and thus the salvation of devout Christians.

It is recorded that the frame that enclosed this painting during the seventeenth century bore words taken from the Old Testament Book of Leviticus (19:35–36): "Ye shall do no unrighteousness in judgment, in meteyard, in weight, or in measure. Just balances, just weights, a just ephah, and a just hin, shall ye have: I am the Lord your God…" This suggests that the moneylender is being warned to be honest as he weighs a client's coins against his weights to ascertain their gold content (and, by extension, that the viewer is, too). In the lexicon of symbolism, scales can also signify justice and the Last Judgment, when, it is said, souls will be weighed by St. Michael, with those who are light being eternally damned, and those who tip the balance being permitted to enjoy everlasting life.

The apple on the shelf may be the moneylender's lunch. Alternatively, it may refer to the forbidden fruit of the Tree of Knowledge of Good and Evil that the serpent tempted Eve to taste in the Garden of Eden, leading to humankind's Fall. As such, it may represent temptation and sin in Christian belief, but also Christ's power to redeem believers from the curse of Original Sin. The apple's color may additionally beg comparison with the golden balls that are the attributes of Avarice personified.

The small wooden box may store weights when the scales are not in use, but, like the ciborium, may also represent the Eucharist and flesh of Christ, for it looks like a pyx, the round box in which communion wafers are transported when a priest is visiting the sick. (Is it mere coincidence that the coins alongside it resemble such wafers?)

The rings on the table are most likely security for a loan. The moneylender and his wife are both wearing rings on their fingers, and it may be that these pieces of jewelry were originally pawned by debtors who were later unable to pay back their loans.

Pearls have monetary value, but may also represent Christ, partly because their shimmering whiteness symbolizes purity, and partly because the manner in which they are created can be equated with the Virgin Birth.

The red-hatted man who is reflected reading a book in the convex mirror at the center of the image may be the artist or a client of the moneylender (or both). Christian details may be discerned in the mirror, however, for the stained-glass quatrefoils in the window that looks out on the outside world are reminiscent of those in churches, and the mullion and transom together form the shape of the cross on which Christ was crucified.

The lady's illuminated, or illustrated, prayer book, or book of hours, is clearly an expensive aid to piety.

Rather than devoting herself to its contents, and to the Madonna and Child that is just coming into view as she turns the page, she gazes intently at the symbols of transient, material wealth in front of her husband.

The candle may be standing ready to provide light at nightfall.

Yet because a burning flame symbolizes spiritual illumination, its darkened wick may be suggesting that this is lacking in the moneylender's house. It may also warn, in the manner of a *memento mori*, that one day the life will be snuffed out of us all.

THE RENAISSANCE WORLD

All art is propaganda…On the other hand, not all propaganda is art.

George Orwell, "Charles Dickens" (1939)

Above: *Detail from* The Miracle of the Relic of the True Cross on the Rialto Bridge *(c.1496). See pages 174–177.*
Right: *Alfonso d'Este's piety is emphasized in this portrait by Dosso Dossi of his patron, who was the Duke of Ferrara.*
Far right: *The sun and moon both appear in Albrecht Altdorfer's* The Battle of Issus *(1529), providing a symbolic celestial mirror of the 333 BC battle between the armies of Alexander the Great and Darius.*

The Renaissance world was a far from tranquil one. During this period, there was barely a part of Europe that was not being fiercely fought over, or at the very least coveted, by emperors, kings, princes, dukes, and mercenary opportunists hungry for territory, power, and plunder. At the same time, a discredited papacy struggled to maintain its nominal spiritual authority over secular rulers, many of whom resented being dictated to, even if it was by God's representative on earth in Rome. Add to this turbulent state of affairs the Protestant rebels against the religious status quo, in Germany and elsewhere, who instigated the divisive Reformation during the sixteenth century, and it is a wonder that this was an exceptionally fertile period for the making of art, rather than its destruction.

In fact, the combination of the humanist emphasis on culture, education, and learning, combined with the fiercely competitive atmosphere that pervaded the courts and cities of Europe, provided both the spark and the fuel that together ignited a rare creative spirit that, once lit, spread like wildfire. And with leading lights of Italian artistry like Michelangelo Buonarroti and Raphael spreading their talents between such Italian beacons of civilization as Florence, Perugia, and Rome, Leonardo da Vinci ending his days in France, and the German artist Albrecht Dürer traveling to Italy and the Low Countries, while his compatriot Hans Holbein the Younger opted for England, it seemed that the adventurous spirit of the Renaissance knew no bounds.

While the primary focus of Renaissance artists, like that of their medieval predecessors, continued to be on the heavens above, and on what awaited humankind in the afterlife, the influence of humanism increasingly prompted their gaze to shift both inward and outward. Looking inward resulted in a greater understanding of the human psyche—of its emotions, fears, aspirations, strengths, and weaknesses—and this growing interest and self-knowledge was reflected in allegories that, on the one hand, commented critically on human nature (Hieronymus Bosch's *The Ship of Fools*, see pages 137 to 139, for instance), and, on the other, painted a wistfully wonderful picture of what an ideal world might look like (see, for example, Botticelli's *Primavera*, pages 122 to 126). Armed with such awareness, Renaissance artists were well equipped to add hidden depths and telling details (at least to those who understood their symbolism) to portraits when patrons instructed them to immortalize their features in paint or bronze. So while, on the face of it, a Renaissance portrait may present itself as a simple likeness, look closer, and you may sense that a tantalizing puzzle lurks beneath the surface, and that if you could only decode the meaning of the details—a strategically placed butterfly, perhaps, or maybe the apparently inexplicable presence of a starling—you would become privy to a fascinating secret. And you would be right.

Below: A view of Giulio Romano's spectacular fresco in the room of the giants in Mantua's Palazzo del Tè. Constructed from 1524 to 1534 for Federico II Gonzaga, these magnificent rooms hosted many of the most illustrious Italian figures of their era.

Above: Vittore Carpaccio's Two Venetian Ladies (c.1495, detail) is replete with animal symbolism.

Broaden your outlook from portraiture to include the history paintings, battle scenes, images of pageantry, study, industry, and domesticity, as well as the townscapes and landscapes so realistically rendered with breathtaking skill by the era's artists, and you will be rewarded by an enthralling insight into the rich diversity, passion, and vibrancy that characterized the Renaissance world.

POWER AND POLITICS

Realism may have pervaded Renaissance art to an extent that made it almost incomparable to that of the Middle Ages, yet this realism did not always represent reality. After all, patrons wanted to impress their contemporaries and rivals by commissioning art that showed them in the best possible light, while the painters that they employed needed to eat and were therefore anxious to please, so that in a sense, much—and perhaps all—Renaissance art was propaganda. Yet the brutal reality of lives lived in the upper strata of Renaissance society included loveless marriages made for purposes of strengthening political, national, and dynastic ties, bloody warfare, and, between battles, ruthless political machinations. Indeed, it was the pragmatic advice that he gave in his book *Il Principe* (*The Prince*, 1512) that caused the Florentine-born Niccolò Machiavelli (1469–1527) to inspire a word—Machiavellian—that is commonly used today to describe an amoral, cunning, and opportunistic approach to life. So although Renaissance art includes stirring martial scenes and portraits of heroic *condottieri* (commanders of mercenary companies), such images represent a glamorized version of reality. Thus Paolo Uccello's *The Battle of San Romano* (see pages 170 to 173), for instance, appears curiously stylized and bloodless, while because Federigo da Montefeltro was invariably painted in profile from his "good side" (see pages 160 and 191 to 193), viewers would not be aware of the duke of Urbino's missing right eye, a sacrifice to war, and ultimately to his ambition.

*Above: One of at least four similar portraits of Giuliano de' Medici painted during the 1470s by Botticelli. One of the later versions shows the somber figure in front of an open door, symbolizing the transition from life to death; the portrait was commissioned in the aftermath of Giuliano's assassination in 1478. **Below:** Influential Venetian artist Giorgione's* Gentleman in Armor *(c.1510).*

Privileged though they may have been by the standards of ordinary citizens, the rulers of Europe's realms and, in Italy's case, city states, were engaged in a constant struggle to wrest more possessions and power from each other, by force if necessary. And it was during the Renaissance era that England lost its territory across the English Channel to France; that the French king, François I (1494–1547), was captured on the battlefield at Pavia, in Italy, by troops of the Holy Roman Emperor Charles V (1500–58) in 1525; and that Pope Clement VII (1478–1534) was forced to take refuge in the Castle of Sant' Angelo while Rome was sacked by Charles V's army in 1527.

Pope Clement was born Giulio de' Medici, into a Florentine family of erstwhile physicians whose members had made a fortune in banking, and had then exploited their wealth and position in Florentine society—largely through political maneuvering rather than battlefield bludgeoning—to become effectively the hereditary rulers of Florence, in theory a republic. It was Giovanni di Bicci de' Medici (1360–1429) who first began to spend some of the money that he had amassed through banking on commissioning works of architecture and art, his son Cosimo (1389–1464) then following in his father's footsteps, and so on, with the symbiotic relationship between Medici patron and Italian artist achieving its most spectacular flowering under Lorenzo the Magnificent (1449–92).

Their rise to riches and influence may have been less spectacular than that of the Medici family, but many merchants throughout Europe were steadily accumulating wealth, too, usually through banking, or moneylending (see *The Moneylender and his Wife*, pages 150 to 153), or through trade, so that the number of individuals with money to spare to spend on commissioning paintings was widening. And for those who regarded such an expenditure as an investment rather than a frivolity, it was money well spent.

PATRONAGE AND PRESTIGE

That the nature of the relationship between patron and artist was symbiotic, or mutually beneficial, was without doubt, even if the benefits to the patron were rather more intangible than the cash that the artist pocketed (and maybe also the board and lodging supplied during the duration of the period of creation).

Humbler patrons—sometimes collectively, as in the case of the confraternities, see, for instance, *The Miracle of the Relic of the True Cross on the Rialto Bridge*, pages 174 to 177—tended to commission works that expressed their piety (often literally, if their likenesses were incorporated into a religious scene) or their pride in their family members and family name (see *Lady with a Squirrel and a Starling*, pages 194 to 195), or, indeed, both (see *Pieter Jan Foppeszoon and his Family*, pages 196 to 199). The expense of paying for a painting was considered justified because it contributed to the purchaser's soul's salvation or, in those dynastically conscious times, created an heirloom to be to cherished by later generations.

That there was an element of boastfulness or posturing in commissioning a painting—any type of painting—was undeniable, however, and in this respect those who belonged to the higher echelons of society upped the stakes dramatically, with every prince or pope with cultural pretensions seeking to outdo his rivals. One way of coming up trumps was to hire the most in-demand and accomplished artist, and in his *The Lives of the Artists*, Giorgio Vasari tells of the clamor for Michelangelo's services, especially after the death of Pope Clement VII, when:

Michelangelo then thought himself truly free to attend to completing the tomb of Julius II [for the duke of Urbino, Julius's nephew], but after the creation of the new pope, Paul III, not much time passed before he, too, summoned Michelangelo, and after offering him

Above: *This portrait of Smeralda Bandinelli (1471), by Botticelli (or his school), represented a new way of portraying women on canvas. It is thought to be the first portrait of a woman looking directly at the viewer; female portrait subjects were previously painted in profile.*

special signs of affection and proposals, he tried to convince Michelangelo that he ought to serve him and that he wanted him nearby.

Another way of provoking the envy of one's peers, as well as, it was hoped, the respect and admiration of future generations, was to request a work of art that reflected well on the commissioner. And thanks again to the humanist influence, this usually resulted in an image that suggested that the artist's patron was a person of great taste, education, and a multitude of intellectual, sensual, and physical interests and talents—in short, that he was an *uomo universale* ("universal man" in Italian), or what we would today call a "Renaissance man." The concept of the *uomo universale*, which was expanded on in *Il Cortegiano* (*The Courtier*, 1528), by Italian writer Baldassare Castiglione (1478–1529), was exemplified in Pedro Berruguete's portrait of Federigo da Montefeltro (see pages 191 to 193), in which the then duke of Urbino was simultaneously represented as a battle-hardened soldier, an enlightened man of learning, a champion of the pope and pious person, a ruler who had earned the friendship and respect of European kings, and a kindly and protective father figure to the people of Urbino, as well as to his son and heir. Similarly, Hans Holbein's *The Ambassadors* (see pages 200 to 203) speaks volumes about how two well-to-do Frenchmen wished to be perceived. Often included in such portraits, or on the reverse of portrait medals, and even within a room's newly commissioned decorative scheme, were emblems or symbolic devices (*imprese*) that alluded to the identity of the "owner" and to his or her erudition, in a manner whose subtleness or wittiness was intended to elicit an admiring smile of recognition from those in the know.

PERSONAL, DYNASTIC, AND PAPAL EMBLEMS

Imprese (Italian for "devices") were personal emblems used by prominent individuals to symbolize the essence of their character, and usually consisted of a pictorial symbol (the *corpo*, "body" in Italian) and a motto (the *anima*, "spirit" in Italian, for the text was said to give the *corpo* meaning). The motto was typically in a language different to that of the *impresa*'s deviser or owner, presumably to show off his or her learning. An *impresa* may sometimes make an appearance in a Renaissance painting in its entirety, although the separate use of the *corpo* or *anima* may also allude to the owner.

Other personal devices that make reference to a patron's identity include the badge—a simple image, perhaps an animal, such as the ermine, which could denote the noble house of Brittany, in France, which had adopted this creature, a symbol of purity, as its emblem—and the rebus (a pictorial representation of something that acts as a pun on a person's name).

Coats of arms, either inherited from medieval forebears or awarded as a sign of ennoblement, usually signify dynasties, but can be "differenced," or modified according to the rules of heraldry, to denote an individual or branch of the family.

Just a few of such symbolic devices that point toward particular individuals in Renaissance art are outlined below.

See also *The Wedding Feast*, pages 140 to 143; *Giovanna Tornabuoni, née Albizzi*, pages 188 to 190; *Lady with a Squirrel and a Starling*, pages 194 to 195.

Above: Isabella of Portugal, Queen of Spain and Empress of the Holy Roman Empire, painted by Titian in 1544. Below: Hans Holbein the Younger's c.1537 masterpiece of King Henry VIII was one of the first officially commissioned state portraits of any British sovereign.

England

The Tudor dynasty of monarchs— Henry VII (1457–1509), Henry VIII (see below), Edward VI (1537–53), Mary I (1516–58), and Elizabeth I (1533–1603)—a Tudor rose.

King Henry VIII (1491–1547) *Corpo:* a heart. *Anima (French):* Loyal, "Faithful."

France

The Valois dynasty of monarchs (1368–1589): a stag, sometimes with wings, sometimes with a crown around its neck; the fleur-de-lis, a symbol of France (but note that a stylized lily may also represent the Italian city of Florence).

King Louis XII (1462–1515) *Corpo:* a bristling porcupine, sometimes with its spines shooting outward, sometimes wearing a crown. *Anima (Latin): Cominus et eminus,* "Hand to hand and from a distance."

King François I (1494–1547) *Corpo:* a salamander surrounded by flames. *Anima (Latin and Italian): Nutrisco et extingo,* "I nourish and extinguish," or *Notrisco al buono, stingo el reo,* "I nourish the good and extinguish the bad."

Diane de Poitiers (1499–1566) *Corpo:* a spear. *Anima (Latin): Consequitur quodcunque petit,* "Whatever he follows, he aims at."

The Holy Roman Empire

The Habsburg dynasty, members of whom were almost invariably elected Holy Roman emperor between 1440 and 1806: a double-headed eagle.

Emperor Charles V and King Charles I of Spain (1500–58) *Corpo:* two pillars rising from the sea. *Anima (Latin): Plus ultra,* "Even farther."

The Papacy

The most common papal emblems were: two crossed keys, one gold and one silver; the papal tiara (a conical headdress displaying three crowns).

See also the Medici and Rovere families, below, and *The Legend of St. Ursula,* pages 91 to 93.

Pope Leo X (Giovanni de' Medici, 1475–1521) *Corpo:* a yoke. *Anima (Latin): Suave,* "Pleasant."

Italy
The Este Family

The Este family ruled Ferrara, Modena, and Reggio from the late thirteenth century until the late sixteenth century. Its emblems included: a blindfolded lynx; a palm tree, occasionally with a unicorn; an eagle. *See Portrait of Ginevra d'Este,* pages 182 to 183.

Isabella d'Este (1474–1539) *Corpo:* a burning candle in a triangular candelabrum. *Anima (Latin): Sufficit unum [lumen] in tenebris,* "One [light] is enough in the darkness."

The Farnese Family

One of the emblems of the noble Farnese family was a woman and unicorn.

Cardinal Alessandro Farnese (1520–89) *Corpo:* a shield, with an arrow in the middle, hanging from a tree. *Anima (Greek characters):* "Shoot in this way."
Alessandro Farnese (1545–92) *Corpo:* cannon firing at a city. *Anima (Latin): Invitus invitos,* "I reluctantly conquered the unwilling."

The Gonzaga Family

The Gonzaga family ruled Mantua from 1328 until the early years of the eighteenth century. It could be denoted by an eagle, as well as by a maze (sometimes with a mountain at the center), occasionally with water surrounding it, accompanied by the Italian motto *Forse che si, forse che no,* "Maybe yes, maybe no." One Gonzaga *impresa* had a mountain for a *corpo,* sometimes with an altar or tomb on top,

Above, left: A portrait of Cardinal Alessandro Farnese of Parma by Titian, 1546. Above, right: Isabella d'Este, the subject of this Titian portrait of 1534, was highly educated and among Italy's most influential patrons of the arts.

and sometimes at the center of a maze, with Greek characters spelling out "Olympus" for its *anima,* or the Latin word *Fides,* "Faith."

Ludovico II (or III) Gonzaga (1412–78) *Corpo:* a sun. *Anima (French/Latin): Par un sol désir,* "For a single wish."
Gianfrancesco Gonzaga (1466–1519) *Corpo:* a blazing crucible containing gold ingots. *Anima (Latin): Probasti me, Domine, et cognovisti,* "Lord, you have searched me and known me."
Federico II Gonzaga (1500–40) *Corpo:* a salamander. *Anima (Latin): Quod hic deest me torquet,* "That which is lacking torments me."

The Medici Family

The Medici family effectively ruled over Florence, albeit with enforced interruptions, from 1434 until the eighteenth century. The family's most commonly seen emblems include: five to twelve red balls (*palle*) on a golden background; after 1465, five red balls and a blue ball containing three gold fleurs-de-lis; red or golden balls; a diamond ring, often accompanied by the Latin word *Semper,* "Always"; three interlinked rings, each set with a diamond stone; a diamond shape; three feathers, sometimes a white, a green, and a red one, held together within a ring (used by Pope Leo X, born Giovanni de' Medici, and Pope Clement VII, born Giulio de' Medici, 1478–1534).

See *The Journey of the Magi to Bethlehem*, pages 29 to 31; *Primavera*, pages 122 to 126; *The Wedding Feast*, pages 140 to 143.

Cosimo I de' Medici (1389–1464) *Corpo:* a tortoise with a sail on its shell. *Anima (Latin): Festina lente*, "Make haste slowly." *Corpo:* the goat–fish of Capricorn. *Anima (Latin): Fidem fati virtute sequemur*, "I shall pursue with courage the promise of fate." *Corpo:* a tree with a missing branch. *Anima (Latin): Uno avulso non deficit alter*, "With one removed, the other is not missing."

The Montefeltro Family

The Montefeltro family ruled Urbino almost uninterruptedly from 1234 to 1508, and may be represented by an eagle.

Federigo da Montefeltro (1422–82) *Corpo:* a stork. *Anima (German): Ich kann verdauen ein grosses Eisen*, "I can digest a big iron."

As featured in: *Portrait of Federigo da Montefeltro, Duke of Urbino, and his son Guidobaldo*, pages 191 to 193.

Below: Piero della Francesca's Portraits of Federigo da Montefeltro and His Wife Battista Sforza *(1465–66). Federigo da Montefeltro was one of the most successful condottieri of the Italian Renaissance, and lord of Urbino from 1444 until his death in 1482.*

Piero I de' Medici (1414–69) *Corpo:* a falcon clutching a diamond ring in its talons. *Anima (Latin): Semper*, "Always"; or *Fa con dio amante*, "Do it for the love of God."

Lorenzo de' Medici (1449–92) *Corpo:* a laurel bush. *Anima (Latin): Ita ut virtus*, "So is virtue." See *The Wedding Feast*, pages 140 to 143.

Piero II de' Medici (1471–1503) *Corpo:* two flaming rods crossed to form an "X." *Anima (Latin): In viridi teneras exurit medullas*, "In youth, [love] burns to the marrow."

The Montefeltro Family
See left.

The Rovere Family

The primary emblem of the Rovere family was an oak tree (*rovere* in Italian), or else oak leaves and acorns. Two Rovere popes, Pope Sixtus IV (Francesco della Rovere, 1414–84) and Pope Julius II (Giuliano della Rovere, 1443–1513), were identified with these emblems in art.

REFLECTIONS OF THE RENAISSANCE WORLD

Portraiture therefore flourished during the Renaissance, but so, too, did other types of painting, all of which reflected in some way the values and preoccupations of the time. This was an era of learning, enabled by an ever-increasing body of knowledge, thanks to the printing press, and as people read more Roman literature or immersed themselves in the teachings of the ancient Greeks, so historical figures from the ancient past were increasingly portrayed in art, as were architectural details dating back to Classical times. And because, partly due to the humanist mindset and partly due to the plague, people were also far more interested in the here and now than ever before, contemporary townscapes, landscapes, and genre scenes began to supplement portraits in reflecting the many facets of life in the Renaissance world.

HISTORICAL FIGURES IN RENAISSANCE ART

Many Renaissance paintings incorporated historical characters who were admired for their achievements or morality. These included philosophers and poets, as well as monarchs and martial men. Their clothing and attributes usually provide a clue as to when they lived and the nature of their fame, which may in itself be symbolized by a glittering crown or laurel wreath (the latter usually in the case of writers and artists). Some of the most notable such personages are listed below, along with their usual attributes.

See also *School of Athens*, pages 162 to 166.

Constantine the Great (c.274–337) *Appearance:* a mature man, dressed either as an emperor or as a soldier. *Attributes:* a crown; a scepter; soldiers; a cross in the sky; a flag (the labarum) with a red cross on a white field or a *chi-rho* symbol; a model of a church. See *Allegory of the Old and New Testaments*, pages 132 to 136.

Dante Alighieri (1265–1321) *Appearance:* a middle-aged man in fourteenth-century clothing. *Attributes:* a laurel wreath; a book (usually the *Divina Commedia*, or the *Divine Comedy*); an older man in Roman garments (Virgil). See also *Dante and his Poem the "Divine Comedy,"* pages 178 to 181.

Homer (c.800 BC) *Appearance:* an old man with a white beard, often crowned with a laurel wreath, clearly blind. *Attributes:* a scroll or book or books; a musical instrument; human helpers.

Socrates (?470–399 BC) *Appearance:* an older, white-bearded man. *Attributes:* a cup; a mirror.

Publius Cornelius Scipio Africanus Major (237–183 BC) *Appearance:* a mature man dressed in the uniform of a Roman soldier. *Attributes:* a tent; a plethora of golden objects and other treasure.

Publius Cornelius Scipio Africanus Minor (c.185–129 BC) *Appearance:* a sleeping man in the uniform of a Roman soldier. *Attributes:* a book; a sword; myrtle; three women offering gifts.

Virgil (70–19 BC) *Appearance:* an older man, often wearing white Roman robes and crowned with a laurel wreath; a man in a basket. *Attributes:* a scroll or book; a middle-aged man (Dante). See also *The Adoration of the Mystic Lamb*, pages 55 to 58; *Dante and his Poem the "Divine Comedy,"* pages 178 to 181.

Below: Botticelli's 1495 portrait of Dante Alighieri features his most important attribute, the laurel wreath.

School of Athens

Raphael

1510–11, fresco, Vatican Museums and Galleries, Vatican City, Italy

Not only is the *School of Athens* a High Renaissance *tour de force*, but Raphael's suggestive use of symbolism and sly portrayals make it a masterpiece of ingenuity, too. Indeed, one of the many details that cause this fresco to be so intriguing was marveled at by the artist's near-contemporary Giorgio Vasari, who revealed, in *The Lives of the Artists* (1568): "…next to him [the figure holding a globe of the heavens] is the portrait of Raphael, the master of this work, who painted himself by looking in a mirror. He has a youthful head and a very modest appearance coupled with a pleasant and gentle grace, and he is wearing a black beret."

Raphael was a mere twenty-five years of age when he traveled to Rome in 1508 to join a band of artists who had been commissioned to decorate a suite of private rooms at the Vatican for the della Rovere pope Julius II (1453–1513). The *School of Athens* gradually took shape in the room that was destined to become Julius's library (and later Leo X's study, whereupon it was renamed the Stanza della Segnatura, or "Room of the Signature"). Befitting a library, the overall theme of the decorative scheme was the intellect, illustrated by four separate subjects—philosophy, theology, jurisprudence, and poetry—with Raphael's *School of Athens* (which was originally entitled *Causarum Cognitio*, or "*Knowledge of Causes*") representing philosophy, and his *Disputà* ("*Dispute*"), theology. They may have been illustrated on opposite walls, but philosophy and theology were not regarded as being in opposition, but rather as complementary, with the theories of the Classical philosophers revealing aspects of God's divine truth.

Plato and his pupil, Aristotle, are the venerable Greek philosophers that stand at the center of this virtuoso demonstration of perspective painting, before its vanishing point. They are flanked by thinkers who had sympathy with their ideas, and whose own contributions to the ever-growing tapestry of human knowledge still have relevance today.

See also The Seven Liberal Arts (page 101), The Rovere Family (page 160).

Classical architectural and decorative features emphasize that the personalities depicted, and the philosophies that they represent, predate the Christian era. A statue of Apollo, the Greco–Roman god of light, learning, reason, and music, can be identified by his traditional attribute of a lyre. The Peripatetic School founded in Athens by Aristotle, whose adherents theorized as they strolled, was based at the Lyceum, whose name was derived from a nearby temple dedicated to Apollo Lukeios.

The mathematician Pythagoras (?580–?500 BC) is depicted copying a diagram that sets out his influential ideas on music and harmony. In the language of symbolism, Pythagoras can represent the liberal arts of arithmetic and music.

The Platonic (natural) philosophers portrayed on Plato's side of the fresco are thought to include Zeno of Citium (?336–?264 BC), the founder of Stoicism, shown here as an old man with a luxuriant white beard. The younger man by his side, wearing a wreath of leaves and absorbed in writing, is considered to be Epicurus (341–270 BC).

Although it is not clear exactly who this man represents—some believe that it is Democritus (?460–?370 BC), and others, Heraclitus (?500 BC)—the face is thought to be that of Michelangelo Buonarroti (1475–1564), who was working on the Sistine Chapel at the same time as Raphael was creating this work of art.

In the lexicon of symbolism, the square denotes the Earth.

Because Plato (c.427–348 BC) believed that everything in the universe reflects, albeit in inferior form, an exalted model on a parallel spiritual plane, he is depicted pointing toward heaven. He is holding a copy of his work *Timaeus*, which discusses the nature of the universe. Some claim that Raphael borrowed the features of Leonardo da Vinci (1452–1519) for this depiction. Aristotle (384–322 BC), who is carrying a heavy-looking copy of his *Ethics* (which advises that happiness can only be found in pondering philosophical truths), gestures toward the ground,

as if making the point that we should look around us for existential insight. Symbolically speaking, Aristotle can personify the liberal art of logic.

Diogenes of Sinope (?412–?323 BC), the Cynic philosopher, is portrayed here sprawled on the steps, his clothes in careless disarray. The cup by his side may represent a beggar's cup or may refer to a story that after seeing a child drink from cupped hands, Diogenes threw away his own drinking vessel, considering it superfluous to his requirements.

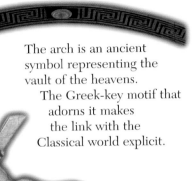

The arch is an ancient symbol representing the vault of the heavens.
   The Greek-key motif that adorns it makes the link with the Classical world explicit.

Vasari says that this is "the portrait of Federigo II, Duke of Mantua, who was in Rome at that time." A member of the Gonzaga dynasty, Federico (1500–40) would not rule Mantua until 1519.

It is thought that this figure is either Zoroaster, or Zarathustra (?628–?551 BC), the Persian founder of the Zoroastrian, dualistic system of sacred belief, who is balancing a globe representing the heavens on his fingertips, or else the Greek geographer Strabo (c.58 BC–AD 24).

Raphael's face looks out at us, alongside that of fellow artist Giovanni Antonio Bazzi (1477–1549), nicknamed Il Sodama.

Her armor and spear, along with her shield (the *aegis*), which bears the gorgoneion, or head of the Gorgon Medusa, leave us in no doubt that this statue has been fashioned in the image of the Greco–Roman goddess Athena/Minerva. As well as being the patron of the martial arts, Athena promoted learning, wisdom, and the Seven Liberal Arts (grammar, logic or dialectics, and rhetoric, these three being the *trivium*, or "three roads"; and the *quadrivium*, the "four roads" of geometry, arithmetic, astronomy, and music).

Among the Aristotelian (moral) thinkers depicted enjoying a lively exchange of ideas is the mathematician Euclid, who is demonstrating one of his theorems with the help of a pair of compasses. Euclid (who can personify geometry, one of the seven liberal arts) may have lived during the third century BC, but Raphael has given him a sixteenth-century face, namely that of the architect Donato Bramante (?1444–1514), who had been working on the basilica of St. Peter's since 1506 and had recommended Raphael to Pope Julius.

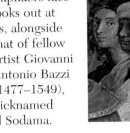

Ptolemy, the second-century-AD Alexandrian deviser of the Ptolemaic system, which held that the planets revolve around the Earth (a theory that was accepted in Raphael's time), grasps a globe symbolizing the Earth. Ptolemy may signify the liberal art of astronomy.

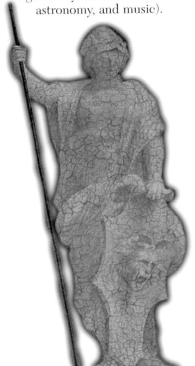

Portrait of a Knight

Vittore Carpaccio

1510, oil on canvas, Thyssen-Bornemisza Collection, Madrid, Spain

Among the small number of undisputed statements that can be made about Vittore Carpaccio's *Portrait of a Knight* is that it is one of the first instances in European art in which the whole of the subject is portrayed in life-sized dimensions. Another is that it concerns the ideal knight or Christian soldier (*miles christianus* in Latin). Yet while the symbolic clues with which this image is packed underline this "perfect-knight" theme, they fail to resolve the perplexing issue of the knight's identity, if, indeed, Carpaccio depicted a real-life individual rather than an imaginary or allegorical figure.

The launching point for most who embark on the challenge of unraveling this knotty puzzle is typically the two text-bearing signs that can be seen on the right and left of the painting. On closer scrutiny, the text that they present is written in Latin, with that on the right giving the artist's name and the date of the painting's completion, and that on the left displaying the motto of the Order of the Ermine, a chivalric order named after the creature that Carpaccio has depicted nearby. Because the Order of the Ermine was associated with the Aragon kings of Naples, some researchers believe that the inclusion of these details indicates that this is a posthumous portrait of King Ferdinand II of Naples (1469–96), for many of the painting's features furthermore have funerary associations. Others, guided by the portrait's date and military theme, believe the knight to be Francesco Maria della Rovere (1490–1538), who, in 1510, was both the duke of Urbino and the captain, or commander, of the papal army. Still further names have been proposed, another theory being that the young knight may represent a saintly soldier of the Lord, with favored candidates being St. Hubert and St. Eustace, both of whom are traditionally depicted alongside stags and—particularly in Hubert's case—hunting dogs.

*See also **The Vision of St. Eustace** (pages 80–82), **water spout detail** (page 104).*

A hawk with dark plumage is getting the better of a gray crane (or heron) in an aerial battle. Not only does color symbolism suggest that the bird of prey represents evil, while the fishing bird denotes good, but in Christian allegory, the crane signifies vigilance, a virtue traditionally required of rulers. Was Carpaccio encouraging viewers to equate the knight with the soon-to-be-vanquished crane?

An equine sign hangs from the castle. Both horse and fortress underline the painting's emphasis on knighthood, and may also pinpoint the young man's starting-out point on his final quest or short journey through life as a soldier of Christ. In short, the painting's background may be a literal representation of the knight's background story.

The water gushing from the pipe may symbolize spiritual sanctification and eternal life.

It is likely that the knight in the background and the knight in the foreground are one and the same. It may be significant that his steed is the color of death.

The text above the ermine reads *MALO MORI QUAM FOEDARI*, which means "I would rather die than be sullied." This motto of the Order of the Ermine is based on the once prevalent belief that the ermine (a stoat whose coat turns white in winter, apart from its tail) really does prefer death to dirtiness, which is symbolically associated with sin.

In the Christian context, the peacock symbolizes regeneration, incorruptibility, and immortality, partly because it was said to renew its feathers each spring; partly because its flesh was believed not to decay after death; and partly because its displayed tail feathers resemble the starry sky, or heaven.

White rabbits were popular attributes of the Virgin Mary at this time, their white fur linking them with her spotless virtue, and their fecundity, with her position as the mother of Christ. They may also denote victory over lust and promiscuity.

The iris gave rise to the stylized fleur-de-lis, which is in turn the emblem of the kings of France and the city of Florence. Could this flower therefore be read as another clue to the knight's identity?

Both St. Eustace and St. Hubert had life-changing encounters with stags that represented Christ, and it may be that the background knight is about to experience such an event. Stags (whose lightning-resembling, regenerating antlers link them with light and renewal) are often represented standing by fountains, streams, or pools in Christian art, when the water symbolizes life's source and sustenance, and thus God.

The vivid red berries next to the knight may represent his lifeblood, shed in battle. It may also be significant that these fruits are poisonous, and that the roots of the *Arum maculatum* plant that bears them yields a starch that was once used to bleach freckled skin, giving us three possibly relevant keywords: fruition, death, and spotlessness.

Swords signify armed action.

Is the knight sheathing his, suggesting that he has fought his last fight? Or is he unsheathing his weapon, indicating that he stands ever ready to battle against the forces of evil?

As well as being an attribute of St. Hubert, dogs represent fidelity, and thus also the knight's faithfulness to God.

Like the iris on the left, the white lily is an emblem of the Virgin Mary and represents spiritual purity, beauty, and goodness in the lexicon of Christian symbolism.

The felled tree may represent the knight, who has been cut down in his prime. If the path that wends its way through the painting, starting at the castle's gate, represents his journey through life, or his spiritual quest, that same tree (that is, he) may first be seen in full leaf, or flourishing (by the lake), and then shedding its foliage, or in decline (directly behind him).

Carpaccio has signed and dated his work in Latin: *VICTOR CARPATHIUS FINXIT MDX* ("Vittore Carpaccio made this, 1510").

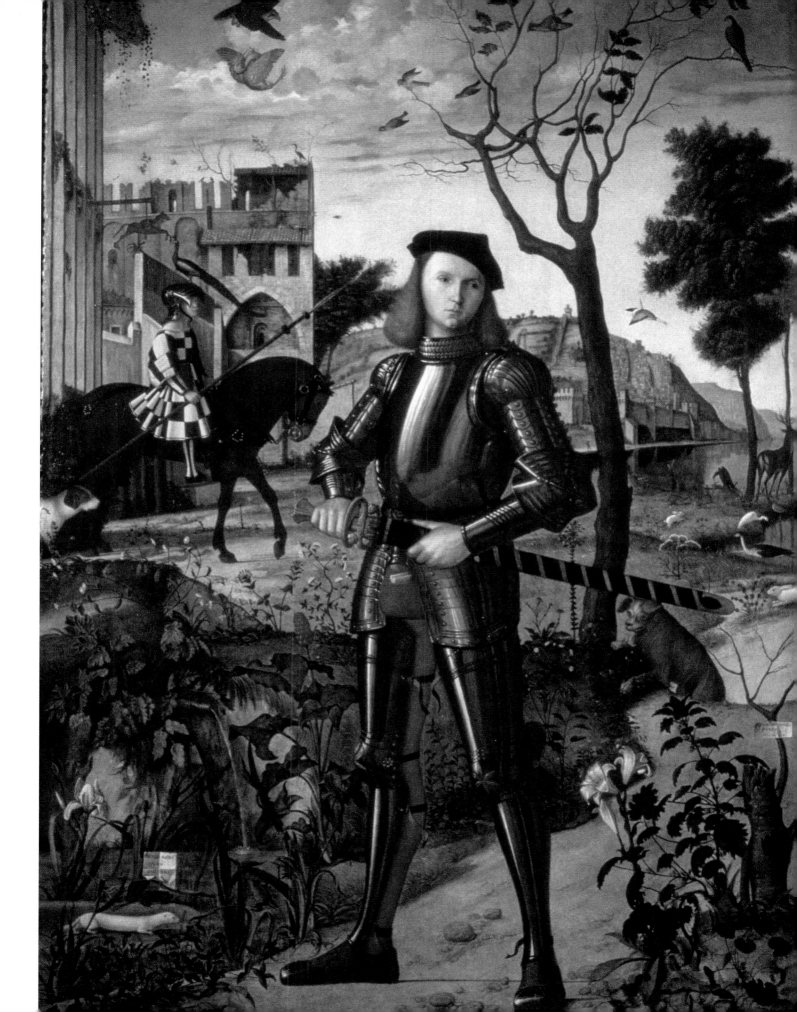

The Battle of San Romano

Paolo Uccello

c.1456, oil on panel, Musée du Louvre, Paris, France

Paolo Uccello was renowned—even notorious—for his pioneering obsession with perspective. Indeed, in his *The Lives of the Artists* (1568), Giorgio Vasari opens his chapter on the Florentine artist with the faintly damning words: "Paolo Uccello would have been the most delightful and inventive genius in the history of painting…if he had spent as much time working on human figures and animals as he lost on problems of perspective…" Certainly, his horses seem copied from a merry-go-round, while the angles at which the lances bristle in this, one of Uccello's three scenes of the Battle of San Romano, along with the foreshortening of his warhorses, are evidence of his experimental quest to represent reality.

One of the realities that characterized life in fifteenth-century Italy was warfare, for the unification of Italy was centuries away, and in the meantime, bitter rivalry was poisoning relationships between the Italian city-states. Mutual hostility and power struggles often boiled over into warfare, prompting, for example, the Battle of San Romano to be fought between Florence and Siena on June 1, 1432, near Lucca. Florence ultimately won the day, and around twenty years later, Uccello was commissioned to commemorate the victory for the Florentine palace of the Bartolini Salimbeni family. Uccello produced three panels, which were subsequently acquired by the de' Medici and have since been separated. The first scene, now in London, England, focuses on Florentine *condottiere* (mercenary commander) Niccolò da Tolentino's desperate defense of the tower of San Romano; the second is this portrayal of Florentine *condottiere* Micheletto da Cotignola in the act of launching a counterattack on the Sienese; and the third, which is still in Florence, depicts the unhorsing of the Sienese *condottiere* Bernadino della Ciarda.

As well as serving as a historical document of sorts, this painting provides an interesting insight into the symbolism of arms and armor, quite literally from a Renaissance-world perspective.

See also **Popular Personifications in Renaissance Art** (pages 99–101), **Power and Politics** (pages 155–56).

The horse is traditionally regarded as combining animal power with nobility of mind, while a knight astride a horse represents the rational mind firmly in control of such animal passions as lust.

Uccello has used artistic licence in portraying da Cotignola wearing a huge, turbanlike headdress (called a *mazzocchi*), for this would have marked him out as a target, without providing a helmet's protection. (Soldiers returning from the Crusades popularized the turban in Italy, albeit at court, rather than on the battlefield.)

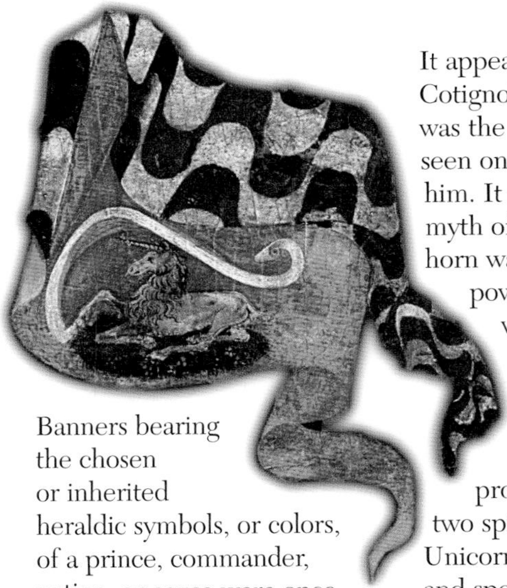

Banners bearing the chosen or inherited heraldic symbols, or colors, of a prince, commander, nation, or cause were once used both for identification and as rallying points on battlegrounds.

It appears as though da Cotignola's personal emblem was the unicorn that can be seen on the pennant behind him. It is speculated that the myth of the unicorn, whose horn was said to have the power to detect poison in water, was propagated by Crusaders who had seen the wild antelopes of the Middle East in profile, and mistook their two spiraling horns for one. Unicorns could symbolize lust and speed, but by the time that this picture was painted, usually instead signified purity, chastity, or Jesus Christ, as well as St. Justina of Antioch and St. Justina of Padua.

Because a black horse usually denotes the negative energies of destruction and death, it is likely that Uccello depicted da Cotignola's steed as being as dark as night for no other reason than to add drama and depth.

The sword that he is swinging behind his head signifies that he is a cut above the other horsemen, whose lances restrict their freedom of movement.

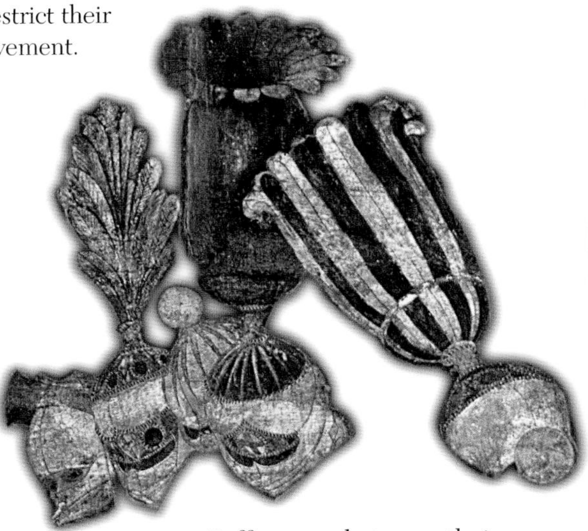

Differences between their helmets' styles and adornments helped to identify individual knights in the thick of battle, although these showy examples are more reminiscent of those worn for chivalric tournaments than for war.

Centuries ago, the distinctive heraldic emblems emblazoned on a shield signaled the identity of the warrior safeguarding his body behind it. The symbol depicted here represents the sun, which in turn denotes such qualities as light and life, strength and fiery energy, invincibility, and thus victory.

Shields represent protection, and, in artistic representations, may symbolically defend the virginity of such virtuous figures as chastity personified.

The lancers on the left begin their attack. As well as signifying aggression, most weapons, the lance included, can be interpreted as phallic symbols. The lance is typically carried by rank-and-file cavalrymen and is regarded as a lesser weapon than the sword. In a Christian context, the lance can represent St. Longinus and St. Jude.

The helmet generally symbolizes a warrior figure, such as Ares/Mars, the Greco–Roman god of war, but may also signify protected thoughts, and, as such, may represent Athena/Minerva, the Classical goddess of wisdom and the martial arts. In Christian iconography, the helmet may furthermore signify the cardinal virtue of fortitude, as well as the theological virtue of faith.

The Miracle of the Relic of the True Cross on the Rialto Bridge

Vittore Carpaccio

c.1496, oil on canvas, Galleria dell' Accademia, Venice, Italy

The title of this painting is somewhat misleading, implying as it does that we should feast our eyes on the bridge that spans the right-hand side of the picture. In fact, the miraculous action is taking place on the loggia, or balcony, of the building on the far left, where the power of the True Cross is restoring a possessed, or lunatic, man to sanity.

By the Middle Ages, an elaborate legend had sprung up around the True Cross, or the cross on which Christ was crucified. Across Christendom, it was believed that after Adam died, a branch from the Tree of Knowledge was planted on his grave. This was felled during the time of King Solomon, but proved unsuitable for building purposes, so was laid across a stream and used as a bridge, where the queen of Sheba encountered it and had a vision that this was no ordinary tree. Indeed, before it was erected at Golgotha in order for Christ to be nailed to it, the waters in which it floated became renowned for their healing powers. Centuries after Christ's crucifixion, it was identified in Jerusalem as the "True Cross" by Helena, the mother of the Emperor Constantine. Following this "invention," part of the True Cross was seized by King Chosroes II of Persia, later being recaptured by Emperor Heraclius, who returned it to Jerusalem, where it was "exalted."

In 1369, Philip de Mézières, chancellor of the kingdom of Cyprus and Jerusalem, presented a fragment of the True Cross to the Scuolo Grande di San Giovanni Evangelista (the great "school," or confraternity, of Saint John the Evangelist) of Venice. And was this wealthy body of pious laymen that commissioned nine paintings (created between 1494 and 1501) from various notable artists to celebrate the miracles associated with their True Cross. That said, Carpaccio's creation is today acclaimed more as fascinating snapshot of late fifteenth-century Venice than as a reverent homage to a holy relic.

See also tree and bridge details (page 48), Patronage and Prestige (page 157).

On the right of the balcony, members of the Scuolo Grande di San Giovanni Evangelista kneel in awe. This event took place in 1494, so would have been fresh in the collective Venetian memory.

On the balcony of the Palazzo Querini, or Querini Palace, Francesco Querini, the Patriarch of Grado, who is recognizable from his red cap and white vestments, holds up the reliquary that contains the splinter of the True Cross. Before him, a black-clad man writhes as the demon that has possessed him is driven away: simple color symbolism makes it clear that its dark power of evil is no match for the bright force of good that is concentrated in the True Cross above the unfortunate's head.

The *Ponti di Rialto* (Rialto Bridge) once provided the only means of crossing the *Canal Grande* (Grand Canal) on foot. The wooden, shop-lined bridge recorded here is at least the third incarnation, having been built during the mid-fifteenth century to incorporate a drawbridge in the middle that could be pulled back to allow tall vessels to pass through.

(The bridge that stands here today is of stone, and dates from 1592.) The procession that can be seen wending its way across the bridge is actually the same company of people that is portrayed on the balcony, having arrived at its destination.

People can be seen going about their business in the Rialto, Venice's oldest marketplace and bustling center of commerce. Architectural historians have identified some of the buildings that Carpaccio has included in this section of his cityscape; certain of them, such as the Fondaco dei Tedeschi, La Ca'baglioni da Mosta, the Palazzo dei Camerlenghi, and the Santi Apostoli church, still grace this stretch of the Grand Canal, although most have since been renovated or rebuilt, so that they look rather different.

Strict, hierarchical dress codes prevailed in Venice at this time, according to which senators were required to dress in red damask robes, to which procurators, who outranked senators, were permitted to add black stoles.

A multitude of funnel-shaped chimneys crowds the skyline. Land being at a premium in water-surrounded Venice, its houses are tightly packed together. This makes it vital that smoke be encouraged to disperse upward, into the sky, rather than downward, where it would create a sooty, choking atmosphere.

The oval sign affixed to the side of a building alongside the bridge advertises the Sturion hotel (which still exists, trading as the Hotel Antica Locanda Sturion).

One of the gondoliers plying his trade on the Grand Canal is of African origin, illustrating the cosmopolitan character of Venetian society.

Dante and His Poem the "Divine Comedy"

Domenico di Michelino

1465, tempera on panel, Duomo, Florence, Italy

His masterpiece the *Divine Comedy* (1306–21) is largely responsible for Dante Alighieri's reputation as one of the world's greatest poets. And because Dante was born in Florence (in 1265), his hometown has for centuries basked in his reflected glory, with Domenico di Michelino's painting, which can still be seen on the north wall of Florence's Duomo (cathedral), for instance, being commissioned to mark the two-hundredth anniversary of his birth. How Dante would have relished this glorification, having been banished from Florence on pain of death during his lifetime.

During the thirteenth and fourteenth centuries, many politically active Italian families aligned themselves with either the pro-papal Guelphs or the Ghibellines, whose allegiance was to the Holy Roman emperor. The Alighieris supported the Guelphs, who were in turn divided into two passionately opposed factions in Tuscany: the Bianchi ("Whites"), who wanted an independent, democratic Florence, and the Neri ("Blacks"), who were prepared to accept a measure of papal influence. As a committed Bianchi, Dante was banished from Florence in 1302, shortly after the Neri took control of the city, never to return.

Dante composed his *Commedia* ("Comedy"—it did not gain its *Divina*, or "Divine" honorific until the sixteen century) during his long years of exile, completing it shortly before his death in 1321. This epic, and allegorical, poem, which he sets in 1300, is remarkable on many levels, not least because, unusually for its time, it was written in the Tuscan vernacular, rather than in the Latin that was considered the mark of educated and cultured men. Following an introductory *canto* (section of verse), Dante leads the reader—as he himself is led by first Virgil, who symbolizes reason, and then by Matilda, who signifies the ideal active life, and finally by Beatrice, who represents the ideal contemplative life or divine revelation—through Hell (*Inferno*), Purgatory (*Purgatorio*), and Paradise (*Paradiso*). All three realms of the Christian afterlife are illustrated in this painting, as is Florence, the city that once barred one of its most illustrious sons from setting foot inside its walls.

See also **Charon Crossing the River Styx** (pages 112–15).

QVI COELVM CECINIT MEDIVMQVE IMVMQVE TRI
ENSIT CONSILIIS AC PIETATE PAT   EM   NII

LVSTRAVIT QVE ANIMO CVNCTA POETA SVO · DOCTVS ADEST DANTES SVA QVEM FLORENTIA
IT TANTO MORS SAEVA NOCERE POETAE · QVEM VIVVM VIRTVS CARMEN IMAGO FACIT

In the *Paradiso* section (XXV, 1–9) of the *Divine Comedy*, Dante wrote of longing to return to his baptismal font to receive a poet's crown. Domenico di Michelino has granted his wish—in paint, at least—by portraying him wearing a laurel wreath, the traditional mark of a "laureate," or someone deserving of honor. This symbolic association dates back to Greco–Roman times, when the laurel was dedicated to Apollo, the god of light, lyricism, and music.

The *Divine Comedy*'s opening lines can just be discerned: *Nel mezzo del cammin di nostra vita…* ("Midway on the journey of our life…")

Echoing the astronomical beliefs of the day, the planets, sun, and moon are depicted revolving around the earth, which was then considered to be at the center of the universe.

One of this painting's alternative titles is *The Comedy Illuminating Florence*, and the halolike rays of light that emanate from the copy of the *Commedia* that Dante is holding, spotlighting his home city, could be interpreted as either illuminating Florence in a golden glow of glory or as highlighting its connection with the characters and contents of his epic.

The heavens were thought to consist of nine spheres, each of the first seven being dominated by a heavenly body (their astronomical signs are shown alongside their representations here), that of the moon being nearest to the earth, followed by that of Mercury, Venus, the sun, Mars, Jupiter, and Saturn. The eighth sphere was the realm of the fixed stars (including the constellations). In the ninth sphere, Dante tells of encountering first the nine orders of angels, and then the Empyrean, a radiant stream of light at the heart of which the Virgin Mary and saints surround the dazzling Holy Trinity.

Dante envisages Purgatory (*Purgatorio*) as a water-surrounded mountain consisting of seven levels, up which those whose souls are to be purified must labor, struggling along each successive terrace weighed down by the heavy burden of punishment for their sins of pride, envy, wrath, sloth, avarice, gluttony, and lust. The higher they progress, the lighter their loads become, until the purifying fire that will cleanse their souls is at last in sight.

The sword-wielding Archangel Michael guards the doorway to Purgatory's path, which in turn leads to Earthly Paradise. He will allow only truly repentant supplicants to pass.

DVI COELVM CECINIT MEDIVMQVE
ENSIT CONSILIIS AC PIETATE PATI

The Latin inscription praises Dante's wisdom and his enduring legacy.

Adam and Eve are portrayed before the Fall in their Earthly Paradise, or the Garden of Eden, at the summit of the mount of Purgatory.

QVE TRIBVNAL LVSTRAVIT QVE ANIMO CVNCTA POETA SVO DOCTVS ADEST DANTES SVA QVEM FLORENTIA SAEPE
NIL POTVIT TANTO MORS SAEVA NOCERE POETAE QVEM VIVVM VIRTVS CARMEN IMAGO FACIT

 According to Dante, the gates of Hell bear an inscription that culminates in the words, "Abandon all hope, you who enter here."

In his *Inferno*, Dante describes Hell as consisting of nine levels descending deep into the earth.

From the top down, it is inhabited by those whose only fault is to have been unbaptized at death, ranging through those who committed mortal sins to heretics and those who were violent in life, all of the damned eternally suffering hellish torments enthusiastically administered by Satan's demonic minions. The ninth level is reserved for traitors, who are devoured by the three-headed Lucifer, who squats evilly at the center of the earth.

Florence Cathedral—the Duomo, or Basilica di Santa Maria del Fiore—is identifiable by its octagonal dome, baptistery, and campanile, or bell tower. An iconic landmark, this revolutionary Renaissance dome was designed by Filippo Brunelleschi (1377–1446) and was constructed between 1420 and 1436.

Portrait of Ginevra d'Este

Antonio Pisanello

c.1435–49, oil on panel, Musée du Louvre, Paris, France

As one of its alternative titles, *Portrait of an Este Princess*, suggests, the exact identity of the elegant lady depicted in profile by Antonio Pisanello has long been disputed, as has the date on which the artist laid down his brush for the final time. What is not in doubt, however, is the lady's close affiliation with the ruling Este family of the northern Italian city of Ferrara, which is why Margharita Gonzaga, the wife of Leonello d'Este (who was born in 1407 and ruled as lord of Ferrara from 1441 until his death in 1450), one of Pisanello's patrons, has been considered a likely candidate, another being Margharita's sister, Cecilia Gonzaga. Yet the twenty-first-century consensus is that Pisanello's ethereal young noblewoman portrays neither of the Gonzaga sisters, but is instead the likeness of Ginevra d'Este, Leonello's sister.

Decode the clues in the painting, and it is difficult to disagree, not least because the Italian name of the sprig of juniper—*ginepro*—tucked somewhat incongruously into the ornate piping at the top of the lady's sleeve sounds rather like Ginevra (and its Dutch name, *genever*, even more so). Further symbols in this International Gothic/early Renaissance painting can be interpreted as pointing to love and death, and, indeed, having married Sigismondo Pandolfo Malatesta (1417–68), Ginevra died, poisoned, it was said, by her husband's hand in 1440, at only twenty-one years of age. (It seems that Malatesta was something of a Bluebeard, for in 1442, the widowed "Wolf of Rimini" remarried Polissena Sforza, who died under equally shady circumstances in 1449.) If Leonello commissioned this image, which could have been painted any time between 1435 and 1449, it is therefore likely that he did so in the spirit of mourning and remembrance, and that this was therefore both a memorial piece intended to preserve Ginevra's likeness on earth and a prayer in paint that her soul would enjoy eternal life.

See also **The Este Family** (page 159), **chalice and pearl details** (page 152).

In the language of symbolism, the butterfly signifies the immortal soul. Having started life as a caterpillar, the butterfly then cocoons itself in a shroudlike chrysalis, from which it eventually emerges in all of its glorious beauty, a cycle that has been likened to life, death, and resurrection since ancient times. (Indeed, in ancient Greece, the word *psyche* signified both "soul" and "butterfly.")

A prominently placed sprig of juniper (*ginepro* in Italian) hints strongly at the lady's name: Ginevra. As an evergreen, the juniper can also signify eternal life, and its wood was furthermore once thought to be incorruptible.

Pisanello is notable for his finely observed naturalism, and has certainly depicted white carnations here, possibly to symbolize pure love. According to an old Christian tale, carnations sprang from the tears that the Virgin Mary shed at the foot of the cross while witnessing Christ's crucifixion.

The columbine was regarded as a funerary flower in Renaissance times, largely because it was thought to resemble doves, and the dove (*columba* in Latin) is in turn a Christian symbol of the Holy Spirit. An alternative common name for the columbine (*Aquilegia vulgaris*) is aquilegia, which is derived from the Latin word for "eagle," *aquila*, on account of the similarity between the curving shape of the flower's petals and the bird of prey's talons or beak. Was it sheer coincidence that eagles featured on the Este coat of arms at the time that this portrait was painted?

Apparently confirming the theory that the mystery lady is Ginevra d'Este, not only do her facial features closely resemble those of Leonello, as depicted by Pisanello in a portrait of 1441, but the vase embroidered on her gown matches one that appears on a portrait medallion that Pisanello created for his patron, also in around 1441. In addition, containers such as this may represent the human body, the fragile "vessel" that contains the immortal soul, and although this vessel has cracked and broken, it has done so to enable the life within—or soul, here represented by a vigorous plant—to break free of its earthly confines and thrive. The pearls that decorate this motif may be equated with both purity and tears.

Portrait of
Luca Pacioli   Jacopo de' Barbari

*1495, oil on panel, Museo de Gallerie Nazionale
di Capodimonte, Naples, Italy*

That Renaissance artists were becoming increasingly aware of the apparently magical effects that could be achieved through an understanding of mathematics is demonstrated by Jacopo de' Barbari's portrait of Luca Pacioli (*c*.1445–1517). For although de' Barbari has depicted the friar in the habit of his Franciscan order, the objects that surround him make it clear that the Venetian artist is paying tribute to Pacioli's mastery of mathematics rather than to his piety.

A peripatetic teacher of mathematics to noble pupils, Pacioli is especially remembered for his friendly collaboration with two towering figures of Renaissance art, namely Piero della Francesca (*c*.1415–92), who, like Pacioli, was born in Borgo San Sepolcro, Tuscany, and Leonardo da Vinci (1452–1519). Indeed, between 1496 and 1499, while both Pacioli and da Vinci were employed at the Milanese court of Ludovico Sforza (1451–1508), it was da Vinci's "ineffable left hand," according to Pacioli, which was "most fitted for all the mathematical disciplines," that created the illustrations for Pacioli's *De Divina Proportione* ("*On the Divine Proportion*"). Although it was in this tome, published in 1509, that Pacioli introduced readers to the "golden ratio," which he considered to have been divinely created, his best-known work was *Summa de Arithmetica, Geometria, Proportioni et Proportionalita* ("*Sum of Knowledge of Arithmetics, Geometry, and Proportions*") (1494). In true Renaissance-man style, Pacioli spread his interests and talents, and is credited with popularizing the double-entry book-keeping system, described in his *Summa*, that is still used in accounting today.

Pacioli was not without his critics, however, particularly in respect of his borrowing of other mathematical thinkers' ideas for his publications. Giorgio Vasari, writing in *The Lives of the Artists* (1568), even accused him of downright plagiarism: "when Piero…died after having written many books, the said Master Luca usurped them for his own purposes and had them printed as his own work."

See also **The Seven Liberal Arts** (page 101),
Euclid detail (page 166).

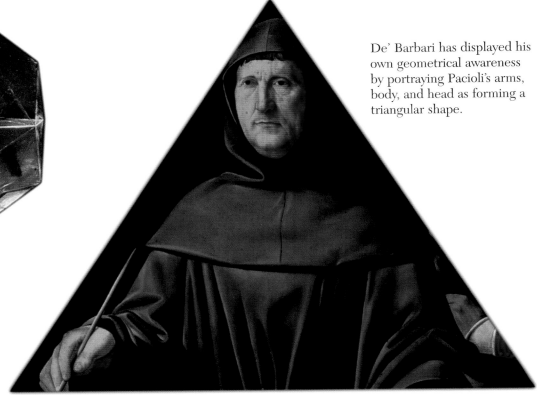

De' Barbari has displayed his own geometrical awareness by portraying Pacioli's arms, body, and head as forming a triangular shape.

The polyhedral model that hangs alongside Pacioli, at head level, is a twenty-six-faced rhombicuboctahedron, made of glass and half-filled with water. Because it is as difficult to create as its name is to spell and pronounce, the rhombicuboctahedron represents the height of geometrical knowledge and achievement. Some claim that it is so well rendered that the artist responsible must have been Leonardo da Vinci; another theory holds that the Palazzo Ducale, or ducal palace, at Urbino is reflected in one of its faces.

The objects on the table include a set-square, an inkwell, a container for writing implements or mathematical instruments, chalk, and a pair of dividers. Together, they represent learning, knowledge, and the tools of creation.

Pacioli is depicted drawing a diagram on a slate. The name "EUCLIDES" that has been inscribed on the slate's wooden frame indicates that the diagram's inspiration is the third-century-BC Greek mathematician Euclid, and, indeed, it is thought that Pacioli is following Euclid's instructions in order to replicate an equilateral fifteen-sided figure. Symbolically speaking, an equilateral triangle enclosed by a circle like this can represent matter contained within an eternal cycle, as well as the Christian concept of the Holy Trinity at the center of the Church Universal. Yet it appears as though Pacioli is in the middle of describing a pentagon, which, when completed, will include a triangle that demonstrates the golden ratio. The pentagon is a significant shape symbolically because it is likened to the human microcosm of the universal macrocosm.

A model of a regular dodecahedron, a twelve-sided, solid figure whose faces are made up of regular pentagons, sits on top of an ornately bound book.

The number twelve signifies cosmic order, for there are, for example, twelve months of the year, twelve signs of the zodiac, twelve hours in a day, and twelve in a night. The book is a copy of Pacioli's *Summa de Arithmetica, Geometria, Proportioni et Proportionalita,* and the Latin characters that face the viewer— "LI.R.LUC.BUR."— signify *Liber Reverendi Luca Burgensis,* or "The Book of the Venerable Luca of Borgo."

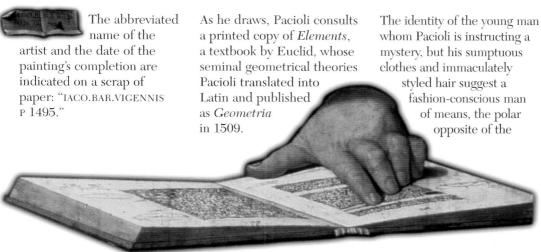

The abbreviated name of the artist and the date of the painting's completion are indicated on a scrap of paper: "IACO.BAR.VIGENNIS P 1495."

As he draws, Pacioli consults a printed copy of *Elements*, a textbook by Euclid, whose seminal geometrical theories Pacioli translated into Latin and published as *Geometria* in 1509.

The identity of the young man whom Pacioli is instructing a mystery, but his sumptuous clothes and immaculately styled hair suggest a fashion-conscious man of means, the polar opposite of the ascetic, unworldly monk, who has taken a vow of poverty. Some believe that this is the likeness of Guidobaldo da Montefeltro, Duke of Urbino (1472–1508), to whom Pacioli dedicated his *Summa*; others, that it is de' Barbari; and still others, that it is Albrecht Dürer (1472–1528), whom de' Barbari is known to have introduced to the principles of perspective and proportion during the German artist's mid-1490s' trip to Italy.

Giovanna Tornabuoni, née Albizzi Domenico Ghirlandaio

1488, oil on panel, Thyssen-Bornemisza Collection, Madrid, Spain

The beautiful young subject of Ghirlandaio's painting died in the same year that it is dated, leading some scholars to claim that this is a posthumous, memorial portrait. That may indeed be the case, but a closer reading of the symbols secreted within this apparently straightforward portrayal reveals that, above all else, it is the depiction of a trophy wife.

The lustrous lovely pictured here in profile was born Giovanna degli Albizzi in 1468, into a well-to-do and influential Florentine family. Her wedding, on June 15, 1486, to Lorenzo Tornabuoni, the son of Giovanni—whose sister had married into the Medici family, and who held important positions as a Medici banker and Pope Sixtus IV's treasurer—was not only a lavish, expensive affair, but represented the creation of a mutually advantageous dynastic tie between the Albizzi and Tornabuoni families.

By 1488, the date that appears in Roman numerals in this painting, Giovanna had done sterling duty in producing Giovanni's first grandson, who was named after his grandfather, but she died on October 7 of the same year while giving birth to her second child. A similar representation of Giovanna, albeit full length, can be seen in the "Visitation" scene of a fresco cycle commissioned from Ghirlandaio by Giovanni Tornabuoni for the chapel of Florence's church of Santa Maria Novella (where Giovanna was laid to rest), which was executed between 1486 and 1490. All in all, it is unclear whether Ghirlandaio's portrait of Giovanna predates or postdates her death, or whether it was painted from life or was based on his earlier inclusion of her likeness in the fresco. What is unmistakable, however, is the intention that we should be dazzled by Giovanna's good looks; that we should approve of her modesty and piety; and that we should be impressed by the obvious wealth and taste of the Tornabuoni family.

See also **Personal, Dynastic, and Papal Emblems** (pages 158–60).

Although the intention may have been to convey Giovanna's meekness (and, perhaps, the prettiness of her profile and artfully arranged hair, the sign of a married woman) by showing her side on, with her eyes averted, the overall effect makes it seem as though we are being encouraged to admire an exquisite, inanimate, object, or a prized possession, rather than to engage with an individual character.

To Giovanna's right, the side that represents her conscious mind and public, worldly face, lies a magnificent jewel, whose golden setting, ruby, and pearls are complemented by the pendant that decorates her bosom. Although these ostentatious jewels were probably primarily wealth-flaunting Tornobuoni family pieces, they may also have signified Giovanna's "gemlike" qualities. For while pearls symbolize purity, virtue, and the feminine ideal, yet tears, too, rubies represent love and passion, generosity and enthusiasm, and, more poignantly, given Giovanna's premature death, health, vitality, and longevity. The golden dragon that can be discerned above the ruby represents a mythological guardian of treasure, and therefore the quality of vigilance. Ghirlandaio may have been aware of these connotations, and may additionally have had a special interest in depicting jewelry, for in his *The Lives of the Artists* (1568), Giorgio Vasari informs us that he was the son of a goldsmith, and that "he was apprenticed to a goldsmith, but he did not find that profession to his liking and did nothing but draw continuously…"

ARS VTINAM MORES
ANIMVMQVE EFFINGERE
POSSES PVLCHRIOR IN TER
RIS NVLLA TABELLA FORET
MCCCCLXXXVIII

The orange-pink string of lustrous beads that emphazises Giovanna's delicate curves, as well as her upright posture, is actually a coral paternoster, or rosary. Because the Roman Catholic use for these beads is to count off "Our Father" and "Hail Mary" prayers, rosaries convey piety, also making a link with the Christian ideal of womanhood represented by Mary, the "Virgin of the Rose Garden." Coral has been credited with the power to avert illness, evil, sterility, and harm since ancient times, and red coral was thought to strengthen the blood. Indeed, contact with a *pater de sang* ("blood rosary") was believed to ensure that its owner would never suffer a hemorrhage, an important precaution at a time when many women died from blood loss in childbirth (which begs the question, did it fail Giovanna?)

Like the rosary, the prayer book signifies devoutness.

By positioning both aids to religious devotion to Giovanna's left, the side that is associated with the unconscious mind and a person's private, inner life, Ghirlandaio may have been signaling her true, unfeigned spirituality and unworldly nature.

The "L" that can be seen woven into the brocade on Giovanna's shoulder stands for "Lorenzo," her husband's name.

In the language of symbolism, the simple, white-petaled, daisylike flowers that adorn Giovanna's sleeve allude to her purity of spirit, or virtue, as well as to her fresh, unspoiled beauty.

The diamond, or rhombus-shaped, motif that forms part of the pattern on Giovanna's sumptuous gown is an emblem of the Tornobuoni family.

When interpreted from the Latin, the inscription behind Giovanna reads: "Oh Art, if you could portray her manners and her spirit, no picture more beautiful than this would exist on Earth. 1488." The words are borrowed from the Roman poet and epigrammist Martial (*c.* AD 40–103)—

they originally appeared in *Epigram XXXII: On a Portrait of Antonius Primus*—and were undoubtedly in part intended to praise Giovanna's superlative qualities, but was Ghirlandaio being boastful or self-deprecating in attaching them to his work?

Portrait of Federigo da Montefeltro, Duke of Urbino, and His Son Guidobaldo

Pedro Berruguete

1480–81, oil on panel, Galleria Nazionale delle Marche, Urbino, Italy

Pedro Berruguete crammed a multitude of messages into this double portrait of Federigo da Montefeltro, Duke of Urbino (1422–82), and his son, Guidobaldo (1472–1508). In it we can discern evidence of the older man's character, achievements, values, and hopes for the future.

When the Spanish-born Berruguete—who had traveled to Urbino to help beautify the library at Federigo's palace—painted his patron, it was only a few years since Pope Sixtus IV (who reigned between 1471 and 1484) had created Federigo duke of Urbino, both in reward for services rendered and to keep his captain of the papal army on his side. For during a period when the Italian city-states were incessantly fighting each other for supremacy, and popes were as political and power-hungry as any secular ruler, Federico was both a vital papal ally and a formidable *condottiere* (commander of a mercenary army). Yet Federigo was far more than a warmonger, also being a cultured man of learning who vigorously promoted the arts at his court and governed his subjects fairly. Federigo may not have been of legitimate birth, but this portrayal speaks volumes about the legitimacy of his leadership, about his wealth and power, about his multifaceted personality, and about the paternal and protective nature of his rule.

His young son Guidobaldo is depicted as a proud princeling who is destined to grow up to inherit his father's legacy and to continue his work, and Guidobaldo indeed not only ruled Urbino after Federigo's death, but presided over a court that was praised to the skies in Italian author Baldassare Castiglione's book *Il Cortegiano* (*"The Courtier"*), which was published in 1528. Yet rather than having portrayed the first in a long line of dukes of Montefeltro, fate decreed that Berruguete should depict the first and last, for Guidobaldo died childless in 1508, whereupon the title that meant so much to his father passed to Francesco Maria della Rovere, his nephew.

See also Portrait of a Knight (pages 167–69).

The pearl-encrusted, conical headdress atop the lectern resembles a papal tiara, minus the three crowns that mark out its wearer as the pope himself. Both his grandfather, Antonio, and father, Guidantonio, had been papal vicars, or representatives, so Federico was following in the family footsteps in serving the pope on succeeding his legitimate half-brother, Oddantonio, as Urbino's ruler in 1444.

The sword is the symbol of the knight, of readiness to fight for a just cause, and consequently also of justice. A sheathed sword, such as this, signals peace, but also the owner's readiness to spring into action at a moment's notice.

Federico wears an English chivalric order below his knee: the Order of the Garter. It is recorded that King Edward IV conferred this high honor upon Federigo in 1474, no doubt in the interests of cementing an alliance.

Having lost his right eye in battle, Federigo was always painted in profile. An old battle scar can be seen just above his jaw, and the extraordinary outline of his nose betrays a badly healed break.

The heavy chain that lies on Federigo's chest, and the ermine (complete with black tails, the only part of the ermine-yielding stoat that doesn't turn white in winter) beneath it, together signify the chivalric Order of the Ermine that King Ferdinand I of Naples bestowed upon Federigo in 1474.

Federigo may be sitting on a ducal throne, a symbol of his worldly power, but the lectern, or bookstand, before him is decorated with the emblem of a far higher, spiritual power, for the three-armed symbol known as the triskele, or triskelion, that adorns it represents the Christian Holy Trinity, with its apparently dynamic, spinning motion denoting the eternal cycle of life.

The book that Federigo is reading suggests literature and learning, and thus his education and wisdom. One of Federigo's aims was to create a world-renowned library in Urbino, and his patronage of the arts, combined with his martial prowess, promotion of the pope's interests, and tolerant style of government caused many to regard him as the ideal Renaissance man.

Federigo's helmet, the embodiment of his martial persona, has been positioned in diametrical opposition to his papal-conferred headdress, his two "hats" representing the very different aspects of his character and authority.

The pearls that crown Guidobaldo's head and adorn his rich robes signify innocence, as well as wealth and privilege.

The scepter that the angelic-looking Guidobaldo is holding symbolizes a ruler's authority. The word *Pontifex* (which is Latin for "pontiff" or "high priest") that has been inscribed on the scepter indicates that power to govern has been delegated to the Montefelto dynasty— as represented by Guidobaldo, the next in line to succeed— by the pope.

The steely gleam of armor can be glimpsed beneath the rich fabric of Federigo's flowing finery, indicating that at heart he is a warrior who stands prepared to defend his faith and those who depend on him.

Lady with a Squirrel and a Starling

Hans Holbein the Younger

c.1526–28, oil on oak panel, National Gallery, London, England

The prominent presence of two wild creatures in a portrait of a respectable-looking Englishwoman had long been a puzzle, especially since, unlike, for instance, the raven or the rabbit, neither the starling nor the squirrel symbolizes any apparently pertinent qualities. Recently, however, researchers have developed a plausible explanation for the inclusion of this bird and beast in such intimate proximity to the matronly lady, and one that is inextricably linked to the identity of the sitter.

Despite having moved to Basel via Lucerne in the quest for work, the Augsburg-born artist Hans Holbein was finding commissions increasingly hard to come by, prompting him to seek employment in England in 1526. There, his talent as a portraitist soon procured him work, and although he returned to Basel for a spell, he would end his days in England, having won the patronage of King Henry VIII. During his first foray across the English Channel, his clients were a little less exalted, however, and it is thought that they included Francis Lovell, an "esquire of the body" to the king and the husband of the lady—Anne—depicted here.

The fashion of the time was to include a rebus—a visual reference to a subject's heraldic emblem or a pictorial pun on a name—in a personal portrayal, and scholars have identified two here: the red squirrel, which was the Lovells' heraldic device or badge; and the starling, whose name is reminiscent of East Harling, in the county of Norfolk, where the Lovell family seat was situated. Francis had inherited this estate on the death of his uncle Thomas, in 1524, while Anne had given birth to his male heir, Thomas, in 1526. It therefore seems likely that Francis commissioned this painting as a proud statement piece.

See also **Personal, Dynastic, and Papal Emblems** (pages 158–60), **pearl details** (pages 152, 182, 188 and 193).

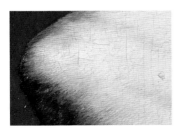

Starlings are vocal and sociable birds (which generally have symbolic significance as messengers), and this bright-eyed example appears to be animatedly addressing Anne's fur-muffled ear. Some authorities have speculated that Holbein intended to suggest that it is saying the name "Anne," so that her first name, her husband's family name, and the name of their domicile are all represented in this painting.

Holbein has probably depicted Anne wearing an ermine cap for practical and pragmatic reasons, that is, it kept her warm while sitting for her portrait in a chilly English room, and it gave him the opportunity to demonstrate his virtuoso skill in painting fur. Its inclusion is furthermore symbolically appropriate, for it was once believed that the ermine-yielding stoat would rather die than dirty its white winter coat, thereby linking it with chastity, spiritual purity, and virtue. The color white shares these connotations, so that Anne's cap, shawl, the modesty-preserving gauzy detail of her gown, and its pearly button are all subtle testimonies to her all-round goodness.

Red squirrels (which are native to the British Isles) were occasionally kept as pets in centuries past. Although their habit of stockpiling food for the winter can be interpreted as prudence, it more often caused them to be associated with greed and gluttony. Its fiery red color, lightning speed, unpredictable movements, and tendency to make mischief and wreak havoc were once all considered Satanic qualities in Christian eyes. These negative associations reinforce the theory that the sole reason for including the squirrel alongside Anne was as a rebus.

Holbein included fig leaves and vine tendrils in the background of many of his paintings. Figs denote fruitfulness in the Classical language of symbolism, and the grape-producing vine is an emblem of Christ, his blood, his sacrifice, and thus the Eucharist, while in Hebrew belief, the fig and vine together signal peace and prosperity. Both fig and vine can, in addition, be equated with the tree of life and salvation. Although these plants can also signify sin and drunkenness, few sitters would quibble with being painted alongside vegetal symbols of tranquility and plenty, earthly longevity, and spiritual immortality.

Pieter Jan Foppeszoon and His Family

Maerten van Heemskerck

1530, oil on panel, Gemäldegalerie Alte Meister, Kassel, Germany

Although this Netherlandish family portrait has long been considered an important precursor of the seventeenth-century Dutch still-life genre, not much was known about it until relatively recently. It was the identification of the heraldic emblem adorning the signet ring worn by the father figure as that of the Haarlem notable Pieter Jan Foppeszoon that was the significant breakthrough that helped to confirm Haarlem-based Maerten van Heemskerck as the picture's painter, rather than his teacher, Jan van Scorel (1495–1562), with whom he worked between around 1527 and 1529. Van Scorel had traveled extensively between 1518 and 1524, and so inspired van Heemskerck with the ideas and techniques that he had learned in Renaissance Italy that his pupil would literally follow in his footsteps between 1532 and 1536.

Further research has revealed the name of Pieter Jan Foppeszoon's wife (pictured at right) to have been Alijdt Mathijsdr, while their three children, portrayed here from left to right, were Jan (who was around five years old in 1530), Cornelia (aged about three), and baby Pieter. We also know that the father of the family was an upright citizen, being a well-off merchant, a civically minded town councillor, and a warden of the church of Saint Bavo. We may never know exactly why Foppeszoon commissioned this portrait from van Heemskerck, but what we have learned about him and his family accords with the symbolic messages signaled by the careful selection and positioning of a number of apparently incidental objects within the painting. By deciphering the codes inherent in the food on the table in particular, it becomes clear that they may have been blessed with healthy children, wealth, comfort, and security. Yet these responsible, God-fearing parents nevertheless recognize that all things on earth are transient, and that true salvation, and thus eternal life, depend on keeping the spirit of Christ alive in their home and hearts.

See also **The Moneylender and his Wife** (pages 150–53), **rosary detail** (page 190).

In the Christian context, wine refers to Christ's blood, a concept that Jesus himself introduced at the Last Supper. Being both the "cornerstone" of this painting and at its forefront, the wine-containing jug emphasizes the fundamental importance of this family's Christian faith, into which the father seems to be welcoming the viewer by means of his raised wineglass and direct gaze.

The halved apple may signify the sin with which Christians believe every person has been born ever since Adam and Eve ate the fruit of the tree of knowledge in the Garden of Eden. Although the scriptures do not specify the type of fruit that grew on the tree, the apple is usually equated with it because its Latin name, *malum*, also means "evil." As well as denoting original sin, the apple can, however, refer to the "new Adam," or Christ the redeemer.

It was the distinctive, if difficult-to-discern, design on his ring that identified Pieter Jan Foppeszoon.

Red grapes, which are used to make wine, symbolize Christ's blood and Eucharistic wine.

The purse hanging at Pieter Jan Foppeszoon's waist represents his material wealth.

The pear's sweetness may be likened to that of Christ's love, and is said to refer to verse 8 of Psalm 34: "O taste and see that the Lord is good: blessed is the man that trusteth in him." Because its shape resembles that of the womb, this fruit also signifies fertility and the bearing of children.

A walnut's three components can refer to the Holy Trinity, or, as explained by St. Augustine, to Christ, with its woody shell denoting the cross on which he was crucified; the green, outer flesh, his body; and the nutty kernel, his divine nature. In some traditions, the walnut also signifies marriage.

Protein-rich cheese may be eaten in Protestant countries during Lent, when observant Christians abstain from meat.

The bright-red hue of the cherry recalls the color of fresh blood, and thus Christ's Passion. Yet because it is so sweet and so savored, it is associated with rewards, which is why it is said to be a fruit that grows in paradise, where it may be enjoyed by the deserving virtuous.

The bread on the table represents the body of Christ, the second component of the Eucharist that Christians take into themselves at the altar in remembrance of their savior's self-sacrifice.

Fruit symbolizes abundance and plenty, and may also refer to the joys of being the parents of thriving children. Plums symbolize fidelity, but because their dark-purple color is similar to that of congealing blood, they may serve as a reminder of Christ's Passion and death.

The blue sky in the background represents heavenly truth, which the clouds obscure, preventing those on earth from seeing God's paradise in its full glory.

It is probably no coincidence that the pose that Alijdt and her baby have adopted is strongly reminiscent of that of traditional Virgin-and-child representations. This visual echo, along with the crucifix that baby Pieter appears to be displaying to the viewer, underline the Christian message subtly conveyed by this family scene. The crucifix is the pendant hanging from the bottom of Alijdt's coral-beaded rosary, which signals her piety. Babies were once encouraged to gnaw on coral beads or rattles, for not only was coral thought to encourage and ease teething, but it was believed to keep malign influences at bay.

The Ambassadors

Hans Holbein the Younger

1533, oil on panel, National Gallery, London, England

I ts title, its subjects, its contents, and the artist who created this picture together speak volumes about the royal courts of sixteenth-century Europe, when learning was prized, when dynastically obsessed monarchs despatched ambassadors to one another to serve as spies, and when the Reformation initiated by Martin Luther (1483–1546) was starting to transform the religious and political face of Europe.

Having arrived in England the previous year, the German-born Holbein had a name to make for himself in 1533, and, indeed, would end his days in the employ of King Henry VIII (1491–1547). In the meantime, he worked hard to create, and fulfill, the increasing demand for his extraordinarily lifelike portraits, of which one of the most complex was this double depiction of two Frenchmen: Jean de Dinteville (*c*.1503–55), a diplomat sent to Henry's court by the French king, Francis I (1494–1547), and his friend, Georges de Selve (*c*.1508–41), the Roman Catholic bishop of Lavaur and occasional ambassador to the Holy Roman emperor, Vatican, and Venice. In portraying these sleek, well-dressed men amid rich furnishings and a wealth of scientific and musical instruments and books, Holbein painted a flattering picture of a pair of prosperous, educated men in their prime, who possessed exquisite taste, enquiring minds, and important positions in society.

There are at least two further, deeper levels of meaning, however. One may allude to the tense situation in Europe, for this was the momentous year in which King Henry divorced his Catholic wife, Catherine of Aragon, and married the Protestant Anne Boleyn (their daughter, Elizabeth, would be born later that year). In a related move, it was also in 1533 that Henry renounced the supremacy of the pope and proclaimed himself head of the Church of England. The other is even more profound, for certain clues communicate the uncompromising message that no matter how privileged we are, death comes to us all, and that if we wish to enjoy an eternal afterlife in heaven, rather than allowing ourselves to be diverted by ultimately transient earthly distractions, we should remain mindful of the central, and simple, Christian message.

See also **The Reformation** (page 17),
Power and Prestige (page 157).

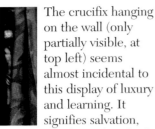

The crucifix hanging on the wall (only partially visible, at top left) seems almost incidental to this display of luxury and learning. It signifies salvation, and thus the hope that death is not the end, as long as one believes in Christ.

A figure—29—can be discerned amid the decorative detail ornamenting de Dinteville's sheathed dagger. This is his age. It may be sheathed, denoting peace, but the presence of the dagger suggests that de Dinteville is a man of action who is ready, willing, and able to mount an armed defense or offense if threatened.

De Dinteville is dressed richly and warmly (surviving letters record that he detested the chilly English climate). He appears to be wearing the medallion of *L'Ordre de Saint-Michel* (the Order of Saint Michael), France's first order of chivalry, denoting his membership of a select band of French nobles who enjoyed their king's trust.

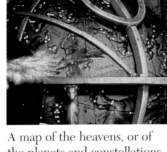

A map of the heavens, or of the planets and constellations, is represented on the celestial globe on the top shelf. As well as signifying heavenly concerns, the globe may symbolize astronomy, one of the seven liberal arts. Scholars have ascertained that the latitude is set to that of Rome, rather than London, suggesting that this is where the men's spiritual loyalties lie.

Like many of the other objects jostling for position next to it, the sundial is an instrument of measurement. Because it also reflects the passing of time, the sundial can, like the hourglass or clock, imply ageing and death.

As befits his status as a "man of God," de Selve is dressed more soberly than his secular friend, albeit no less expensively. His elbow rests on a book—a symbol of learning—on whose compacted leaves his age—25—has been inscribed.

Too good to be trampled on, this costly rug would have been imported from the East. It signifies both spending power and contact with far-flung places.

"As above, so below," and if the top shelf refers to heaven, the bottom shelf represents the Earth, as is emphasized by the terrestrial globe. It is possible to zoom in on the map shown here, into Europe, then into France, and finally, to focus on Polisy, where de Dinteville's *château*, or castle, was located, and which was thus the center of his world. Next to the globe is a pair of dividers that may denote the liberal art of geometry, or may literally signify division.

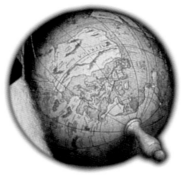

The open book in front of the lute is a Lutheran (Protestant) hymnal, and it may not be a coincidence that "lute" (*Laute* in German) sounds rather like the German pronunciation of Luther ("lut-ter"). Although its inclusion was likely to displease devout Catholics like de Selve (who yearned to heal Europe's ever-widening religious schism), the texts that can be made out—the hymn *Veni Sancte Spiritus* (Latin for "Come Holy Spirit") and the Ten Commandments—are nondenominational, and therefore hint at the universality of certain fundamental Christian beliefs.

The bookmark indicates that de Dinteville is in the process of reading this book, and that he has got as far as the section headed "*Dividirt,*" German for "Divide." Published in 1527 by the German mathematician Peter Apian, the book's title, when translated from German into English, is *A New and Reliable Instruction in All Commercial Calculations.*

Holbein may have made use of the symbolism relating to shapes in his portrayal of the flooring materials, for one of de Dinteville's feet rests on a square (which is equated with the Earth), while the other has been planted on a circle (which represents the heavens). Was Holbein subtly referring to life and death? Or was he suggesting that the French ambassador had a foot in both camps, i.e., the French and English courts?

The lute symbolizes the liberal art of music, as well as harmony. Look closely, however, and you'll see that a string has broken, a detail that hints at discord, the cause of which may be suggested by the book in front of it. Similarly, the set of flutes to the right is incomplete.

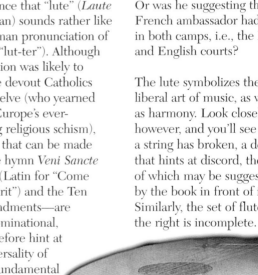

Once you realize that the strange, distorted image in the foreground is actually an anamorphosis, or a dramatically foreshortened skull, an unmistakable symbol of death, it is evident that Holbein has included a *memento mori*, or a reminder that we must all die, in his worldly portrait. The skull can be made out only when viewed from the bottom right, or with the help of an optical instrument, but the artist has accorded it a very prominent position. Making such a vital feature of this portrayal an anamorphosis furthermore raises all sorts of questions relating to enduring truths and ephemeral matters, and to how we perceive, or misperceive, them. *The Ambassadors* therefore contains a veiled warning that during our limited time on earth, we should recognize what is truly important, consequently comport ourselves according to Christian principles, and in this manner, live each day as though it were our last.

INDEX OF ARTISTS

INDEX

BIBLIOGRAPHY

Readers are advised to consult Clare Gibson's *The Hidden Life of Art* (see below for further details) for a wider and deeper understanding of many of the secrets and symbols that can be found in Renaissance masterpieces.

Appiah, Kwame Anthony, & Gates, Jr., Henry Louis (Eds.), *The Dictionary of Global Culture*, Penguin Books, London, 1998.

Aston, Margaret, *The Panorama of the Renaissance*, Thames and Hudson Ltd., London, 1996.

Battistini, Matilde, *Symbols and Allegories in Art*, Getty Publications, Los Angeles, 2005.

Benét, William Rose, *The Reader's Encyclopedia*, Guild Publishing, London, 1988.

Bergin, Thomas G., and Speake, Jennifer (Eds.), *The Encyclopaedia of the Renaissance*, B. T. Batsford Ltd., London, 1988.

Bull, Malcolm, *The Mirror of the Gods*, Penguin Books Ltd., London, 2006.

Carr-Gomm, Sarah, *The Secret Language of Art*, Duncan Baird Publishers, London, 2001.

The Catholic Encyclopedia, 1913, which can be consulted online at: http://www.newadvent.org/cathen/index.html

Chilvers, Ian, *Concise Dictionary of Art & Artists*, Oxford University Press, Oxford. 2003.

Cooper, J.C., *An Illustrated Encyclopedia of Traditional Symbols*, Thames and Hudson Ltd., London, 1978.

Currie, Elizabeth, *Inside the Renaissance House*, V&A Publications, London, 2006.

Douglas, J.D., & Tenney, Merrill C., *NIV Compact Dictionary of the Bible*, Hodder & Stoughton, London, 1989.

Duchet-Suchaux, G., & Pastoureau, M., *The Bible and the Saints*, Flammarion, New York, 1994.

Farmer, David, *Oxford Dictionary of Saints*, Oxford University Press, Oxford, 1996.

Fisher, Sally, *The Square Halo and Other Mysteries of Western Art*, Harry N. Adams, Inc., New York, 1995.

Foister, Susan, *Holbein in England*, Tate Publishing, London, 2006.

Gibson, Clare, *The Hidden Life of Art*, Saraband (Scotland) Ltd., Glasgow, and Barnes and Noble. Inc., New York, 2006.

Hagen, Rose-Marie, & Hagen, Rainer, *What Great Paintings Say, Volume I*, Benedikt Taschen Verlag GmbH, Köln, 2005.

Hall, James, *Dictionary of Subjects and Symbols in Art*, John Murray (Publishers) Ltd., London, 1974.

Haworth-Maden, Clare (Ed.), *The Passion of the Christ*, Saraband (Scotland) Ltd., 2004.

Holy Bible, The, the authorized King James Version.

Impelluso, Lucia, *Nature and its Symbols*, Getty Publications, Los Angeles, 2004.

Kemp, Martin, *Behind the Picture*, Yale University Press, New Haven and London, 1997.

Kenner, T.A., *Symbols and Their Meanings*, Carlton Publishing Group, London, 2006.

Laneyrie-Dagen, Nadeije, *How to Read Paintings*, Chambers Harrap Publishers Ltd., Edinburgh, 2002.

McLeish, Kenneth (Ed.), *Bloomsbury Guide to Human Thought*, Bloomsbury Publishing Ltd., London, 1993.

Mühlberger, Richard, *The Bible in Art: The Old Testament*, Portland House, New York, 1991.

Murray, Peter, and Murray, Linda, *The Art of the Renaissance*, Thames and Hudson, London, 1963.

Oswalt, Sabine G., *Concise Encyclopedia of Greek and Roman Mythology*, Wm. Collins Sons & Co. Ltd., Glasgow, 1969.

Read, Herbert, and Stangos, Nikos, *The Thames and Hudson Dictionary of Art and Artists*, Thames and Hudson, London, 1994.

Roberts, Keith, *Italian Renaissance Painting*, Phaidon Press Limited, Oxford, 1976.

Rynck, Patrick de, *How to Read a Painting*, Thames and Hudson, London, 2004.

Stemp, Richard, *The Secret Language of the Renaissance*, Duncan Baird Publishers, London, 2006.

Thomas, Anabel, *Illustrated Dictionary of Narrative Painting*, John Murray (Publishers) Ltd., London, 1994.

Vasari, Giorgio, *The Lives of the Artists*, Oxford University Press, Oxford, 1998.

Voragine, Jacobus de, *The Golden Legend*, Penguin Books, London, 1998.

ACKNOWLEDGMENTS

The publisher would like to thank Alex Edouard of Bridgeman Art Library for his help in the preparation of this book. All featured paintings are reproduced by kind permission of the Bridgeman Art Library and by courtesy of the institutions named on the relevant pages (and of Peter Willi, pages 87–90 and 91–93); all the images are copyrighted by those institutions.

Grateful acknowledgment is also made to the following individuals and institutions for permission to reproduce the illustrations that appear in the introductory pages to the chapters:

© **2007 JUPITERIMAGES:** 6 b, 12, 96 t, 97 l; **Planet Art:** 4, 6 t, 7 t, 9, 10 t, 11, 13, 14, 15 b, 16 l, 16 r, 17, 94 b, 95 b, 96 b, 97 r, 98, 100, 101, 154 b, 155, 156, 157, 158 t, 159, 160, 161; Saraband Image Library: 7 b, 8, 15 t, 16 l, 95 t, 99, 158 b.